D0848307

Ideas and Ideologies
General Editor:
Eugene Kamenka

Ideas and Ideologies

Already published:

Law and Society:
  The Crisis in Legal Ideals
Edited by Eugene Kamenka, Robert Brown and
Alice Erh-Soon Tay
*Robert Brown, Gordon Hawkins, Eugene Kamenka,
W. L. Morison, Alice Erh-Soon Tay*

Human Rights
Edited by Eugene Kamenka and
Alice Erh-Soon Tay
*Christopher Arnold, Stanley I. Benn,
Nathan Glazer, Eugene Kamenka, John Kleinig,
K. R. Minogue, J. G. Starke, Alice Erh-Soon Tay,
Carl Wellman*

Titles in Preparation:

Intellectuals and Revolution:
  Socialism and the Experience of 1848
Edited by Eugene Kamenka and F. B. Smith
*Leslie Bodi, Tony Denholm, J. H. Grainger,
Eugene Kamenka, G. A. Kertesz, R. B. Rose,
F. B. Smith*

Law and Social Control
Edited by Eugene Kamenka and
Alice Erh-Soon Tay

Justice
Edited by Eugene Kamenka and
Alice Erh-Soon Tay

Imperialism
Edited by Eugene Kamenka

Community
Edited by Eugene Kamenka

Bureaucracy

The Career of a Concept

**Edited by Eugene Kamenka
and Martin Krygier**

St. Martin's Press
New York

© Edward Arnold (Publishers) Ltd 1979

ISBN 0–312–10803–6

Library of Congress Cataloging in Publication Data
Main entry under title:

Bureaucracy: the career of a concept.

(Ideas and ideologies)
Includes bibliographical references and index.
1. Bureaucracy—Addresses, essays, lectures.
I. Kamenka, Eugene. II. Krygier, Martin.
HM131.B77 1979   301.18'32   79–14670
ISBN 0–312–10803–6

2-16-81

Contents

Introduction   vii
Eugene Kamenka

1 State and bureaucracy in Europe: 1
   the growth of a concept
   Martin Krygier

2 Saint-Simon, Marx and the non-governed 34
   society
   Martin Krygier

3 Weber, Lenin and the reality of socialism   61
   Martin Krygier

4 The revolution betrayed?   88
   from Trotsky to the New Class
   Martin Krygier

5 Freedom, law and the bureaucratic state   112
   Eugene Kamenka and
   Alice Erh-Soon Tay

6 Bureaucracy: the utility of a concept   135
   Robert Brown

   Contributors   156

   Index   159

Introduction

The word 'bureaucracy' has become one of the shibboleths of our
time. For many, it signifies a concept that deserves a central place
in the theory and especially in the critique of modern society. The
word is used to identify an institution or a caste, a mode of operation,
an ideology, a way of viewing and organizing society or a way of life.
As such, it has engaged some great minds and a host of lesser ones;
it has become a social category. We find discussions of it in textbooks
of sociology, politics, economics, social psychology and administrative
theory; it is ubiquitous in popular journals and current political invective. For some it is an inescapable trend implicit in the logic of a
developing capitalism; for others it is of the very essence of socialism.
Certainly, a whole new turn in radical socialist thought—the rejection
of 'bureaucratic socialism' and 'obsolete communism'—was dependent on the view that bureaucracy is the new danger, infecting the
socialist revolution as much as, if not more than, advanced capitalist
society. There are those, indeed, for whom bureaucracy has characterized a new, or not so new but alternative, social formation in which
the state is the centre and ultimate controller of all significant activity
and in which the classical dichotomies of bourgeois and proletarian,
of free enterprise and public ownership, become irrelevant. As a term
of abuse, 'bureaucracy' has been hurled against the US Department
of Health, Education and Welfare or any other social agency the
speaker dislikes, against General Motors and the big corporations,
against the Soviet Communist Party and the contemporary Chinese
opponents of the 'Gang of Four'. Retrospectively it has been used
to characterize the ruling caste of the great 'oriental despotisms' of
Egypt, Mesopotamia, India and China and the ruling elites of a host
of countries from Thailand to Meso-America. The concept of
bureaucracy, in brief, works as a Jack-of-all-trades and today it works
overtime.

Bureaucracy, then, is a vast subject and this volume cannot and does not pretend to deal with it in all its aspects, comparative, analytical, empirical and theoretical, examining its operation in the political systems of the past and of the present, in chieftain societies, great empires and modern totalitarian or dictatorial complexes. This volume studies in detail neither the contemporary civil service nor the contemporary firm. It is concerned rather with the emergence and development of the concept of bureaucracy as a conceptual tool for large-scale, macro-sociological, discussions of society, as a tool in the armoury of social criticism, as an idea that betrays and carries with it an ideology. It does so in the context of the great social issues and some of the great social thinkers of the nineteenth and twentieth centuries, in the context, in short, that has shaped our time. Since concepts do not arise out of a vacuum, the volume begins with a sketch of the growth of powerful, hierarchical and centralized administrative institutions in Europe in connection with state-centred absolutism and the theoretical responses to and ingredients in this growth. It notes that the term bureaucracy began with a strong pejorative overtone and that it took a comparatively long time to develop a proper theoretical appreciation of the administrative imperatives to which it pointed and of the social functions that it performed. At the same time a whole new tradition of social criticism inaugurated by Saint-Simon and carried on, in certain respects, by Marx, Lenin and Trotsky put enormous emphasis on social planning and the rational development of social resources while insisting that the government of men would be replaced by the administration of things. The realities of Soviet socialism created more and more difficulties for this view and even for the Marxism that was supposed to give it a solid theoretical foundation. Much of the volume, therefore, is concerned with the way in which the term bureaucracy functions in and raises difficulties for the Marxist view of the world and of the development of contemporary society—a theoretical drama that has occupied the attention and shaped the thought of thinking radical socialists for some forty years. But that drama, while not without its continuing echoes, is to some extent played out and the volume concludes with an examination of new problems that increasingly engage the attention of the present generation—the relationship between law, freedom and the increasing strength and role of bureaucratic-administrative structures and attitudes in the regulation of society as well as the possible disintegration of the ideal type 'bureaucracy', the coming apart of factors that have been lumped together, in the light of new social and technological developments, above all the computer.

Four chapters of this book—the greater part of it—were written by Mr Martin Krygier as he was completing his PhD thesis on 'Marxism and Bureaucracy' for submission in the History of Ideas Unit of the Australian National University and are based on that thesis. It was generous of him to undertake this task in the midst of completing a thesis and beginning his duties as Lecturer in Jurisprudence in the University of Sydney. Miss Margaret O'Neill and Mrs Mary Stefanidaki have typed most of the manuscript; Miss Marion Pascoe has checked the proofs and prepared the index.

Canberra, June 1978   Eugene Kamenka

I

State and bureaucracy in Europe: the growth of a concept

Martin Krygier

Administration as an institutionalized activity has been carried out in all complex societies. However, the ways in which it is carried out, the forms of administrative organization employed, the qualifications required of administrators, their number, and the importance and pervasiveness of administrative agencies have varied greatly from society to society and from one age to another. So too have the amount and kinds of writing about administrative organizations and officials and the extent of public consciousness of their existence, activities and roles.

In all industrially developed societies today, unprecedented numbers of large-scale organizations employ unprecedented numbers of people to deal with an unprecedented range of tasks. As Hans Rosenberg observes:

> Everywhere government has developed into a big business because of the growing complexity of social life and the multiplying effect of the extension of the state's regulative functions. Everywhere government engages in service-extracting and service-rendering activities on a large scale. Everywhere the supreme power to restrain or to aid individuals and groups has become concentrated in huge and vulnerable organizations. For good or for evil, an essential part of the present structure of governance consists of its far-flung system of professionalized administration and its hierarchy of appointed officials upon whom society is thoroughly dependent. Whether we live under the most totalitarian despotism or in the most liberal democracy, we are governed to a considerable extent by a bureaucracy of some kind.[1]

In so-called capitalist societies, state apparatuses have become massive and continue to grow. Government agencies proliferate and spread, and there are no signs that the enormous number of people employed in government offices will diminish. Since the last century,

[1] Hans Rosenberg, *Bureaucracy, Aristocracy and Autocracy: the Prussian Experience 1660-1815* (Boston, 1966), p. 1.

moreover, huge non-state bureaucratic structures have come to assume profound importance in both economic and political affairs. The *soi-disant* socialist countries are managed and directed by central party and government organizations which employ all those who are employed, to such an extent that many believe that the USSR itself is best understood as a large complex bureaucracy. Everywhere 'there is organization, everywhere bureaucratization; like the world of feudalism, the modern world is broken up into areas dominated by castles, but not the castles of *les chansons de geste*, but the castles of Kafka.'[2]

'Bureaucracy' has become one of the most examined phenomena in academic social science: research proliferates on the internal structure of bureaucracies, on what is functional and dysfunctional for efficient bureaucratic performance, on the relationships between different categories of bureaucrats, between bureaucrats and their social, economic and political environment, between bureaucrats and their 'publics', between bureaucracy and socio-economic development. Bureaucrats are studied by psychologists, sociologists and political scientists; bureaucracies are studied individually and comparatively, within and between societies, in government and outside it.

Outside the academy, and often not very far outside, 'bureaucracy' has also had a busy career as a weapon of popular invective. As we shall see, the term may not be conspicuous for its clarity, but its force in such expressions as 'bureaucratic red-tape', 'the bureaucratic runaround' or simply a despairing 'bureaucracy!' is commonly understood. In political argument, opposition to bureaucracy creates strange bedfellows. The vehement opposition of the New Left to bureaucratic forms of organization and those who staffed them is fully shared by writers who have little else in common with that movement. Robert Nisbet, for example, argues that:

> Unhappily, as is now a matter of full record, the bureaucratic instrument has taken command. It is impossible to so much as glance at the thousands of miles of bureaucratic corridors, the millions of file cases, the millions of bureaucratic employees organized in a complexity that gives fresh meaning to Laocoon, as all these become revealed in ordinary human experience, without realizing that once again in history means have conquered end.[3]

But while there has been a massively accelerated growth of large-scale, centralized administrative structures in this century, such structures have a considerable ancestry. Similarly, there is a good deal of continuity between present and past discussion and criticism of administrators and their methods.

[2] Sheldon S. Wolin, *Politics and Vision* (Boston, 1960), p. 354.
[3] R. Nisbet, *The Twilight of Authority* (New York, 1974), p. 54.

I The growth of the administered state

The growth of powerful, hierarchical and centralized administrative institutions in Europe was a crucially important element in the development of the modern European nation-state and in the consolidation of several hundred more or less independent political units in 1500 into twenty-odd states in 1900. On the one hand, huge and centralized administrative structures could not develop in the absence of a powerful centre. On the other, the centre, especially in culturally heterogeneous communities with specific historical traditions was led to rely on such structures to subdue and replace provincial power-holders, establish central authority and collect taxes.

Such developments were especially marked in the European absolute monarchies of the seventeenth and eighteenth centuries. What particularly distinguished these monarchies from their forebears was the increasing concentration of military and administrative power in centrally directed institutions, a concentration which occurred at the expense of the church, corporations and estates, of local aristocrats and provincial centres of power. Moreover, centrally controlled institutions did not simply supersede these 'intermediate bodies' in the performance of existing functions. They and their successors came to perform a whole range of new and more demanding functions.

Nowhere were these developments more strikingly apparent than in France from the early seventeenth century and in Prussia from the mid-eighteenth. France and Prussia were important because of the degree of central dominance achieved by their rulers and because they served as models for other administratively ambitious rulers. In France, effective, centrally controlled administrative institutions began to develop in the second quarter of the seventeenth century, primarily because of the need for effective collection of taxes. The crucial institution in this development was the provincial *intendant*. Royal *commissaires* had existed before the seventeenth century and were known as *intendants* from the mid-sixteenth century. However, they differed from the seventeenth-century *intendants* appointed by Richelieu and Mazarin in three respects:[4] they were not appointed on a permanent basis, but for specific, temporary, purposes; they were not sent throughout France; and they were not administrators but emissaries and inspectors of the activities of local, independent, *officiers*. Between 1634 and 1648, however, *intendants* were sent to every *généralité* in France except for two or three outside Paris, they were established as permanent provincial officials, and, most important of all, 'from an inspector-reformer, the provincial *intendant*

---

[4] See Roland Mousnier, 'Etat et Commissaire. Recherches sur la creation des intendants des provinces (1634–1648)' in his *La Plume, La Faucille et le Marteau* (Paris, 1970), pp. 179–99.

[became] an administrator'.[5] By the mid-seventeenth century, the *intendants* supervised the assessment and collection of royal taxes, the organization of local police or militia, the preservation of order and the conduct of the courts. They were temporarily suppressed after intense opposition from local officials during and after the Fronde, but from 1658 onward they were gradually reintroduced. Louis XIV and Colbert initially tried to limit their powers and the range of their activities, but after France's war with Holland of 1672 the *intendants* acquired an extraordinarily broad range of responsibilities. Apart from their administrative functions, Colbert's insistence on full and accurate reports had the effect of extending the *intendants'* function as information officers and led to the development of a hierarchy of subordinate officials—*subdélégués*, *maires* and *échevins*. At the centre, Louis—*le roi administrateur*—and Colbert reorganized the administrative apparatus into functional ministries with staffs of assistants and secretaries and links to the *intendants*, *parlements* and other officials in the provinces. By the end of Louis XIV's reign, a system of administration had been established which was clearly under the direction of the central authority, and extended virtually over the whole territory of France.

It is important not to exaggerate the efficiency of this burgeoning administrative machine; to say the least, it deviated considerably from Weber's ideal type of bureaucracy, in structure and in performance. The *intendants* constantly vied with independent *officiers*, local notables and local traditions. The extent to which the *intendants* managed effectively to subordinate the latter remains a matter of controversy. Most *généralités* were large and the *intendants'* powers did not always match the range of their responsibilities. Moreover the *intendants* themselves were not always easy to control. The situation is well characterized by Franklin Ford:

> The structure of French government in the eighteenth century has been variously described by a series of metaphors, all of them designed to convey the impression of a complexity bordering on utter confusion. Behind this situation lay the long process of accretion inherent in the crown's efforts to maintain control of its unavoidable delegations of authority. By the time of Louis XV, that process had produced a bewildering array of governmental organs, many of them fallen into contempt and near uselessness, but each still asserting its claim to control over some portion of the conduct, the personal property, the taxes, the disputes or the physical services of the French population.... Moreover, the effects of the long reign just ended were apparent in the tremendously over-expanded bureaucracy, swelled by the thousands of sinecures which the government had sold to increase its monetary income....
>
> To these factors there must be added the infinite number of regional variations, deriving from the manner in which the modern French

[5] *ibid.*, p. 181.

monarchy had been formed. . . . Little wonder that the total effect should
have been one of seeming chaos.

Nevertheless, French government did function. Inefficient, to be sure,
loaded down with overlapping and conflicting features, it still managed
to provide greater power for the king and greater protection for the people
than did any of its rivals on the continent, with the possible exception
of the new Prussian monarchy.[6]

In the years before the French Revolution, central direction of the
intendants became far less effective than under Louis XIV and there
was a great deal of confusion and turnover among central officials.
Moreover, under the *ancien régime* public and private spheres were
inextricably confused, in two senses. First, there was still no clear
conception of the state or nation separate from the person of the king;
officials were the king's servants, not the nation's. Second, as a result of
the widespread venality of public offices, government posts—though,
as Tocqueville emphasizes, not those of the *intendant* and his subordinates—were quite literally the private property of royal officials.
France's finances, for example, were in the hands of

> private businessmen and the crown could control them only by occasional
> legal process, not by continuous administrative direction. . . .
>
> The aristocratic society of the *ancien régime* inevitably undermined
> all general laws and regulations because privileges, *grâces*, favours and
> marks of distinction consisted in personal exemptions and exceptions.
> We know this best, perhaps, in the field of taxation, where any general
> law merely gave the crown fresh opportunities for awarding exemptions.
> But in every other field, too, the personal, the idiosyncratic, or what
> in America today would be called the 'individualistic' always prevailed
> over the general law and the general interest.[7]

The French Revolution changed this situation dramatically, in public
consciousness and to a great degree in fact; it was a profoundly significant landmark in what Barker calls the 'disengagement' of the state.[8]
No longer the king's servants, public officials came to be regarded
as servants of the *nation*—that nation which, the Declaration of the
Rights of Man and of Citizens had proclaimed, was 'essentially the
source of all sovereignty; nor can any individual or body of men be
entitled to any authority which is not expressly derived from it'.
Moreover, as Bosher emphasizes, French officials began to form a
'bureaucracy' in a modern sense: they became public servants who
were paid regular salaries by, and were answerable to, the state.

[6] Franklin L. Ford, *Robe and Sword: the Regrouping of the French Aristocracy after
Louis XIV* (New York, 1965), pp. 35–6.

[7] J. F. Bosher, *French Finances 1770–1795: from Business to Bureaucracy* (Cambridge,
1970), pp. xii, 277–8.

[8] See Ernest Barker, *The Development of Public Services in Western Europe 1660–
1930* (London, 1945).

After the failure of the experiments in local self-government in-
itiated by the Revolution, Napoleon radically reorganized, recentral-
ized and rationalized the administrative structure. The prefects were
the heirs of the *intendants*. Appointed by Napoleon and under absolute
central control, the prefects governed the provinces through *conseils*,
sub-prefects and the mayors of communes. On Napoleon's fall:

> What the Bourbons found to hand in 1814 was a system purged of the
> frustrations, inhibitions and vested interests that had clogged the
> machine before the Revolution and guaranteed its destruction.... No
> government could resist the temptation to exploit this modern instrument
> of political direction and control....
>
> The prefect had been invented for a system to which the Restoration
> was in principle profoundly opposed. Yet he was retained as an indispens-
> able instrument of political control, with, of course, certain modifications
> that reflected the change of regimes....
>
> The post-Napoleonic administrative apparatus is the result of the
> revolutionary rationalization of the inconsistent, irrational, frustrated
> and inhibited centralism of the old regime into a juggernaut of modern
> bureaucracy.[9]

A second great centre and example of bureaucratic development
was Prussia of the seventeenth and eighteenth centuries. The three
great Prussian rulers of those centuries—the Great Elector (ruled
1640–88), Frederick William I (1713–40) and Frederick II (the Great,
1740–86)—bequeathed a remarkably centralized administrative apparatus to nineteenth-century Prussia. In the mid-seventeenth century, the Great Elector drew together the hitherto independent
Prussian Estates under an 'all-Prussian' central government, with
centralized financial and military administration. In 1722 Frederick
William I introduced a centralized supervisory body, the 'General
Directory', and provincial domains boards, and he subordinated local
associations—estates, municipal corporations and provincial courts—
to central direction.

Under Frederick the Great, Prussia became a major European
power and the outlook, role and organization of its administrators
changed markedly, though perhaps neither as quickly nor as dramatically as is often suggested. Beside the enormously increased scale of
the functions which Frederick asked his officials to perform, at least
three profoundly important innovations took place in his reign. First,
there was the large-scale institution of specialist training and the
regularized recruitment of civil servants. Frederick William I had
made some steps in this direction: for example, he set up chairs of
Cameralistics at Halle and Frankfurt in 1727. But recruiting practices
remained haphazard until well into his successor's reign. Though

[9] Alan B. Spitzer, 'The Bureaucrat as Proconsul: The Restoration Prefect and the
police générale', *Comparative Studies in Society and History* VII (1964–5), pp. 371, 391–2.

some of the bureaucrats themselves sought regularity in recruitment and training, Frederick II resisted their attempts until the end of the Seven Years War. Until then, the only major innovation in this field, which served as a model for later reforms, occurred outside the central and traditional bureaucratic structure, in the judicial system. The central bureaucracy and the boards lagged behind the courts and indeed were kept behind as a result of the judiciary's control over education. By 1770, however, the General Directory's chief minister, von Hagen, had persuaded Frederick to support the establishment of a centralized recruiting system for the whole executive corps of the bureaucracy, and in February 1770 a Superior Examination Commission began to operate; with this began the professionalization of the Prussian civil service. By the end of the century a merit system applied to all posts; a degree in cameralistics was required for higher posts, followed by a period of practical training and a further oral and written examination.

A second innovation under Frederick II concerned the mode of *organization* of administrative structures. Prussian administration had traditionally been organized on a principle quite different from that of both modern and eighteenth-century French organizations. In the modern 'monocratic' form of organization, offices are usually responsible, function-related ministries which are organized hierarchically under a single head of department. In the eighteenth-century Prussian, Austrian, Swedish, Russian, and, for much of the century, British monarchies, organization was 'collegial'. The 'colleges' or boards in Prussia were organized on a territorial rather than functional basis. They comprised several members whose 'seat and voice' determined their importance; all affairs were discussed collectively, and all members of the college were responsible for the actions of the majority. The basic purpose of this inherently slow-moving form of organization, together with supplementary devices such as the royal spy, the *Fiscal*, was to enable the king to control and, if necessary, discipline, his functionaries. It was, as Rosenberg remarks, to protect the king 'against idlers, saboteurs, liars, crooks, and rebels on the royal payroll'.[10]

Under Frederick II, collegiality was not abolished in the General Directory and it remained in the seventeen provincial chambers. But, without being overthrown, collegial bodies were being surrounded on all sides, and even subverted from within, by new specialist, functionally based ministries.

Finally, associated with these developments there occurred a profound change in the relations between the king and the proliferating ministries which he had encouraged, set up and supervised. The

[10] Rosenberg, p. 96; see also Reinhold August Dorwart, *The Administrative Reforms of Frederick William I of Prussia* (Cambridge, Mass., 1953), pp. 190–91.

Prussian officials of the reign of Frederick William I and the early part of that of Frederick II, were regarded as the *king's* servants, for the fiction was maintained that it was he, quite literally, who ruled. While the actual situation was far more complicated than that,[11] the king did retain an extraordinarily powerful, pivotal, role.

Frederick the Great himself appeared to favour, and contributed to, the 'disengagement' of public officialdom from the king or dynasty; and, in any case, the 'first servant of the state' was finding it increasingly difficult to control the other servants. The various ministries he had set up, independent of and often in competition with the traditional system, had led to a proliferation of ministries at the centre; these were not easily co-ordinated and were beginning to slip beyond even Frederick's control. The leading officials were very keen to replace royal arbitrariness with general rules and with their own dominance. As Rosenberg observes, the bureaucracy

> almost automatically ... derived great advantage from the impersonal basis of its strength; from its huge size as an organization; from its permanence, functional indispensability, and monopoly of expert knowledge; from its self-consciousness as an aristocratic status group and power elite; and from its patient and oblique obstructiveness.[12]

Moreover, Frederick's successors, Frederick William II and III, had neither the talent nor the inclination to combat the bureaucracy's increasing self-direction.

The Prussian General Legal Code of 1794, which was drafted while Frederick was alive, subjected the monarch to binding rules in matters of personnel administration, curbed his power, placed him under the law and generally 'depersonalized' government. Erstwhile 'royal servants' were now called 'servants of the state' and 'professional officials of the state'. The Code gave them the qualified legal right to permanent tenure and the unqualified right to due process of law in regard to questionable conduct. It recognized them 'as a privileged corporation subject to its own separate jurisdiction, distinct in title and rank, and exempt from many of the ordinary civil obligations'.[13]

The decisive change in the form and the role of the bureaucracy, however, came only after Prussia's catastrophic defeat by France at Jena in 1806. Enlightened bureaucrats were given the job of reforming the Prussian bureaucracy. Though the reform era was shortlived—it ended effectively in 1812—its legacy was a remarkably modernized and rationalized administrative structure. In place of the *Kabinett-*

---

[11] See Hubert C. Johnson, *Frederick the Great and His Officials* (New Haven, 1975), *passim.*

[12] Rosenberg, p. 176.

[13] John R. Gillis, *The Prussian Bureaucracy in Crisis 1840–1860* (Stanford, 1971), p. 23.

System, a rationalized system of departments was established, in which each minister was responsible for a separate area of service. Ministries were reorganized on functional rather than provincial lines, the jumbled, overlapping collection of central agencies was rationalized, and the connections between these ministries and the judicial and administrative agencies of the provinces were clarified and organized in a hierarchical and relatively efficient manner.

This growth of centralized power wielded by permanent bodies of officials, while more conspicuous and further developed in France and Prussia than elsewhere, was, of course, not confined to them. Marc Raeff has pointed to 'the drive for centralization and uniformity, as well as the excessive mania for regulation that we observe in the absolute monarchies of the later seventeenth century'[14] and Brian Chapman, to 'the general tightening of the administrative structure throughout western Europe'[15] about the middle of the eighteenth century. Nor was only western Europe involved. The Petrine reforms in Russia, for example, were closely modelled on the police ordinances of the German states. In Austria, Maria Theresa, and more dramatically Joseph II, promoted secular education, designed modernized curricula for the training of public servants, professionalized the civil service, introduced recruitment on merit, and maintained surveillance over bureaucrats by police agents modelled on the Prussian *Fiscal*. Finally, in the light of the widely-held view that England lagged far behind the absolute states in administrative development, that compared with Frederick William I's Prussia, English civil service was primitive and that the first major 'bureaucratic' developments in Britain were the Northcote–Trevelyan reforms of the 1850s, L. J. Hume's dissenting view should be kept in mind:

> Britain's early achievement of legal unity and centralization, the relative unimportance of 'venality' in appointments to office, the relatively early sloughing off of 'farming' in taxation and the relatively effective control of local authorities by the centre brought the country more rapidly towards the modern bureaucratic state than the Continental monarchies. The latters' claims were repeatedly frustrated or falsified by nobles, the church, provincial courts and estates and recalcitrant officials with financiers whom the state could neither discipline nor do without. The Northcote–Trevelyan reforms were a mopping-up operation, not the start of the campaign.[16]

[14] Marc Raeff, 'The Well-Ordered Police State and the Development of Modernity in Seventeenth- and Eighteenth-Century Europe: an Attempt at a Comparative Approach', *American Historical Review* LXXX (1975), p. 1226.
[15] Brian Chapman, *The Profession of Government* (London, 1959), p. 21.
[16] L. J. Hume, 'The Executive in Eighteenth-Century Thought', a chapter in his forthcoming study of Jeremy Bentham's theory of government. I have benefited greatly from discussion with Dr Hume.

In the nineteenth century, the Napoleonic model and the Prussian example, especially in education, had a profound impact on the administrative and legal systems of other states. This is partly because, as Chapman remarks, 'administrative arrangements can be copied more easily than political institutions, particularly when they are couched in clear and comprehensive terms.'[17] But ease of emulation is inadequate to explain the similarities between, and massive growth of, European bureaucracies in the nineteenth century. For the European states faced, more or less in common, a strikingly novel order and range of social, political and economic changes and difficulties. Growth in continental European population—from 187 millions in 1800 to 401 millions in 1900, and in roughly similar proportions in every European country—led to great expansion in the number of officials required to perform traditional tasks; and governments undertook new tasks. Government expanded into areas formerly managed by others, for example the responsibilities of former serf-owners, and there was an equally important growth of tasks hitherto not performed at all, but stimulated by nineteenth-century industrial, economic, and technological developments:

> In addition to expansion of traditional responsibility for public finance, police, judiciary, the military and foreign affairs—each with its bureaucracy—came functions novel in kind or extraordinary in extent. These functions included responsibility for roads, canals, bridges, harbours, and later, for railways and telegraph and telephone, each requiring a corps of officials with a degree of training. Introduction of military conscription necessitated creation of a civilian bureaucracy to administer details and to provide scientific and technological services for a modern army, and on a smaller scale, for the navy. Education, ecclesiastical affairs, and cultural agencies, with the institutions for commerce, industry and agriculture either entirely new or greatly enlarged, required similar bureaucratic services. Social problems connected with modern industry —factory inspection, legislation for working conditions, poor relief, workers' compensation and insurance, public housing, public health and other services—called for administrative personnel on a large scale, for laws affecting these matters could not be executed entirely by local amateurs, whether elected or voluntary.[18]

Moreover, the Industrial Revolution not only encouraged governments to perform new functions; it made possible the levying of far greater amounts in taxation and the employment of many more officials than ever before. In consequence of such developments, pressures, and new resources, Continental administrative organizations grew enormously in size and in importance and were constantly reorganized and reformed during the nineteenth century.

[17] Chapman, p. 29.

[18] Eugene N. Anderson and Pauline R. Anderson, *Political Institutions and Social Change in Continental Europe in the Nineteenth Century* (Berkeley, 1967), p. 168.

II Early modern sources of 'administrative science'

It would have been extraordinary if these profound changes in the nature, size, organization and role of the state and of its administrative structures, throughout Europe over several centuries, had found no echo in political thought. Indeed these changes were not simply followed, but at times facilitated, by many equally profound changes in the subjects and concerns of persons writing on politics, the state, and, later, administrative functions and functionaries. Hobbes assumed that the political institution which mattered most was the central, sovereign power; the natural rights theorists who followed him and disagreed with him on so much else, shared this assumption. And while Hobbes and Locke were confident that the most important political activity was legislation, Rousseau believed that this should be the case but doubted that it would be, and Saint-Simon had no doubt that administrators would inherit the earth.

Hobbes was still primarily concerned with the supreme lawmaker, though he does make several remarks in *Leviathan* about the role and tasks of public officials. In the eighteenth century, however, many writers began to discuss administration directly, and one form which such writings took throughout Europe was that of observations, especially by officials, about existing administrative practices and also about proposals for administrative reform. The most sustained tradition of such writings existed among the Prussian and Austrian Cameralists, beginning with Osse and Obrecht in the sixteenth century, but similar observations and proposals also proliferated in eighteenth-century England, France and Russia. These writings often discussed problems of administration merely on the way to what were regarded as more important matters, and they rarely put such problems at the centre of political theory (as opposed to administrative advice). Nevertheless, by the end of the century, a substantial body of ideas about the executive had emerged. Nor did these ideas develop in a vacuum. They contributed to, and were influenced by, far broader and more profound movements in attitudes to and expectations of the state, movements which led to increasing demands being made on the state and increasing regard being paid to the state's *means* of satisfying these demands—its administrative apparatus and its officials.

One profoundly 'modern' attitude to the state sees it as capable of deliberately harnessing its resources to promote social and economic development and change. The *philosophes*, with their 'lust for improvement', clearly exhibited this attitude, but it did not begin with them. The mercantilists of the seventeenth and eighteenth centuries sought to maximize the state's wealth and especially its power, and seventeenth-century Protestant eudaemonists, and especially Pietists, insisted that:

The subjects' welfare and prosperity would increase productivity and foster their creative energies and industriousness, which in turn would rebound to the benefit of the state and the ruler's power and provide the proper framework for a Christian way of life. . . .

By the beginning of the eighteenth century the responsibility for this goal was thrust onto the person (i.e. the ruler) or single secular institution (i.e. the state) through the virtual elimination of all other institutions that the middle ages had developed to this same end—the church, monastic orders, and fraternities. As a result, the traditional mandate of government (i.e. rulership) shifted from the passive duty of preserving justice to the active, dynamic task of fostering the productive energies of society and providing the appropriate institutional framework for it.[19]

Given this dynamic conception of the state's responsibilities, the qualities of its administrative structure gained in importance, whether officials were called upon to establish and encourage industries, gather revenues or supply burgeoning armies. This conception might indeed have been sufficient to stimulate writing about administration, without any other changes in attitudes to the nature or proper role of the state; and among the early Cameralists, king's servants all, it appears to have been. In principle, of course, and to a large extent in practice, this dynamic conception could be seen as serving a variety of 'masters' —the ruler himself, the state, the nation or the people. But many of the most significant writers about administration in the second half of the eighteenth century no longer regarded the government as simply incarnate in the ruler and they shared conceptions of the proper role of government which suggested that the quality of administration was a *public* concern, that the purposes which officials served were public purposes, and that such purposes must be served diligently and well.

We have seen already that the interests of the 'state' in Prussia and of the 'nation' in France had been 'disengaged' to a significant degree from those of the ruler by the beginning of the nineteenth century; a similar process of disengagement was inaugurated in Russia by the Petrine reforms.[20] This process did not suddenly reduce the ruler to *primus inter pares* but it did change the status of his servants and in particular, of what were perceived to be their responsibilities. The state or the nation, not to mention the 'people', might remain excluded from participation in politics and administration, but administration and tutelage was to be exercised on their behalf.

One claim repeatedly made by writers in the eighteenth century was that rulers held power in *trust* for their people, and must exercise their power in accordance with the terms of that trust. Hobbes might insist that the sovereign owed his subjects nothing but what Oakeshott

[19] Raeff, 'Well-Ordered Police State', pp. 1225–6.
[20] Marc Raeff, *Plans for Political Reform in Imperial Russia 1730–1905* (New Jersey, 1966), pp. 6–11.

describes as the 'general duty of being successful'[21]—which itself need not always be a small matter—but Locke soon held that the 'supreme legislative authority' had no right to breach the terms of its trust, and Rousseau, by distinguishing sharply between the *sovereign* people and the mere *government* which the sovereign appoints and might peremptorily dismiss, underlined the obligations of the latter to the former. This conception of government as a trust held on behalf of citizens was triumphantly proclaimed in America in 1776 and in France in 1789, and even authors who rejected all talk of 'natural rights' had a similar conception of the obligations of government. Burke was not always consistent on this matter but, at least when he was opposing official policy, he was prepared to invoke this conception in striking terms:

> All political power which is set over men and ... all privilege claimed or exercised in exclusion of them, being wholly artificial and for so much a derogation from the natural equality of mankind at large, ought to be some way or other exercised ultimately for their benefit.... Such rights or privileges, or whatever else you choose to call them, are all in the strictest sense a *trust*: and it is of the very essence of every trust to be rendered *accountable*—and even totally to *cease*, when it substantially varies from the purposes for which alone it could have a lawful existence.[22]

Bentham, similarly, called the central government a 'public trust' and argued that:

> Public powers differ no otherwise from private fiduciary powers than in respect of the scale on which they are exercisable: they are the same powers exercisable on a greater scale.[23]

In itself, this conception only suggests to whom duties are owed, not what they entail. It is equally compatible with a 'night watchman' and a 'service' state, with Seckendorff's or even Catherine II's 'cameralistic' sense of responsibility and Bentham's or the *philosophes*' more adventurous utilitarian claims, with Locke's insistence on rights *against* the state and Paine's prophetic demand that claims from the state by the aged or poor be regarded 'not as a matter of grace and favour, but of right'.[24] The conception of government as a public trust is important for our theme, however, in two respects. First of all, it was connected with an eighteenth-century shift in views of government from what Krieger has called 'an authority of origins' to what

---

[21] M. Oakeshott, 'Introduction' to Thomas Hobbes, *Leviathan* (Oxford, 1957), p. XL.
[22] Edmund Burke, *Selected Writings and Speeches*, ed. Peter J. Stanlis, (New York, 1963), pp. 370–71 (speech on Fox's East India Bill).
[23] J. Bentham, *Of Laws in General*, ed. H. L. A. Hart (London, 1970), p. 86.
[24] *Rights of Man* (reprinted, Harmondsworth, 1976), p. 265. Paine himself, however, was confident that this demand was compatible with a substantial *reduction* in the expense and size of government—a combination of beliefs echoed in Marxist thought.

he calls 'an authority of ends' or, less happily, 'the telic view of politics'.[25] The governments of European states were beginning to be assessed in terms of success in achieving public goals rather than simply in terms of their genealogical or divine claims, and this criterion of assessment placed demands on, and turned attention to, their machinery for achieving these goals.

Secondly, the idea of government as a trust came increasingly, in the second half of the eighteenth century, to be put to the service of a specific kind of end—the welfare, prosperity and happiness of citizens. That government should advance these goals had, as we have seen, already been suggested in the seventeenth century, but they were still frequently regarded as subsidiary, as instrumental to the greater wealth, power or virtue of the ruler, or as obligations owed solely to God, rather than as obligatory secular goals whose performance might be demanded by a ruler's subjects.

In the eighteenth century, however, there appeared what Raeff has called 'the "enlightenment amendment" ... the transformation of felicity from a mere instrument of a transcendental political goal into an end to be achieved for its own sake'.[26] According to the Prussian Cameralist, J. H. G. von Justi:

> The ultimate aim of each and every republic is ... unquestionably the common happiness.... It is unnecessary to enlarge upon the proposition, therefore, that the subjects do not exist for the sake of the ruler.[27]

Justi, who had no intention of attacking absolutism—his book was dedicated to Maria Theresa—clouded the issue on occasion by referring to the interests of the *state* rather than those of the subjects, but in either formulation the ruler was taken to be serving this-worldly interests other than his own. The Austrian Cameralist Sonnenfels also had no intention of criticizing absolutism but he too insisted that the function of administrative 'science' was to increase public welfare.[28] In France, utilitarian doctrines became popular in the second half of the eighteenth century, and the Physiocrats, who disagreed with the Cameralists on so much else, agreed at least that the goal of society was 'the whole sum of happiness and enjoyments possible for humanity'.[29] In England, Bentham, following Priestley, Beccaria, Helvetius and others, enunciated the 'greatest happiness' principle

[25] Leonard Krieger, *An Essay on the Theory of Enlightened Despotism* (Chicago, 1975), pp. 52, 56.

[26] Raeff, 'Well-Ordered Police State', p. 1239.

[27] J. H. G. von Justi, *Staatswirthschaft* ..., in Albion W. Small, *The Cameralists* (Chicago, 1909), p. 319, see also p. 413.

[28] Robert A. Kann, *A Study in Austrian Intellectual History: from Late Baroque to Romanticism* (London, 1960), p. 172.

[29] Le Mercier de la Rivière, *L'Ordre naturel et essentiel des sociétés politiques*, ed. Eduard Depitre (Paris, 1910), p. vii, quoted in Krieger, p. 50.

in 1776, and even in Russia where the interests of the people, the state and the ruler were still far from being sorted out, the influence of Benthamite and French 'enlightened' ideas was considerable. The 'Project for a most graciously granted Charter to the Russian People' which was drawn up by, among others, Count Vorontsov, who later became chancellor, and Michael Speransky, the most important Russian 'bureaucratic' reformer of the nineteenth century, proposed that the Tsar announce that:

> For ourselves, we take as a rule the truth that it is not the people who have been made for the Monarchs, but it is the Monarchs who have been established by Divine Providence for the benefit and welfare of the peoples living under their rule.[30]

For our purposes, the fact that such declarations are often self-serving or not consistent with government practice is unimportant. What is important is that they begin to occur and increasingly to recur in the writings of a wide range of writers who were also paying an unprecedented amount of attention to the role and deficiencies of administrative structures. Moreover, the attachment of both the Cameralists and the Russian reformers to autocracy was *not* inconsistent with these affirmations of the public purposes of government; they dovetailed very comfortably. Johnson has argued, for example, that the early Austrian Cameralists and their successors were well aware that, 'with each attempt to glorify the power and theoretical authority of the prince, the prestige and effective authority of the ambitious bureaucrat also rose,'[31] and the combination of reliance upon the sovereign with an extension of the perceived obligations of government had potent repercussions. Writing of the eighteenth-century German supporters of 'enlightened government'—principally the Cameralists—Geraint Parry comments that:

> Administrative training for 'enlightened government' derived its importance from the central part which administration played in the political task of welding together a disparate and non-political ruled mass. Whatever unity civil society possessed was not contributed by the atomized mass of non-participating subjects but by the organized administration. Society, Frederick the Great argued, had to be lent the unity of a philosophical system, and this was possible only if the system had its source in one place—the sovereign and his administration. To ensure the achievement of this rationalist ideal of unity and uniformity social behaviour was directed towards its single goal of 'happiness' by central planning. The first essential of any wise government was a well conceived plan, which was to be the guide for all state activities. But though a bold welfare plan was essential to the happiness of a society, it was of no avail

[30] Raeff, *Plans for Political Reform*, p. 77.
[31] Hubert C. Johnson, 'The Concept of Bureaucracy in Cameralism', *Political Science Quarterly* LXXIX (1964), p. 387.

without the administration which drew up and implemented the plan. Material resources, size of population or territory were nothing without organization. Administration made the final difference between strength and weakness in a state.[32]

More generally, and even outside the 'enlightened despotisms', the eighteenth century witnessed a novel, often obsessive, concentration on the government's *means* of fulfilling what had come to be regarded as its duties. This concentration initially was expressed by treating legislation as the central activity of government. The eighteenth-century theorists of 'police', of 'economy', and even of 'political economy' all emphasized the role of centrally made and directed laws; and these theorists devoted a great deal of attention to the arrangement, improvement, clarification and organization of bodies of rational laws. Strenuous attempts were made to codify, simplify and make more effective the laws emanating from the sovereign. One implication of this attention to legislation, and to ways of increasing its uniform applicability and effectiveness, became increasingly evident during the eighteenth century: if for Hobbes covenants without swords were but words, it was now becoming obvious that legislation without effective administrative agencies and services was little different. Proposals for governmental reform came increasingly to focus not merely on legislative institutions and reforms, but also on specifically administrative ones. The cast of mind of many such reformers, of thinkers such as Justi and Speransky, or indeed Frederick the Great and Alexander I, is revealed by Sonnenfels in his *Über die Liebe des Vaterlands*—if more candidly in the second sentence than in the first:

> For forms of government, I say with Pope, let fools contest! Whate'er is best administered is best.

Sonnenfels was a member of what Gay has aptly described as a 'tribe of authoritarian rationalists' and kin of this tribe could be found throughout Europe at this time. What Parry observes of the Cameralists is equally true of Bentham and of Alexander I's 'Unofficial Committee':

> Political discussion is of solutions and techniques.... The study of politics became the study of organization, of how given ends of government could be attained with the utmost economy of effort. The theorists of 'enlightened government' regarded themselves as scientists of adminis-

---

[32] Geraint Parry, 'Enlightened Government and its Critics in Eighteenth-Century Germany', *Historical Journal* VI (1963), p. 184; see Raeff's almost identical observation about Alexander I and the 'Unofficial Committee' in his *Michael Speransky: Statesman of Imperial Russia* (The Hague, 1957), p. 44.

tration entering on a new way in the study of politics ignored hitherto by scholars.[33]

One of the most favoured metaphors for administrative institutions throughout Europe was that of machinery. Justi, who made frequent use of this metaphor, wrote that:

> A properly constituted state must be exactly analogous to a machine, in which all the wheels and gears are precisely adjusted to one another; and the ruler must be the foreman, the main-spring, or the soul—if one may use the expression—which sets everything in motion.[34]

In France, as a modern scholar puts it:

> The word 'machine' had been increasingly used to describe administrative organizations. By the end of the eighteenth century the machine had become an obsessive image. Anson used it to describe the projected Ministry of the Interior, Camus to describe the entire administration, Marat to represent municipal administrations, and to sum up, the machine image in the writings of Lebrun, Roederer, Laffon de Ladébat and many others seems to show that this generation thought of administrative and political agencies as analogous to machines. The other possible analogy, comparing the organization to the human body as Hobbes for instance had done, seldom appears in the writings of the late eighteenth-century French reformers and revolutionaries.[35]

In Russia, the 'Principles of Government Reform', drafted by the 'Unofficial Committee' in 1802 explain that:

> Just as radii starting from different points on a circumference converge all at a common centre, so all the parts of the administration are interlocked and must converge to the same goal. If, therefore, the movement of the individual parts is not calculated in terms of this general rule, the general result can only be an incoherence which will hamper their regular performance.
>
> To avoid this defect, those who are entrusted with the task of renovating the shapeless edifice of our social contract according to correct principles must know the structure of the whole machine; and by constantly keeping in view its movement, they shall be in a better position to see the defects of its wheels and gears. This will enable them to have a better grasp of what improvements are required.[36]

The conception of administrative institutions as machinery was particularly apt for rationalist reformers in an 'enlightened' state, for it

---

[33] Parry, pp. 181, 184. For the appositeness of these remarks to Alexander I, Speransky and the 'Unofficial Committee' see Raeff, *Michael Speransky*, p. 44 and *passim*.

[34] J. H. G. von Justi, *Gesammelte Politische- und Finanzschriften* (Leipzig, 1764) III, pp. 86–7. Quoted in Parry, p. 182, and Krieger, p. 40.

[35] Bosher, p. 296.

[36] Raeff, *Plans for Political Reform*, p. 89.

legitimized both their role and that of their ruler. An administrative machine needs to be tended by qualified mechanics, and it can be designed, redesigned and manipulated according to the technical knowledge which these mechanics monopolize. As a machine, it is indeed essentially manipulable by those with appropriate knowledge and skills; it is not, as conservative critics such as Justus Möser maintained, an organic growth which could be altered only with caution, patience and restraint. Viewing administrative institutions as machinery allowed many of these thinkers to distinguish and stress the central, guiding role of the ruler, who was not part of the machine but was required to run and oversee its workings. But it was also appropriate to the increasing attention which was directed to its parts —the officials—to the heightened perception of the importance of their role within it, and to ensuring that they were *good* parts, suited to the tasks they had to perform. Auget de Montyon, one of the earliest and most perceptive French writers on administrative reform, who insisted that 'we must apply to the composition of social power the general rules of mechanics', devoted a chapter of an unpublished manuscript *Des Agents de l'administration*, to officials,

> because, he said, they are such necessary 'administrative instruments' that good ones can bring success to the weakest administrator and bad ones can bring to nothing the decisions of even the most enlightened, or else so overload him with work that he will lose sight of his true objectives.[37]

Montyon was original in France, though not in Europe, in advocating written examinations in administration, and its development as a proper discipline to be studied. The Cameralists, of course, had advocated this long before and constantly attempted to improve the education and recruitment practices of the Prussian and Austrian administrations. Bielfeld in the 1760s, Bentham in his first articles on administrative themes in the 1770s and on a number of occasions thereafter, Necker in the 1780s, all emphasized the importance of recruiting competent officials.

A parallel and possibly related emphasis on the role and importance of officials can be seen in the outpourings of sinophiles in eighteenth-century Europe, outpourings which were frequently intended as thinly veiled recommendations for reforms at home. Already in the sixteenth century, European reports about China, such as Mendoza's, dealt with its administrative system and almost invariably drew attention to the effectiveness of Chinese government, to its provision of social services and courier systems, and especially to the importance and character of its officials, trained in state-supported schools and recruited on the basis of written examinations. In the

[37] Bosher, p. 135.

seventeenth century similar observations were made by the Jesuit missionaries who wrote of China and La Mothe le Vayer, 'the chief precursor of eighteenth-century sinophilism'[38] in France, and tutor to the young Louis XIV, emphasized and praised the role of the scholar-official in China. In eighteenth-century Europe, fascination with China reached its peak and again attention was drawn to the importance of its officials and their mode of training and recruitment.

Along with the increasing attention being paid to the official went a much more definite attention to function, well conveyed in the mechanistic terms that prevailed at the end of the eighteenth century. This concept was at the root of discussion of collegial versus individual responsibility and of territorial versus function-based administrative units, and of the moves in most European countries toward the latter. In France it was reflected in terminology used soon after the Revolution:

> Whereas the posts of officials during the *ancien régime* had been *offices*, *charges* or *places*, they now began to be called *emplois* or *fonctions* and the officials themselves were for the first time described as *fonctionnaires*. . . . This utilitarian vocabulary was used to describe organizations with quasi-mechanical virtues . . . the idea of function became a principle of quasi-mechanical organization.[39]

Finally, mechanical analogies combined easily with the profoundly influential legislative framework on which many of the reformers relied. Legislation was treated as one of the most important means of implementing administrative reforms and administrative institutions were frequently assessed in terms of the criteria traditionally applied to bodies of laws. The European administrative reformers were concerned above all to establish streamlined, simplified, harmonious administrative structures in which all the parts fitted and worked smoothly together. This concern was a central objective of all the schemes of this period, from Bentham to Speransky, and the legislative model was enlisted to this end. Bentham and Speransky exemplified the 'legal-rational' approach of all of these writers whose passion was for simplicity, clarity, order, clear assignment of functions and responsibility, effective and clearly identifiable chains of communication and command.

These schemes and proposals contain a great deal which anticipates Weber's ideal type of bureaucracy, both in the elevation of legal-rational authority and in many of the specific organizational measures proposed and goals served. And within these broader concerns and preoccupations, a welter of specific suggestions and practical measures was advanced for their achievement. Rules were drawn up specifying

[38] Basil Guy, 'The French Image of China before and after Voltaire', *Studies on Voltaire and the Eighteenth Century* XXI (1963), p. 119.
[39] Bosher, p. 297.

how departmental functions were to be performed; venality of offices was condemned in post-revolutionary France and elsewhere long before, and payment by salary was often proposed; the use of records, inspection and reporting as instruments of control was almost universally recommended.

The general character of these writings was that of prescriptive, technical advocacy, not of social theory and certainly not of revolutionary ideology; it was advice to, and often by, those charged with carrying out a broad and increasing range of tasks. It was rarely systematic and was frequently embedded in pedantic discussion of detail and in consideration of other matters, but it was not negligible either in quantity or in intelligent appreciation of the problems and difficulties of large-scale and active administration.

III Nineteenth-century 'anti-bureaucratic' polemic

The administrative thought which began to flourish at the end of the eighteenth century discussed many problems and administrative imperatives which seemed to take twentieth-century revolutionaries by surprise. Revolutionaries, however, were well acquainted with, and contributed much to, a quite different kind of writing about administrative institutions and personnel—polemic against 'bureaucracy'.

The coining of a term is, of course, no sure guide to the importance of, or level of concern about, a phenomenon. Eighteenth-century critics of 'despotism', for example, argued that a despot's power would be lost to his 'vizier' and that this was not accidental but was a basic tendency of despotic states; they did not, however, show any need for terms such as 'vizier-' or 'bur-' 'eaucracy' to express their belief. Again, in 1791, Wilhelm von Humboldt had no need of the term to argue against state intervention for the positive welfare of citizens, on the grounds, *inter alia*, that:

> It arises that in most states from decade to decade the number of the public officials and the extent of registrations increase, while the liberty of the subject proportionately declines.[40]

Moreover, even when a term has come into use, it is not the only possible vehicle for expressing similar thoughts: Saint-Simon to my knowledge never wrote of *bureaucratie* but his complaints about officials are often indistinguishable from those of people who did.

Neologisms are, however, not merely coined; they also need to be received, and the reception accorded some terms is far wider and more enthusiastic than that granted to others. 'Bureaucracy' has had an extraordinary reception since the mid-eighteenth century, and, as

[40] Wilhelm von Humboldt, *The Limits of State Action*, ed. I. W. Burrow (Cambridge, 1969), p. 34.

a Marxist might observe, this is 'no accident' in view of the political, economic, social and administrative developments to which I have alluded above. The pervasiveness of the word, and its strong initial associations with France and Prussia, are clearly related to the concern in Europe, from the eighteenth century onwards, with the pervasiveness of the things which it was being used to describe.

Secondly, notwithstanding the various uses of the term, specific concentration on 'bureaucracy' is interesting for, though natural enough, it is not an inevitable, nor the only possible, response to the development of centralized state power. One might be concerned instead with 'despotism' or liken one's government to an oriental despotism—a *leitmotif* of many eighteenth-century French writings— and be basically concerned with the amount of power monopolized by the despot. One could follow Rousseau in lamenting the inevitable process by which 'all the governments of the world, once armed with the public force, sooner or later usurp the public authority.'[41] And one could direct one's attack against 'the state', as so many nineteenth-century writers did. To direct one's attacks against 'bureaucracy' was to focus on the body of government officials, those who staffed the bureaux.

Finally, there is one specific reason why 'bureaucracy' is of special interest from our point of view. Though the term has, almost from the start, been a vessel into which many different meanings have been poured, etymologically, as Albrow notes,[42] it represents an addition to the Greek classification of governments, suggesting government by a new group of rulers—officials. The word itself, whether used pejoratively or not, elevates the status and potential of officials: they are no longer subordinate 'viziers' who might usurp power from those who should rule, but a social category which might rule in its own right, its own way. The term is often used in quite different senses from this, but this sense has, for example, come to haunt the history of Marxism much as another spectre was once alleged to have haunted Europe.

The term 'bureaucracy' appears to have begun its career with this meaning. The term is usually attributed to Vincent de Gournay, a Physiocrat and mentor of Turgot, who is alleged to have also coined the phrase *laissez-faire, laissez-passer*.[43] It would be appropriate if both attributions were accurate, for the chief vice of which bureaucracy was initially accused was an inability to leave anything alone. De Gournay is said to have coined the term in 1745; from the start its use appears to

---

[41] Jean-Jacques Rousseau, *The Social Contract* (1762), translated and introduced by Maurice Cranston (Harmondsworth, 1968), p. 147.

[42] Martin Albrow, *Bureaucracy* (London, 1970), pp. 16–17.

[43] See Gustav Schelle, *Vincent de Gournay: Laissez-faire, laissez-passer* (Paris, 1897); also Joseph A. Schumpeter, *History of Economic Analysis* (New York, 1954), pp. 244–5.

have been pejorative and its focus to have been on government officials. In July 1764, Friedrich Melchior von (or Baron de) Grimm wrote to Diderot advocating the free export of grain. He complained of the multitude of public officials to whom, because they would be robbed of the opportunity to regulate, 'free trade in grain must be an abominable hydra.' France, he wrote, was 'obsessed by the spirit of regulation, and our Masters of Requests do not want to understand that there is an infinity of objects in a great State with which a government ought not concern itself.' One who had so understood was 'the late M. de Gournay ... who ... sometimes used to say: "We have an illness in France that appears likely to ravage us; this illness is called bureau-mania." Sometimes he used to invent a fourth or fifth form of government, under the title of *bureaucracy*.'[44] A year later, Grimm complained in a similar vein: 'Not to over-govern is one of the great principles of government which has never been known in France.... The true spirit of the laws of France is that bureaucracy of which the late M. de Gournay used to complain so much; here the bureaux, clerks, secretaries, inspectors, *intendants* are not established to benefit the public interest, indeed the public interest appears to have been established so that there might be bureaux.'[45] Here bureaucracy is seen as a *form* of government, government by officials, characterized by its tendency to meddle, to exceed its proper functions.

It was in this sense, or in the claim that officials were the real locus of governing power, whatever the superficial form, that complaints about bureaucracy began to appear in France in the 1780s. In 1787 one writer complained of the General Control of Finances that:

> The clerks do everything and give a twist to everything according to whether they are honest or paid by interested parties. From this, the frightful *Bureaucratie* which exists and which is such that what made seven or eight departments under Abbé Terray now makes twenty-seven or thirty.[46]

And Mercier explained in 1789 in *Le Tableau de Paris*:

> Bureaucracy is a word created in our time to designate in a concise and forceful manner the extensive power of mere clerks who in the various bureaux of the ministry are able to implement a great many projects which they forge themselves or quite often find in the dust of bureaux, or adopt by taste or by whim.

Early uses of the word outside France appear to have been con-

[44] Baron de Grimm and Diderot, *Correspondance littéraire, philosophique et critique 1753–69* (Paris, 1878 edition) VI, p. 30.

[45] *ibid.*, pp. 323–4.

[46] Jean-Louis Carra, *Un Petit Mot de réponse* (1787), p. 48, quoted in Bosher, pp. 45–6.

sistent with its French meaning. In Prussia, apart from press reports of the French Revolution, the first recorded use of the word appears to have been by Christian Kraus, a colleague of Kant. 'The Prussian state', he wrote with reason in 1799, 'far from being an unlimited monarchy ... is but a thinly veiled aristocracy ... which blatantly rules the country as a bureaucracy.'[47] An 1813 edition of a German dictionary of foreign expressions defined bureaucracy as:

> The authority or power which various government departments and their branches arrogate to themselves over fellow citizens.[48]

Similarly, the earliest English use of the term which I have found (1818) refers to 'the *bureaucratie* or office tyranny by which Ireland had been so long governed'.[49]

In all of these uses, bureaucracy is seen as rule or arrogation of power by officials. In complaining of the ways in which bureaucracy rules, attention is focused on its relations with and effects on citizens and their activities. Another theme which recurs in many of the early accounts of bureaucracy is concerned with the nature and working style of bureaucrats. Here the focus is not on the relationship between bureaucrats and subjects, but on what kinds of people bureaucrats are, and on bureaucratic predilections. In this usage, 'bureaucracy' is not necessarily confined to a certain kind of government, but, like 'aristocracy', used to characterize a group of people or a life style. In early nineteenth-century France, the bureaucrat was frequently the butt of ridicule and satire. For example, Henry Monnier published two volumes of lithographs, the first, *Moeurs administratives, déssinées d'après nature* in 1828, the second, *Scènes de la vie bureaucratique*, in 1835. In these volumes Monnier portrayed a day in the life of a bureaucrat: at nine o'clock the employees arrive at the ministry and warm themselves around an excessively hot stove; at ten they have tea and sharpen their quills; at ten-thirty they chat; at one they have lunch; at two they go for walks inside the ministry. The only time they work is midday, when the head of their division makes his tour of inspection.[50] In his novel *Les Employés*, published in 1836, Balzac, too, poured scorn on bureaucracy. He linked his attack with the first theme by distinguishing bureaucracy from officials and restricting it to the situation where the official was overweeningly powerful in government:

> Under the monarchy, the bureaucratic armies did not exist at all. Fewer

---

[47] C. Kraus, *Vermischte Schriften* (Königsberg, 1808) II, p. 247.
[48] Quoted in Albrow, p. 17.
[49] Lady Morgan, *Florence Macarthy* II, p. 35, quoted in C. A. M. Fennell, *The Stanford Dictionary of Anglicized Words and Phrases* (Cambridge, 1892), p. 176.
[50] Jean-Hervé Donnard, *Balzac: les réalités économiques et sociales dans la Comédie Humaine* (Paris, 1961), pp. 354-5.

in number, employees obeyed a minister who was always in communication with the king, and thus they served the king almost directly.... Since 1789, the State, *la Patrie*, if you prefer, has replaced the Prince ... clerks have become, despite our beautiful ideas of *la patrie*, *Government employees*, and their chiefs float with every breath of a power called the Ministry which never knows one day whether it will exist the next.... Thus, Bureaucracy, a gigantic power set in motion by dwarfs, is born. Possibly Napoleon retarded its influence for a time, for all things and all men were forced to bend to his will.... It is definitely organized under constitutional government, the natural friend of mediocrity with a penchant for categorical statements and reports, a government as fussy and meddlesome as the wife of a *petit bourgeois*.[51]

In Germany bureaucracy was also attacked as much for its attitudes, style and characteristic modes of behaviour as for what it did to its subjects. The German picture was different, however, and altogether more solemn. In 1821 Freiherr vom Stein who, of all people, should have known, complained:

We are ruled by salaried, book-taught, disinterested propertiless *Bureaulisten*.... These four words express the spirit of our own and similar spiritless governmental machines: salaried, therefore they strive after maintenance and increase of their numbers and salaries; book-taught, therefore living in the printed, not the real world; without interests, since they are tied to no class of citizens of any consequence in the State, they are a class for themselves—the clerical caste [*Schreiberkaste*]; propertiless, therefore unaffected by any change in property. It may rain or the sun may shine, taxes may rise or fall, ancient rights may be destroyed or left intact, none of this worries them. They receive their salary from the state treasury and write, write in silence, in the *Bureaux* behind specially provided locked doors, unknown, unnoticed, unpraised, and again they cultivate their children for equally useful state machines— I saw one machine (the military) fall on the 14th October, 1806. Perhaps the writing-machine will also have its 14th October! That is the ruin of our dear fatherland: official power [*Beamtengewalt*] and the nullity of its citizens![52]

In the late 1830s the Prussian government became increasingly unpopular, and, as Gillis notes, 'the target of political agitation in the decade before 1848 was not the monarchy itself but the form that the monarchy had assumed since the late eighteenth century. Bureaucratic absolutism, not royal despotism, was the issue.'[53] In 1844 an anonymous pamphlet, *Bureaukratie und Beamtenthum in Deutschland*, (*Bureaucracy and Officialdom in Germany*) appeared in Hamburg. The author, who claimed to be an English visitor, endorsed Stein's remarks

---

[51] Honoré de Balzac, *Les Employés* (reprinted Paris, 1950), p. 16.
[52] *Die Briefe des Freiherrn vom Stein an den Freiherrn von Gagern, 1813–1831* (Stuttgart, 1833), pp. 90–92.
[53] Gillis, p. 15.

and agreed with him (and with the young Marx) that bureaucrats formed a caste with purposes of its own, 'a people within the people, a state within the state'. He insisted, as so many other critics have, that bureaucracy was of no productive use but, on the contrary, was 'a powerful cancer [which] feasts voraciously, insatiably, and lives off the marrow and blood of the people'. He emphasized the hierarchical nature of bureaucratic organization, intended to produce craven obedience to anyone who controlled the bureaucracy and unfeeling domination of those under its sway, and he attacked bureaucratic devotion to authority and secrecy:

> Bureaucracy can as well be compared with a military system as with a hierarchy, and is often compared with it. The three are parallels: military, hierarchy, bureaucracy: all rest upon the divine right of despotism, which wills no exception, no leniency, no progress, but only blind devotion and the eternally unchangeable acknowledgement of its infallibility. The three maintain themselves by unconditional obedience; the means by which obedience is maintained is fear; and this is maintained by dependence. The dependence of Prussian Civil Servants is rigidly secured by two devices: secret reports and the strict maintenance of official secrecy. The former reminds officials every moment of their superiors; the latter of the office.[54]

Like so many opponents of bureaucracy, this author insisted that there was an excessive number of bureaucrats and he arrived at a figure of 700,000 for Prussia. In 1845 Karl Heinzen, the radical friend and later foe of Marx and Engels, published *Die preussische Bureaukratie*, in which he made the excessiveness of bureaucracy, in numbers, authority and activity, his central thème. Heinzen also quoted Stein's remarks, substituting 'bureaucrat' for 'bureaulist'. He contrasted bureaucracy with popular sovereignty, and claimed that it had developed out of Prussian absolutism and that it had reached its apogee under Frederick William III, who 'had allowed bureaucracy to become a system'. The essence of bureaucracy, Heinzen explained, was:

> what has generally come to be understood as bureaucracy; the excess of officials and their activity, the abuses and evils of domination by officials and bureaus. The word bureaucracy is one of those words of invective which, like, for example, despotism, canaille, etc., cannot be properly translated into our mother tongue.

It should be evident already that, beyond its usual pejorative core and its focus on officials, 'bureaucracy' is a peculiarly malleable and adaptable word, and this was clear to Robert von Mohl who in 1846

---

[54] Anon., *Bureaukratie und Beamtenthum in Deutschland, I. Preussen* (Hamburg, 1844), pp. 34–5. This passage is quoted in Herman Finer, *Theory and Practice of Modern Government* (New York, 1949), p. 738. I have followed Finer's translation.

made the first academic analysis of the concept.[55] Mohl noted that
'since a relatively short time ago, in every place and on the most varied
occasions, talk has been about "bureaucracy"' but, besides being
about 'a social power or a system of rule', the content of this talk varied
greatly within and between social groups. Nobles complained about
denial of their privileges and the inconsiderateness of officials; indus-
trialists complained 'on the one hand about indolence and apathy and
on the other about unnecessary and harmful overgoverning'. Some
of them alleged 'ignorance of life and of industry' while others complained of 'clumsiness and pedantry in administration'; churches
complained that the bureaucracy interfered with a 'free and autonomous religious life'; artisans of useless paperwork; scholars of bureaucrats' ignorance; municipalities of interference; and statesmen of delay
and obstructionism. Notwithstanding this bewildering variety, Mohl
insists that 'bureaucracy' does refer to something real and that what it
really means is:

> the false conception of the tasks of the state accomplished through an
> organism of numerous professional officials, in part composed of very
> mediocre members satisfied with purely formal conduct and liable to
> much personal incivility.

Typically, Mohl is more successful in distinguishing between existing
conceptions of bureaucracy than in devising a satisfactory and inclu-
sive definition which links them.

Criticisms of both the nature and characteristics of bureaucracy and
its effects on citizens were prominent in early English accounts. As
Albrow has noted,[56] they were joined by a peculiarly British theme—
bureaucracy was foreign. De Gournay's and Balzac's assessment of
French government was endorsed with special fervour by English
writers. Throughout the century 'bureaucracy' was referred to as the
unfortunate 'Continental' (usually meaning Prussian or French) way
of doing things, which the English were wise to avoid. An article on the
French education system published in 1836 suggests some of the
manifold evils of bureaucracy. Bureaucrats are omnipresent, and in
universities, 'the obscure power of the *Bureaucratie*, that is, of the
menials of the university, is . . . felt in all appointments except the very
highest.' They are the instruments of French centralizers whose
doctrines Englishmen abhor 'because they know that by them is
formed the most complete, the most rigorous, and the most complicated, system of despotism the world has ever known'. On the other
hand, the bureaucracy is inefficient, but to the French, 'if the
machinery is found to be inefficient the remedy is add more

---

[55] Robert von Mohl, 'Ueber Bureaukratie', *Staatsrecht, Völkerrecht und Politik*
(reprinted Graz, 1962) II, chap. 2, pp. 99–130.
[56] Albrow, pp. 21–6.

machinery. It never occurs to Frenchmen, who have a lead in this matter, that the plan is inefficient, simply because it is machinery, as far as men can be changed into tools'. In large governmental organizations men 'having no other original *esprit du corps* than what their salaries and officers excite ... will not sink into but will never rise out of the character of a *bureaucratie*'.[57]

Similar points were made about Prussian bureaucracy in an unrelieved attack on 'Prussia and the Prussian System' which appeared in 1842.[58] Again, the bureaucracy is seen as all-powerful and everywhere 'the King of Prussia through his hundred armed bureaucracy literally manufactures everything in his dominions'; 'as there is no church even now better organized externally than the Romish, so there is no government which, by virtue of an all-insinuating bureaucracy, is more complete in its machinery and more strong physically in its framework than the Prussian.' The effects of the bureaucracy are insidious: 'For this grand privilege of being governed by a scientific bureaucracy the Prussians make a sad sacrifice; they sacrifice the independence, the energy, the enterprise, of the great mass of the people. The governors govern well, but the governed, by overmuch cherishing, are made weak; they are mere clods; political nullities; children certainly in every sense.' Finally, much of the bureaucracy's work is simply self-generated: 'The principle being ... that the people shall be allowed to do nothing for themselves, it follows as a necessary consequence that a vast multitude of men must be paid at the public expense for doing that which in other countries nature is allowed to do spontaneously, as the rain falls and the wind blows.'

British opponents of centralization frequently linked its sins with those of bureaucracy: Joshua Toulmin-Smith, the leading member of the Anti-Centralization Union founded in 1854, attacked centralization as 'the system of Functionarism and Bureaucratic control', and the Union's objects were:

> to resist the adoption, renewal or extended powers, of Boards or Functionaries for controlling local or independent action; to oppose Bureaucracy as a Government system; and to promote practical measures for developing and extending municipal and parochial self-government, guaranteed by and responsible to unevadible and certain law.[59]

Hostility to bureaucracy ran deep, even among those who saw an important role for the state. Thomas Carlyle, in a series of articles

[57] Arnaut O'Donnel, 'State Education in France', *Blackwood's Edinburgh Magazine* XL (1836), pp. 580, 583.

[58] J. S. Blackie, 'Prussia and the Prussian System', *Westminster Review* XXXVII (1842), pp. 135–71.

[59] J. Toulmin-Smith, *Government and its Measures* (London, 1857), p. 2, quoted in W. H. Greenleaf, 'Toulmin-Smith and the British Political Tradition', *Public Administration* LIII (1975), pp. 25–44 at p. 42.

published in 1850, exhorts government to be more intelligent and intelligently active. He insists that 'the State is a reality and not a dramaturgy; it exists here to render existence possible, existence desirable and noble for the State's subjects,'[60] and he strenuously attacks 'the notion that any Government is or can be a No-Government without the deadliest peril to all noble interests of the Commonwealth'. Nevertheless, whatever the new and active government he hopes for will be, it will not involve bureaucracy: 'Of the Continental nuisance called "Bureaucracy",—if this should alarm any reader,—I can see no risk or possibility in England. Democracy is hot enough here, fierce enough; it is perennial, universal, clearly invincible among us henceforth. No danger it should let itself be flung in chains by sham-secretaries of the Pedant species, and accept their vile Age of Pinchbeck for its Golden Age!'

The themes I have outlined recur constantly in the nineteenth century, but they are also joined by more specialized, discriminating uses of the term. 'Bureaucracy' maintained the pejorative connotations I have described. Indeed, these connotations could be called on when required, just as in contemporary polemics, an attack on 'bureaucracy' appears to have more force than the same attack directed at 'officials'. But conceptions do emerge which recognize that there are differences other than those of power and size between groups of officials and modes of organization.

One of the most important of these conceptions transfers attention from officials as a social group to the mode of organization of the institutions in which they serve. This use of 'bureaucracy' is important as a forerunner of the widespread twentieth-century habit of applying the terms 'bureaucracies' or 'bureaucratic' to institutions rather than to the officials employed in them; these latter are thus called bureaucrats as much because they work in the institutions as because they are members of a social group. In Germany especially, the transformation of the civil service from collegial to monocratic organization led to the use of 'bureaucracy' by many writers to refer to the monocratic organization into bureaux as distinct from collegial administration. Heinzen accepted that bureaucracy arose in organizations of this form, though he quickly added that he was more interested in its essence than its form. In 1846, Mohl suggested wrongly that this sense had historical priority over the pejorative, less discriminating uses of the term. Even in 1873 the French *Dictionnaire générale de la politique* explained to Frenchmen that this was the German use of the term. By the nineteenth century it was generally agreed that monocratic ministries were more efficient and potentially more powerful than colleges; defining bureaucracy as a form of organization could therefore easily slide

[60] Thomas Carlyle, 'Downing Street' and 'The New Downing Street', reprinted in *Collected Works* (London, 1898) XX, pp. 87–171.

into polemic against bureaucracy as rule by officials. The link between the two conceptions is clearly brought out in a passage which Albrow quotes from the Brockhaus encyclopedia of 1819:

> The modern form of public administration executes with the pen everything which previously would have been done by word of mouth. Hence many pens are set into motion. In every branch of administration bureaux or offices have multiplied, and have been accorded so great a power over citizens that in many countries a veritable bureaucracy, rule by offices, has developed. This bureaucracy becomes increasingly dangerous as the previous custom of conducting business through *collegia* falls into disuse. The directors of a bureau, in addition to their authority over its personnel, have acquired an often inordinate amount of power over citizens at large.[61]

Albrow suggests that 'the identification of the bureau system and bureaucracy made an extremely useful polemical point' for opponents of the German state, who could begin with an apparently neutral definition of bureaucracy as monocratic administration, and then ascribe to it all the negative connotations of bureacracy as government by officials.

A similar leap from analysis of a form of administrative organization to exploitation of the many polemical advantages of 'bureaucracy' was taken in 1864 by the French sociologist, Frédéric le Play, whose *La Réforme sociale en France* contained a long chapter condemning what he called bureaucracy in European government. He apologized for introducing into social science 'this hybrid word created by a light literature', but nonetheless used it. Rather than choose the common approach of defining bureaucracy as the *cause* of sundry ills, le Play identified it with the ills themselves, with what in Soviet discussion is often called 'bureaucratism'. He regarded bureaucracy as a 'vice', an 'illness' which occurred when actual power in government was wielded by anonymous middle- and lower-level functionaries who were accountable to no one. It could only be avoided by making heads of bureaux *actually* responsible for what was done within them, as happened, le Play claimed, in England. From this relatively modest beginning, le Play goes on to attribute most conceivable dangers of government, and some not so conceivable, to this diseased form of administration. Bureaucrats are not only inefficient, arrogant, irresponsible and lazy, but they indirectly encourage revolution by weakening respect for authority; they erode the role of parents, especially by their proliferation of complex examinations for which special training is necessary; they encourage communism; they destroy individual initiative and keep subjects as children (a common

---

[61] *Allgemeine deutsche Real-Encyclopaedie oder Conversationslexicon* (Leipzig, 1819) II, p. 158, Albrow, p. 28.

nineteenth-century criticism); and because of their power lust they are in fact the cause of excessive centralization.

This looseness, not to say wantonness, of the term was as common in nineteenth-century uses of 'bureaucracy' as it is today. Nevertheless, a writer's response to the growth or increased importance of state power did not have to be expressed as a response to 'bureaucracy' or have much to do with what he understood by that word. This is especially true of a greater and more rigorous thinker than we have yet discussed, John Stuart Mill.

Though he contrasted England favourably with the 'bureaucracy-ridden nations of the continent',[62] Mill was less interested than his contemporaries in drawing facile polemical contrasts between England and Europe. While he used the concept 'bureaucracy' and used it suggestively, he did not use it simply as a blanket characterization of continental over-government but as a specific, almost technical description of one way of governing. According to Mill, this way of governing occurs where 'the work of government has been in the hands of governors by profession; which is the essence and meaning of bureaucracy' (*ibid.* p. 245).

For Mill, 'bureaucracy' has to do with expertise and professionalism. He has often been taken to be saying far more about bureaucracy than he actually is, however, because this has been ignored. For example, in the *Principles of Political Economy* Mill puts forward a number of arguments against the growth of governmental functions and powers, and Robson says of these that they include 'almost every consideration advanced by opponents of bureaucratic growth'.[63] This may be true of later (and earlier) writers, but only one of the six arguments Mill advances has to do with what *he* calls bureaucracy. The other arguments are directed against the growth of governmental activity *in general* and have nothing specifically to do with 'bureaucracy' or bureaucratic government. Nor does Mill suggest that they do. In the *Principles* only one sort of problem is raised which, while not necessarily confined to bureaucracies, is necessarily faced by them. Mill considers this problem of central importance, and raises it first of all as his final argument for *laissez-faire*; several pages later, he repeats it to deal with a supposed exception to the principle, and uses the word 'bureaucracy' for the first time in these pages. Anticipating James Burnham, Mill concedes that where individuals manage concerns only 'by delegated agency' as in joint stock companies, the interested persons (the share-holders) are no closer to the power exercised by directors than individuals would be to enter-

[62] *Representative Government* (1861), in John Stuart Mill, *Utilitarianism, Liberty, Representative Government* (London, Everyman reprint, 1964), p. 227.

[63] J. M. Robson, *The Improvement of Mankind: the Social and Political Thought of John Stuart Mill* (Toronto, 1968), p. 208.

prises managed by public officers. Nevertheless, Mill rehearses the arguments against government intervention, and pre-eminent among them is 'the [still greater]⁶⁴ inexpediency of concentrating in a dominant bureaucracy, all the skill and experience in the management of large interests, and all the power of organized action, existing in the community; a practice which keeps the citizens in a relation to the government like that of children to their guardians, and is a main cause of the inferior capacity for political life which has hitherto character-ized the over-governed countries of the Continent, whether with or without the forms of representative government.'

In the light of Mill's definition of bureaucracy it is not hard to see why excessive concentration of talent and initiative was regarded as a likely consequence of it. But while over-government of any kind presented dangers for Mill, not every kind of over-government was bureaucratic and not every kind of danger was a bureaucratic danger. Some writers have considered it significant that in *On Liberty* (1859), 'the dangers of bureaucracy were singled out for the peroration of that immensely influential essay.'⁶⁵ But Mill himself says: 'I have reserved for the last place a large class of questions respecting the limits of government interference, which, though closely connected with the subject of this essay, do not, in strictness belong to it. These are cases in which the reasons against interference do not turn upon the principle of liberty.'⁶⁶ And Mill is again talking generally about the limits of *governmental* rather than *bureaucratic* intervention. Within this discussion, what Mill held to be the 'third and most important reason for objecting to government interference' was not the danger of bureaucracy but the dangers, already referred to in the *Principles*, involved in adding unnecessarily to governmental power. This is a general problem. What *is* true is that powerful governments become particularly dangerous if they are staffed in the most efficient way by the ablest men in society. For in those *special* circumstances, a specific and important problem would arise: 'All the enlarged culture and practised intelligence in the country, except the purely speculative, would be concentrated in a numerous bureaucracy, to whom alone the rest of the community would look for all things' (*ibid.*, p. 166). It would become the focus of all ambition, and the people outside the bureaucracy would fail to be 'accustomed to transact their own business.... Where everything is done through the bureaucracy, nothing to which the bureaucracy is really adverse can be done at all' (p. 167). Part of one of the arguments in *On Liberty*, then, has to do with bureaucracy, and it is clear that it is important to Mill. But he is dealing with much besides bureaucracy when he discusses the limits

⁶⁴ These words were omitted after the 1848 and 1849 editions of the *Principles*.
⁶⁵ Albrow, p. 22.
⁶⁶ *On Liberty*, in John Stuart Mill, pp. 163–4.

of government intervention, and it is a distortion of his view both of the dangers of such intervention and of the specific problems associated with bureaucracies to run the discussions together.

Moreover, despite Schaffer's claim that Mill's 'opposition to bureaucracy was unambiguous',[67] the truth is that his attitude to bureaucracy is quite ambiguous. Mill moved, I believe, between at least three uses of 'bureaucracy', and while none of these is ruled out by his definition he comes to reject claims for bureaucracy in two of the uses while advocating its cultivation in the third sense. Crudely stated, the distinction is between bureaucracy as a *form* of government, to be contrasted with democracy, oligarchy and so on; as the real locus of governing power, whatever the form; and as an *instrument* of government, to be contrasted with non-professional administration. Since Mill does not bother to made these distinctions explicit, the sense in which 'bureaucracy' is used must be gleaned from the context in which it appears.

Mill clearly used 'bureaucracy' to refer to a form of government. The definition I have quoted occurs in the context of a discussion of the claims of rivals to representative government as the 'ideally best polity', and Mill concludes that 'the comparison as to the intellectual attributes of a government, has to be made between a representative democracy and a bureaucracy; all other governments may be left out of account.' But though bureaucracies are expert, operate by 'well tried and well considered traditional maxims' and are staffed by people trained in the practical requirements of their tasks, 'the disease which afflicts bureaucratic governments, and which they usually die of, is routine. They perish by the immutability of their maxims; and, still more, by the universal law that whatever becomes a routine loses its vital principle, and having no longer a mind acting within it, goes on revolving mechanically though the work it is intended to do remains undone.'[68] Bureaucracies need elements of free opposition, for otherwise they will become stultified over time.

The same defects will exist where the bureaucracy is powerful enough to be the *real* governing power. We have already seen the effects of a dominant bureaucracy on citizens' capacities for self-reliance, but the point is also made, in *On Liberty* and elsewhere, that an overpowerful bureaucracy will of necessity do its job badly. Unless a governing body can receive informed criticism from outside itself, it will occasionally be entranced by 'some half-examined crudity which has struck the fancy of some leading member of the corps',[69]

---

[67] B. Schaffer, 'The Idea of the Ministerial Department: Bentham, Mill and Bagehot', in his *The Administrative Factor: Papers in Organization, Politics and Development* (London, 1973), p. 17.

[68] *Representative Government*, p. 246.

[69] *On Liberty*, p. 168.

but usually it will simply be trapped by routine.

However, in the third sense in which the concept is used, bureaucracy is a prerequisite to good government. While Mill argues that the bureaucracy must not absorb all available talent, it is this absorption which is dangerous, rather than the mere existence of a bureaucracy itself. Indeed, in this third sense, bureaucracy is the thing endangered, for, 'if we would possess permanently a skilful and efficient body of functionaries ... if we would not have our bureaucracy degenerate into a pedantocracy, this body must not engross all the occupations which form and cultivate the faculties required for the government of mankind' (*ibid.*, p. 168).

One of the central dilemmas for Mill was to reconcile the need for freedom with the need for skilled government. He valued both and indeed thought that neither was attainable without the other; 'to secure as much of the advantages of centralized power and intelligence as can be had without turning into governmental channels too great a proportion of the general activity—is one of the most difficult and complicated questions in the art of government' (p. 168). In the 'ideally best polity', governments would be selected, watched and 'when needful' controlled by their constituents; the actual business of governing, however, had to be done, or at the very least closely supervised, by the skilled—skilled legislators and bureaucrats.

Mill's respect for expertise and professionalism was, of course, not particularly exceptional in the nineteenth century. Given the contrast between the highly professionalized Prussian bureaucrat, with whom the word was in any case associated, and the English civil servant, for whose training schemes were only beginning to be devised, the association of bureaucracy with professionalism was not rare.[70] But Mill was less concerned than many of his contemporaries to fill the word with purely polemical ballast. He also paid attention to distinctions between circumstances in which bureaucracy might be useful and circumstances in which it might do harm. Unfortunately, making distinctions has not always been the strong suit of writers on bureaucracy.

[70] Bagehot also made this association but he was far more suspicious of purely 'expert' bodies than Mill was. See Walter Bagehot, *The English Constitution* (reprinted London, 1966), esp. pp. 195–9.

2

Saint-Simon, Marx and the non-governed society

Martin Krygier

A perfect society has not a government, but an administration.

Wilhelm Weitling, *Guarantees of Harmony and Freedom* (1842).

Europe in the nineteenth century was crowded with theorists and ideologues who agreed that 'society', rather than politics, was fundamental in human affairs, that societies evolved and changed greatly over time, and that therefore, political arrangements had to be adjusted to such changes. Moreover, these writers, and especially the revolutionaries among them, were extraordinarily confident that they knew the *direction* of historical change and the stage which had been reached: they shared a profound faith in progress and a belief that the goal of this progress—a transition from existing society to a new and in every way better society—was very near.

I Saint-Simon and the organization of industrial society: administration without bureaucracy

Politics in the old society

In their critiques of existing political and administrative arrangements, nineteenth-century revolutionary social theorists contributed a good deal to anti-bureaucratic polemic, but their conviction that a totally new society was attainable, indeed inevitable, and that political forms were malleable derivatives of society, frequently resulted in the dissolution of many conventional problems of political organization and leadership. Common to much revolutionary social theory and to much nineteenth-century sociology was the belief that politics as commonly understood would be irrelevant to and transcended in the new society, the birth of which they were witnessing. As Wolin observes:

> In the nineteenth century the anti-political impulses nurtured by classical liberalism took on a depth and pervasiveness unmatched in previous centuries. 'The irksome situation' of today, Proudhon declared, was due to *'une certaine maladie de l'opinion ... qu'Aristote ... a nommé politique'*. The abolition of the political was proclaimed by almost

every important thinker, and most projects for a future society excluded political activity from the routine of daily life.[1]

The thought of the French social theorist and visionary, Claude-Henri de Rouvroy, Comte de Saint-Simon (1760–1825), is striking in that he shared his contemporaries' order of priorities, their faith in progress and contempt for the political, and yet did not allow his vision of a new society simply to dissolve all the problems that had so preoccupied earlier writers on politics and administration. Instead he took seriously, and devoted considerable attention to, the kind of central administrative organization appropriate to the coming society. Saint-Simon is exceptional, too, in the amount of attention he pays to the *administrative imperatives* of modern society, the need for co-ordination of a 'non-political' kind and its characteristics, the permeation of government by industrial concerns and requirements, and the necessity for the state to utilize managers, scientists, technicians, engineers.

Saint-Simon is not a consistent thinker, or even, at times, a particularly coherent one. His works are full of bad history, bad philosophy and bad applied science. Yet they have the effect of a kind of intellectual catherine wheel. Again and again one is startled by bright and sometimes astonishingly prescient *aperçus*, which often appear fleetingly and disappear again, undeveloped or even contradicted by their author. Saint-Simon's work embodies many of the themes and preoccupations, strengths and weaknesses, ambivalences and tensions which recur in later revolutionary social theory. But more than much of the latter, it points to central and pervasive characteristics of the modern world.

Saint-Simon believed that the society in which he lived was undergoing, and also approaching the end of, a profound crisis, a crisis, he wrote, in which 'society today presents this extraordinary phenomenon: *a nation which is essentially industrial, yet whose government is essentially feudal*'.[2] In putting forward that paradox, he was making two implicit claims—one about the general relationship between societies and the institutions which exist within them, and another about the specific incompatibility between feudalism and industrialism.

Saint-Simon's general claim—later, in revised and sharpened form, made even more familiar by Marx—is that political institutions cannot endure or even operate effectively unless they mesh closely with the state of 'social forces' in their epoch. The particular predicament of Western society stemmed, for Saint-Simon, from the co-existence and

[1] Sheldon Wolin, *Politics and Vision* (Boston, 1960), p. 414.
[2] *Oeuvres complètes de Saint-Simon et Enfantin* (Aalen, 1963–4) [henceforth cited in the text as *OC*] XXXVII, p. 33.

competition of two quite different kinds of forces—feudal and industrial. Even after the French Revolution (which he considered a failure for this reason) feudal institutions and elites still persisted, if falteringly, and sought to retain their dominance. The ostensible temporal and spiritual leaders of society were feudal left-overs, relics. But the 'real', 'positive' forces were not feudal, they were industrial.

One difference between feudal and industrial societies lay in the *goals* they served. Feudal society was devoted to military conquest. Military government, dominated by men of the sword (*sabreurs*) organized for war and conquest and ruling by authoritarian command backed by force, was therefore appropriate to it. Such government is quite inappropriate to the goal of industrial society, which is production. Industrial society is essentially pacific; its development is impeded by precisely those activities that are most characteristic of the military way of working.

A second difference between feudal and industrial forces could be seen in the classes associated with each, and one of the clearest indices of the current crisis was the absolute uselessness of the feudal, and ostensibly ruling, class. For classes are of quite fundamental importance in Saint-Simon's theory, as they were to be in Marx's. Class position is determined by social function, and carries with it characteristic ways of acting, values, competence and beliefs. Except for one mention of individual anomalies such as Saint-Simon himself, whom the 'hazards of birth' had placed in the class of nobles, there is no discussion in Saint-Simon's work of people betraying their class, or of sources of individual action that stem from something other than class position. There is throughout the unruffled assumption that all one needs to know of a person's worth and usefulness can be got from knowing his class. In one of his most famous sallies, and the first, if for perverse reasons, to gain him notoriety, since it led to his prosecution for sedition, Saint-Simon wrote:

> Let us suppose that France were suddenly to lose her fifty best physicists, chemists, physiologists, mathematicians, poets, painters, sculptors, musicians, writers; her fifty best mechanical engineers, civil engineers, artillery experts, architects, doctors, surgeons, pharmacists, seamen, clockmakers; her fifty best bankers; her two hundred best merchants; her six hundred best farmers [he lists a wide array of artisans] ... and one hundred other persons of unspecified occupations, the most capable in the sciences, fine arts, arts and professions, making in all the three thousand leading scholars, artists and artisans of France.

> Since these men are the Frenchmen who are the most essential, those who direct the enterprises most useful to the nation, and those who render it productive in the sciences, fine arts, arts and professions, they are really the flower of French society; they are of all Frenchmen the most useful to their country, they gain for it the greatest glory, they hasten most

its civilization and its prosperity. The nation would become a body without a soul as soon as it lost them.... France would require at least a whole generation to repair this misfortune, for men who distinguish themselves in works of positive utility are real anomalies and nature is not prodigal of anomalies, especially those of this kind.

Let us pass to another assumption. Suppose that France preserves all the men of genius that she possesses in the sciences, fine arts, arts and professions but has the misfortune to lose in the same day M. the King's brother, M. le duc d'Angoulême [etc.]. ...

Suppose that France loses at the same time all the great officers of the crown, all the ministers (with or without departments), all the councillors of State, all the *Maitres des requêts*, marshals, cardinals, archbishops, bishops, vicars-general and canons, all the prefects and sub-prefects, all the government employees, all the judges, and in addition the ten thousand richest proprietors of those who live as nobles.

This accident would certainly distress the French, because they are good people.... But this loss of thirty thousand individuals, reputed to be the most important in the State, would only grieve them for purely sentimental reasons, for no political harm to the State would result from it [*OC* xx, pp. 17–21].

The simple test of political institutions and political people for Saint-Simon here is whether they are useful to industry. None of the second group was, and consequently none was of any use to France. And since men of industry were in fact subordinated to princes and other *dominateurs* and *routiniers*, one obviously had a *monde renversé*. Moreover, feudal officials were not simply the least useful of men, while the *industriels* were the most useful; the carriers of feudalism did actual harm. So far as I know, Saint-Simon never called them *bureaucrates* nor derided them collectively for being a *bureaucratie*. But he did complain that these government officials treated their positions as theirs by right and not as sources of duties, that they governed in their own interests instead of those of the governed, that they therefore sought high pay for themselves and exacted high taxes from the people. They were not merely useless but were an immense, growing, and expensive crowd of incompetent parasites. Since they had the same needs and desires as producers, but produced nothing themselves, 'these people necessarily live on the work of others, either they are given or they take; in a word, they are idlers, that is to say, thieves' (*OC* xviii, p. 130).

For Saint-Simon the fault did not lie primarily with the members of the feudal classes as individuals, but in the institution and activities of pre-industrial government itself. In a society devoted to production, the needs of industry and commerce are of pivotal importance. But control or regulation by *government* is inherently and absolutely inimical to those needs, and to attempt, as feudal government does, 'to control everything, to submit everything to rules, to calculations, is the greatest of human follies' (*OC* xviii, p. 77). For, as *l'immortel* Adam Smith had shown, industry develops spontaneously by an 'interior force', and to meddle with this development from outside is to destroy it. In his earlier writings Saint-Simon is prepared to allow government a slightly greater role than in his later works, but at all times, if government is necessary, it is only a 'necessary evil' to prevent anarchy.

In industrial society, then, the proper role of government is to be an agent not a principal, the *'chargé d'affairs* of society' and not in any sense its directing power. Government functions should be extremely circumscribed—all that it is appropriate for government to do is to protect workers from the unproductive activities of idlers and to maintain order, security and freedom in production. Even this policing function, Saint-Simon suggests, may become, with the development of industrial society, 'almost totally the collective responsibility of all the citizens' (*OC* xx, p. 202). Government at such time will merely prevent disorder, and since disorder will be rare, the task will not be onerous.

Administration in the new society

Saint-Simon is not merely a critic of existing institutions. He is an ideologist with a vision of the good society, certain that it is attainable. His critique of contemporary society forms only the backdrop for his portrayal of the inevitable future course of history and for his demonstration that what is presently inappropriate will become non-existent.

Some of the characteristics of this final system will not surprise anyone familiar with the prophecies of European ideologists or, for that matter, of Melanesian cargo cultists. When industrial society is fully developed, the whole basis and rationale of governmental domination will have disappeared. For industrial society is a co-operative activity of producers, all of whom play some productive role and all of whom have worth by virtue of their active participation. In the words of *L'Organisateur*, the leaders of this industrial co-operation do not need to regiment or command subjects, they combine with and give direction to partners (*associés, sociétaires*) and collaborators. The only commands exercised by the new leaders will be those strictly necessary 'to maintain good order in work, that is to say very few. Industrial capacity of its nature loathes to exercise arbitrariness as much as to support it. . . . Besides, in a society of workers, everything tends naturally to order, disorder comes always, in the last analysis, from idlers' (*OC* xx, pp. 151–2). National hatreds will disappear, since 'this spirit of discord and of hatred is essentially contrary to the industrial spirit; it is nothing but the result of feudal influence' (*OC*

XIX, pp. 62–3). Industry, he explains in another passage, 'is one, all its members are united by the general interests of production, by the needs that they all have for security in work and freedom of trade' (*OC* XIX, p. 47).

Notwithstanding this idyllic vision, Saint-Simon does turn his attention to the problem so many of his contemporaries ignore or merely hint at. For Saint-Simon never suggests that the coming decline in the role of government implies or is likely to lead to any decline in the need for organization and co-ordination of the extremely complex and interconnected affairs of industrial society. Government, he frequently says, will give way to administration, and in his scheme of things administration is no small affair. Industrial society *must* be well administered by those most talented to do so, for otherwise it will fall into anarchy, and this is a fate even worse than that of being governed. Administrative capacity, then, is the 'first capacity in politics' (*OC* XIX, p. 201); once a nation is well administered, the form of government is of little moment (cf. *OC* XX, p. 191).

To what extent is Saint-Simon's aphoristic contrast between government and administration a mere verbal sleight of hand, and to what extent does it represent distinct ways of conducting public affairs? A large part of what Saint-Simon has in mind is suggested by his famous prediction that in industrial society the government of men will be replaced by the administration of things (see *OC* XX, pp. 126–7 and 192). The contrast here appears to be that between military government or command of men by the explicit or implicit use of coercion and the activity of, say, an artisan who is directly related through his work to his raw materials and his product.

But there must be a good deal more to the story than this, for Saint-Simon's schemes are riddled with men instructing, exhorting, managing and organizing other men. *Savants*, for instance, are responsible for educating everyone, and in one scheme they are to devise and organize the teaching of a national catechism in which every Frenchman must pass an examination before being admitted to citizenship. Artists are required to explain the benefits of the new system and the horrors of the old; businessmen must manage large numbers of people in factories and on farms. Those key figures responsible for the *haute administration* of society have, in one way or another, to run the whole national enterprise. The men administering things, in other words, have themselves to be administered. And what is this if not government?

Elements of Saint-Simon's answer are scattered through his writings. He allowed 'administration' of men where it was 'secondary' and 'co-operates in the exercise of a greater action on nature' (*OC* XX, p. 192). Industrial management is an example of this sort of activity. The cohesive, harmonious, nature of industrial society eliminates in large part the need for force; and it is force, above all, which for Saint-Simon characterizes the activities of government.

A third difference between the new and the old is of central importance in Saint-Simon's argument. Once more it can be approached through a Saint-Simonian aphorism. 'In the old system', Saint-Simon writes, 'society was essentially governed by men; in the new it is governed by nothing but principles' (*OC* xx, p. 197). Here the technocratic strain in Saint-Simon emerges particularly clearly. The goal of industrial society is given: it is to increase production and prosperity through utilization of the sciences, fine arts, arts and professions. For Saint-Simon there is no room for dispute about the goal: it is clear and unambiguous and capable of generating open and precise criteria for the judgement of performance. What is required of the people is that they cultivate the talents best suited to such judgement. There is no need and indeed no place for blind obedience to a ruler; there is only a place for deference to tested and acknowledged expertise. It is in this context that Auguste Comte's prophetic insight into the role of the engineer in industrial society occurs, and it is in the same context that he writes, as Saint-Simon's secretary in Saint-Simon's name: 'I do not say a new power rises beside each of the two old powers [temporal and spiritual], but a *capacity* rises beside a *power*' (*OC* xx, p. 86). Given the goal, all that remains to be done is to adjust the means available for attaining it, and this is a purely technical matter, a matter of reasoning, of expertise, not of will or of power. 'The action of governing', Saint-Simon himself writes, 'is then at nought or next to nought, in so far as it signifies the action of commanding. All the questions which ought to suggest themselves in such a political system . . . are eminently positive and judgeable; decisions can only be the result of scientific demonstrations, absolutely independent of all human will, and susceptible of discussion by all those who have the degree of instruction sufficient to understand them' (*OC* xx, pp. 198–9). Politics, in other words, gives way to technique.

Saint-Simon is not, however, prepared to leave it at that. For production and the application of technique must be organized and co-ordinated in the most useful way by the class of people best suited to this task. And it is therefore of crucial importance to determine what is the best form of organization and who is best fitted for it. It is in his thoughts on how best to organize the application of technique that the *industrial* focus of Saint-Simon's thought is most apparent. For what Saint-Simon does is take completely seriously his claim that the nation *is* industry. When he says that 'France has become a great factory and the French Nation a great workshop' (*OC* xxiii, p. 91), he is not merely indulging in metaphor, nor is he simply saying that the nation is absolutely dependent on industry, though he certainly believes this. He is also pointing, as Max Weber later pointed, to the tremendous similarities in the operations and management of state and non-state enterprises. If the state really is thought of as a factory, then it becomes more plausible to argue that the problems to be coped with by a state will have a lot in common with those facing industry, that therefore the skills involved in coping with the latter will be required to cope with the former, and that if some men have these skills and others do not, this fact should be socially recognized.

Saint-Simon frequently says that government by the *désoeuvrés* will be replaced by administration by the *industriels*, but this latter concept is somewhat rough around the edges. Especially in his earlier writings, 'industry' is used in a very broad sense to include 'every kind of useful work, theory as well as application, works of the mind as well as those of the hand' (*OC* xviii, p. 165). Elsewhere, and particularly later, it suffers an unannounced narrowing to include only the works of practical men as distinct from those of artists and scientists. All are useful but not all are *industriels*. Other distinctions and imprecisions muddy the picture further, and in any case, whatever precision can be given the term, it is clear that Saint-Simon does not intend the leaders of industrial society to be co-extensive with it. For the idea of a proper industrial hierarchy pervades Saint-Simon's work. As with so many words used by him, the 'equality' he favours must be understood in a quite special sense; it is apparent that in industrial society some *industriels* will be more equal than others. Industrial society, Saint-Simon writes, allows 'the greatest degree of equality possible' (*OC* xxxvii, p. 35). But what is possible, and Comte adds, desirable (*OC* xx, p. 151), is not *l'égalité turque*, 'the equal admissibility to the exercise of arbitrary power', but its 'contrary ... true equality ... industrial equality which consists in each deriving benefits from society exactly proportionate to his social contribution, that is to say to his positive capacity, to the useful employment he makes of his means' (*OC* xxii, p. 17). The meritocratic judgement implicit in this definition is consistent both with his attack on privileges of birth and with his constant appeals to and praise for 'the most important', 'the most capable', 'the most positive' *industriels*, those who should direct 'the general interests of society ... [since their] capacities are of the most general and most positive utility to society' (*OC* xxxix, pp. 3–4). To grant status on grounds of birth is, on Saint-Simon's theory, quite irrational since the criterion is irrelevant to one's productive potential. But those performing important roles deserved their high status, and were the only persons who did. 'There are today', he wrote, 'no other *notables* in France, with the exception of *savants* and artists, than the heads of works of agriculture, of manufacture and of commerce.' He goes on to explain:

(I understand here by *heads* [*chefs*] of different works, all the *industriels* who are not purely *workmen* [*ouvriers*], that is to say executants, and who take a more or less major part in the direction of works). It is exclusively with them that the power to act on the people is found, because it is to them that the people is habitually subordinated in its day-to-day relations [*OC* xxii, pp. 217–18].

Saint-Simon stresses the importance of educating the masses and increasing their capacity for choice and self-reliance, and there is good reason to think that he would welcome upward mobility among the men of industry. But the national enterprise will be run by the most talented, selected by a process left opaque. And while a worker might somehow rise to leadership, the distinction at any point of time between leaders and led will be clear.

However, it is far from clear how much 'administration' these talented leaders will be required to do. Saint-Simon speaks, as it were, with two voices. One voice constantly explains the cheapness and efficiency of having national affairs managed by *industriels*. Essentially their function is reduced to preparing the budget of industrial administration. One is reminded again and again of 'the fundamental truth in finance: *that the budget should be made by those who are interested in economy and in the good employment of public monies*' (*OC* xxi, p. 142), and there is never any doubt that Saint-Simon is referring to the leaders of industry. Beyond their particular skills within a branch of industry, 'there is a capacity which is common to all of them; it is the administrative capacity; it is the capacity necessary to make a good budget, and they are the only ones who possess this capacity; they were its creators' (*OC* xxi, p. 137). They alone 'make a permanent application of it, and at their personal risks. Thus when the temporal power is entrusted to them, the only impulse of their habits, eminently economical, will lead them to reduce the costs of management and administration to the lowest rate possible' (*OC* xxii, p. 178).

Saint-Simon has variously been seen as the precursor of fascism, socialism, and of what the contemporary Israeli historian Jacob Talmon calls 'totalitarian technocracy'. It is therefore important to keep in mind the *modesty* of central administration as he characterizes it. When asked whether the *industriels* will lose their all-important talents if they devote themselves to national administration, he explains that the public functions of the heads of industry can be discharged on a part-time basis and need not interfere with their private industrial enterprises. This, he points out, is the way in which they already participate in chambers of commerce and manufacture. Anyway, 'in all times those who have directed public affairs, are those who have the fewest occupations.... [In] all Europe ... [it is] the supreme directors of public affairs who hunt the most, give the most festivals, balls, grand repasts, who frequent the most spectacles etc.' (*OC* xxi, p. 149). Elsewhere he explains that the most important *in-*

dustriels will prepare the budget free of charge, and therefore 'this function will only be weakly desired'; in the interests of economy functionaries will be paid only moderately, and thus government places will not be much sought after and their number will diminish considerably. Finally, an order will be established in which a great number of places will be exercised free of charge 'because the rich *oisifs* will find no other means of procuring consideration for themselves' (*OC* XXXVII, p. 10).

But this is not Saint-Simon's only way of speaking. He has another, insistent, voice which rings particularly loud in some of the detailed descriptions he gives of the central authorities of the new society, and of some of the functions they are to perform. The detail of each scheme is deceptive, since it is never the same from scheme to scheme. But there is enough here to bother Adam Smith. In one scheme, admittedly the most detailed, we find that projects of public works are to be drawn up 'to increase the wealth of France and ameliorate the lot of its inhabitants under every heading of utility and amenity' (*OC* XX, p. 51), and these will be carried out by a chamber of execution staffed solely from among the 'principal heads of industrial houses'. The most important activities will be drainage, clearing, cutting of roads, and opening of canals. By the roads and canals will be parks with museums of natural products and industrial products of surrounding countries, facilities for artists who wish to stop, and always there will be musicians inflaming the inhabitants' passion 'for the greatest good of the nation' (*OC* XX, p. 52). These schemes are part of a general programme of redistribution of luxury. Hitherto, 'luxury was concentrated in the palaces of kings, the residences of princes, in the mansions and chateaux of a few powerful men.... The present circumstances are favorable to rendering luxury national. Luxury will become useful and moral when it is the entire nation which enjoys it' (*OC* XX, pp. 52–3).

In what Saint-Simon calls the spiritual sphere—science, education and morality—the amount of work to be done and the amount of control to be exercised is also considerable. This is the sphere of the *savants* and in later works the moralists of the *New Christianity*, and it includes, among other things, complete responsibility for education. These leaders will ensure the observance of ordinances such as the following:

> Considering that the strongest link which can unite the members of a society consists in the similarity of their principles and of their knowledge and that this similarity can only exist as a result of the uniformity of the instruction given to all the citizens, we have directed what follows:
> ARTICLE I   The Institute will be responsible for the surveillance of public instruction; nothing will be taught in the schools contrary to the principles established in the national catechism.

ARTICLE II   The ministers of different cults will be submitted, for their preaching as well as for their teaching of children, to the surveillance of the Institute (*OC* XXII, pp. 238–9).

Even leaving out of the account the various propaganda activities of the artists and the new moralists, the activities of the leaders of industrial society lend a busyness to the central authority which Saint-Simon's first voice does not suggest at all. How is this to be explained? How is it that Saint-Simon could use *both* voices so frequently, apparently with equal conviction? I have no confident answers, only a few tentative suggestions. One is that there may be no real problem at all: to hold someone of Saint-Simon's scattiness of mind responsible for inconsistencies among his desires might be to ask for too much. This may be all that one can say, but if so it should be kept as a last resort, failing more adequate explanation. A second possibility is that Saint-Simon has sufficient faith in the natural harmony of industrial society, the natural deference within it to its leaders, and the obviousness of the principles on which decisions are made, to believe that decisions once taken will not need to be implemented by the central authority, that they will simply be implemented by the populace. Saint-Simon does not say this, but it is, at least, consistent with much that he does say. Third and most important, there is a striking *lacuna* in Saint-Simon's work: Saint-Simon, the ideologist of organization and administration and the withering critic of existing bureaucracies, had no conception of the role and consequence of administrative structures and officials in the new society. There are extraordinarily few references to functionaries in the new society: on one occasion, he explains that *industriels* will not scramble after government places because, *inter alia*, they 'will feel themselves less appropriate to exercise government than those who have become accustomed to this kind of work' (*OC* XXI, p. 134). But if the functionaries are not the old *fainéants*, who are they? Elsewhere, as we have seen, he explains that they will be moderately paid and that therefore their numbers will diminish. What is completely lacking in Saint-Simon is a sense of the pressures which the tasks of the state will exert on its central apparatus, and of the possibility that these tasks will distort the nature of this apparatus beyond recognition. It is an insufficiently remarked upon lapse by this otherwise most modern of men. Yet, the paying of scant attention to the role of functionaries and function-performing institutions in the new society, combined with eagerness that such functions be performed better than ever before, was destined to be far more than a specifically Saint-Simonian idiosyncrasy.

II Marx and the elimination of bureaucracy

There are many fundamental differences between the thought of Saint-Simon and that of Marx. Saint-Simon, for example, paid little attention to conflicts between industrial employers and employees; Marx put such conflicts at the centre of his analysis of modern society. Saint-Simon hoped for a society dominated by industrial managers; Marx, as the world knows, did not. Nevertheless, Marx and later Marxists absorbed,[3] or at least duplicated, to a striking extent central elements of Saint-Simon's thought. In the Marxist tradition, as in Saint-Simon, we repeatedly find Manichaean dichotomies between the old society and the new: command and co-operation; conflict and harmony; government and administration; parasitism and production. Marx and Saint-Simon shared the belief that existing forms of government and of political organization were totally inappropriate to the new society and they shared the faith that they could be readily dispensed with there. In his hopes for, and understanding of, the role of government in the new society, Marx retained the ambivalence and tensions which pervaded Saint-Simon's thought.

Bureaucracy in contemporary society

When Marx wrote of 'bureaucracy' he used the word in the pejorative sense familiar to his contemporaries and to ours: it is probably significant that in his unpublished critique of Hegel's *Philosophy of Right*, Marx explicitly substitutes the word *Bürokratie* for Hegel's *Regierungsgewalt* and *Staatsbeamten*. The pejorative connotations of the word made it a suitable vehicle for Marx's attitude to the institution. In his first explicit attack on bureaucracy, in 1843, Marx complained of the 'presumptuous officiousness' of government officials, and 'the contradiction between the real nature of the world and that ascribed to it in *Büros*'. The individual official, according to Marx, is convinced that 'whether the administrative principles and institutions are good or not is a question that lies outside his sphere, for that can only be judged in *higher* quarters where a wider and deeper *knowledge* of the *official* nature of things, that is, of their connection with the state as a whole, prevails.' Senior officials, on the other hand, 'are bound to have more confidence in *their* officials than in the persons administered, who cannot be presumed to possess the same official understanding'. The result in the Mosel district is that the administration

has everywhere, alongside the actual reality, a *bureaucratic* reality which retains its authority however much the times may change. In addition, the two circumstances, namely, the law of the office hierarchy and the principle that there are two categories of citizens, the active, knowledge-

[3] cf. Georges Gurvitch, 'Saint-Simon et Karl Marx', *Revue Internationale de Philosophie* XIV (1960), pp. 399–416.

able citizens in the administration, and the passive, uninformed citizens who are the object of administration—these two circumstances are mutually complementary.[4]

Marx repeats and expands all of these points in his first critique of the *Philosophy of Right*, where he develops his most extended characterization of bureaucracy and of what Maoists have called the bureaucratic working style, and of what Marx calls the bureaucratic mentality (*Gesinnung*). Although Hegel did not use the word bureaucracy, he described the institution in strikingly Weberian terms, and argued that it played a unique and necessary co-ordinating role between the particularity of civil society—'the battle-field of the individual private interests of all against all'—and the universality of the state, which represented the common, universal interests of all citizens. The bureaucracy is a 'universal estate' which, though itself an estate within civil society, sees to 'the *maintenance* of the *general state interest* and of *legality*'. Its uniqueness as an estate lies in its *function*—not to serve the interests of its members but those of society as a whole. Moreover, this function shapes the consciousness of bureaucrats, whose motivations and orientations to the world are dominated by it.

Like Hegel, the young Marx believed that the rational state must represent the universal interests of the community, but he insisted that the existing state did not do so, and that the prominence of the bureaucracy within it was one of the major reasons why it could not do so. Marx did not quibble with Hegel's description of the structure of bureaucracy. However, Marx insisted that Hegel, and the bureaucracy too, completely distorted its nature, self-conception and modes of behaviour. Far from being a universal estate, bureaucracy is 'a *particular, closed* society within the state',[5] serving its *own*, not the general interest.

Moreover, hierarchy, the central organizing principle of bureaucracy, is not, as Hegel claimed, protection against abuse, but a powerful source of it. It encourages subordinates to rely only on their superiors for rules and policy, superiors to trust only their officials and both to present a united and impassable barrier against outsiders. The bureaucracy shrouds all of its actions in secrecy preserved internally by hierarchy and against the community by its closed, corporate nature. And when it *does* interact with the world, the relationship is essentially, not accidentally, manipulative. The world is clay to be moulded, resistance to be overcome.

Despite the harshness of these remarks, it is clear that, in his Hegel critique, bureaucracy is not Marx's first interest. Already in 1843, well before the materialist interpretation of society had crystallized,

---

[4] Karl Marx and Friedrich Engels, *Werke* (Berlin, 1964) I, p. 186.
[5] Karl Marx and Friedrich Engels, *Collected Works* (London, 1975) III, pp. 45–6.

Marx argued that the 'bureaucracy' which he attacked grew not from any functional imperative or from pressures generated by or within bureaucracies, but primarily as a result of external, and pathological, social divisions. Marx insists, that however independent it appears, bureaucracy *depends* on existing divisions within society. First of all, it depends directly on the separation between civil society and the state, without which it would have no *raison d'être*. Secondly, it rests on the existence of divisions within civil society, of corporations, each concerned with its particular interests. But this second relationship, as Marx explains it, is a more complicated one. On the one hand, the bureaucracy considered other corporations as rivals and fought against them. On the other hand, it *presupposed* the existence of corporations, or at least 'the spirit of corporations',[6] for like them it sought simply to serve its *particular* interests; it tried, therefore, to defeat them, but could not do without them.

In his famous preface to the *Critique of Political Economy*, published in 1859, Marx recalled that his early work on the critique of Hegel had convinced him[7] that law and state were neither autonomous nor emanations from 'the human mind', but stemmed from 'the material conditions of life', civil society, which in turn had to be analysed in terms of political economy. There is, in fact, no evidence of political economy yet in the 1843 critique of Hegel, but there are hints of Marx's later analysis of Bonapartism in his suggestion that the bureaucracy might suppress but still depends on the fundamental groupings in society, that, in a convoluted way, it serves and must serve the groups it oppresses. However, the parallels should not be pressed too far, for in 1843, with his historical materialism not yet fully developed, Marx allowed the bureaucracy more autonomy than he was later prepared to concede. For, while the bureaucracy discussed in 1843 can be said to be serving the corporations in a weak sense, by preserving their existence, Marx does not make the stronger claim that it merely serves their interests. The objection to its control over the state is not that other estates thereby control the bureaucracy, but that the bureaucracy is itself a *particular* interest and that no particular interest should have such control over a state supposed to represent the *whole* of society.

By 1845, however, the doctrine usually taken to characterize 'traditional' or 'classical' Marxism had been developed. For the remainder of his life, Marx insisted that productive economic activity is fundamental in human affairs, that the 'bearers' of relations of production are social classes, and that their conflicts are the motor of historical change. Within each 'mode of production' a funda-

---

[6] *ibid.* p. 45.
[7] 'led to the result that . . .', Karl Marx, *Selected Works* (Moscow, 1951) [henceforth cited in the text as *SW*] I, p. 328.

mentally important distinction exists between that class which owns
the means of production and that which does not; these two classes
are the fundamental actors in each society, and their relationship and
conflict are at the root of the definition and capacity for change of
the society. In this theoretical context, neither bureaucratic activity
nor bureaucrats were or needed to be central foci of attention. In class
societies, bureaucracy was not a class but the servant of classes;
not basic, but, ultimately, subordinate to the ruling class. In capitalist
society, that class is the bourgeoisie.

In *The Holy Family* Marx argued that Napoleon I, who 'still
regarded the *state* as an *end in itself*' represented 'the last battle of
revolutionary terror against the *bourgeois society* which had been proclaimed by this same Revolution', but even he had appreciated and
protected 'the essence of the *modern state* . . . the unhampered development of bourgeois society'.[8] By 1830, the bourgeoisie had matured,

> its *political enlightenment* was now *completed* . . . it no longer considered
> the constitutional representative state as a means for achieving the ideal
> of the state, the welfare of the world and universal human aims but,
> on the contrary, had acknowledged it as the *official* expression of its own
> *exclusive* power and the *political* recognition of its own *special* interests
> [*ibid*. p. 124].

In the *German Ideology* of 1845–6, the argument is extended. Marx
and Engels claim that the state in bourgeois society is simply 'the
form of organization which the bourgeoisie are compelled to adopt
. . . for the mutual guarantee of their property and interests'.[9] The
independent state, they insist, is an anomalous and pre-bourgeois
phenomenon which only remains where estates have declined but
classes are still not fully developed, and where no one group has the
power to overcome the rest.

This tidy and uncomplicated formula dominated Marx's writing
about the modern state until 1851, and while it did so, Marx had
very little to say about bureaucracy. Indeed, the *only* times when Marx
wrote at any length about bureaucracy were when it seemed to him
to be, or to appear to be, independent. When Marx portrayed the
state as clearly subaltern, he had little to say about its bureaucracy;
he was more interested in its commanders and in the activities in which
they were involved. But neither the relationship of bureaucracy to
economic classes, nor Marx's appraisal of it, remained so unproblem-
atic. In particular, Louis Napoleon's *coup d'état* of 2 December 1851,
led to a fundamental shift in Marx's thought and to a deepening of
his analysis of the relationship between a heavily bureaucratized state
and the class structure. The success of the *coup*, the eclipse of
bourgeois representatives, and later, the stability in power of Louis

[8] *Collected Works* IV, p. 123.
[9] *The German Ideology* (Moscow, 1976), p. 99.

Napoleon, would appear to sit uncomfortably with the view of the modern state expressed in *The German Ideology*, and clearly the phenomenon of Bonapartism caused Marx some difficulty. Marx recognized that the result of the *coup* appeared to be a triumph of Napoleon and the bureaucracy over society, a triumph of the executive over social classes. But Marx refused to rest content with these appearances, and the theoretical burden of *The 18th Brumaire of Louis Bonaparte* is to reconcile the materialist conception of history and its emphasis on classes with the apparent omnipotence of a dictator and his bureaucratic machine.

Marx clearly believed that, in France, political power was in the hands of the bureaucratic state. It is equally clear that Marx's attitude to bureaucracy had not mellowed since 1843. In *The 18th Brumaire* he complained of:

> this executive power with its enormous bureaucratic and military organization, with its ingenious state machinery, embracing wide strata, with a host of officials numbering half a million ... this appalling parasitic body, which enmeshes the body of French society like a net and chokes all its pores.... Every *common* interest was straightway severed from society, counterposed to it as a higher, *general* interest, snatched from the activity of society's members themselves and made an object of government activity [*SW* I, p. 301].

Given the strength, massive size, spread and intrusion of such a bureaucracy, Marx argues, a loss of ministerial power will inevitably result in loss of 'all real influence' unless administration is simplified, the number of soldiers and bureaucrats reduced and 'civil society and public opinion' are allowed to set up their own organs independent of the government (*ibid*. pp. 257–8). But the French bourgeoisie could do none of these things. Its economic interests depended directly on a huge bureaucracy, for it offloaded its surplus population there and received in salaries 'what it cannot pocket in the form of profit, interest, rents and honorariums' (p. 258). *Politically*, and therefore indirectly economically, the bourgeoisie was compelled to build up the power of the state, in order to defeat the classes which it oppressed economically. But the sword it had honed was obviously two-edged; the stronger the executive became, the more precarious was the bourgeoisie's hold on it, and the more threatening would be its capture by anyone else.

Just at this point, where Marx had advanced powerful grounds for belief in the possibility of an autonomous bureaucracy, he reasserted a somewhat modified form of historical materialism and its class analysis. Marx had already suggested that where the bourgeoisie was weak, it might prefer less rather than more political power, because of the camouflage which diluted control could afford. It was thus that he explained the attacks by bourgeois royalists on the bourgeois republic. Though the republic was 'the unlimited despotism of one class over other classes' (p. 232), the royalists yearned 'for the former, more incomplete, more undeveloped and precisely on that account less dangerous forms of this rule' (p. 248). Bonapartism represents a more extreme example of weakness being, as it were, a source of strength. Where the class struggle is severe, the bourgeoisie's *economic* position must be secured by a strong state, notwithstanding that the bourgeoisie is too weak to control this state. Materialism is thus vindicated by the phenomenon which most appears to threaten its validity:

> The bourgeoisie confesses that its own interests dictate that it should be delivered from the danger of its *own rule*; that, in order to restore tranquillity in the country, its bourgeois parliament must, first of all, be given its quietus; that in order to preserve its social power intact, its political power must be broken, that the private bourgeois can continue to exploit the other classes and enjoy undisturbed property, family, religion and order only on condition that their class be condemned along with the other classes to like political nullity; that in order to save its purse, it must forfeit the crown, and the sword that is to safeguard it must at the same time be hung over its own head as a sword of Damocles [p. 261].

In the Bonapartist state, then, a class may rule economically without ruling politically; indeed, its lack of political power is, in these circumstances, a *condition* of its economic dominance.

But Marx is not satisfied simply to portray Bonaparte as a somewhat erratic bourgeois lieutenant. There was, first, a theoretical need to explain Bonaparte's position, to ground this individual's apparent independence in a material base. But there was also a very practical need to explain Louis Napoleon's extraordinary electoral and plebiscitary successes. The material base which Marx chose, the small-holding peasantry, required little ingenuity, for it was the most numerous class in France. But Marx's explanation of their choice is ingenious. Marx argues that the small-holding peasants were a class of a special sort, a vast mass of people living under similar economic conditions but isolated from each other and lacking the internal connections or sense of community which would enable them to organize to protect their class interests. They require to be led and dominated.

Marx argues further that a dispersed peasantry forms the ideal soil for the growth, not merely of a dictator, but of bureaucracy. In a passage which contains striking but, in regard to bureaucracy totally undeveloped parallels to Marx's later analysis of oriental despotism, and which, with the substitution of 'democracy' for 'small-holding property', might have come from Tocqueville or Weber, Marx explains:

> By its very nature, small-holding property forms a suitable basis for an all-powerful and innumerable bureaucracy. It creates a uniform level of relationships and persons over the whole surface of the land. Hence it also permits of uniform action from a supreme centre on all points of this uniform mass. It annihilates the aristocratic intermediate grades between the mass of the people and the state power. On all sides, therefore, it calls forth the direct interference of this state power and the interposition of its immediate organs. Finally, it produces an unemployed surplus population for which there is no place either on the land or in the towns, and which accordingly reaches out for state offices as a sort of respectable alms, and provokes the creation of state posts [*SW* I, p. 306].

French Bonapartism, then, is a regime which, in times of bourgeois weakness and fierce struggle within and between classes, serves the bourgeoisie's economic interests without being in their control. Moreover, it is not an example of a truly autonomous state or bureaucracy but a response to the special nature of its class base.

This is Marx's most extended attempt to account for the apparent independence of a modern bureaucratic dictatorship. It is, therefore, not surprising that it should figure prominently in attempts by contemporary Marxists to account for the modern bureaucratic state and, in particular, for dictatorships such as those of Hitler and Stalin.[10] Recently, indeed, a number of writers have gone further to argue that Bonapartism is the central model for Marx's analysis of the relationship between classes and the modern state in general.[11] This latter argument faces formidable difficulties, for Marx continually emphasized that Bonapartism was inherently a response to severe crisis. In *The 18th Brumaire* itself, Marx argued that, as the archaic small-holdings were inevitably undermined, the bureaucracy which was based on them would collapse. In his journalistic writings throughout the Second Empire, Marx 'seems at every moment only to see the symptoms of crisis, and he does not weary of predicting the imminent (*prochain*) collapse of the regime.'[12] On Marx's account, Bonapartism is

> the only form of government possible at a time when the bourgeoisie

---

[10] The model of Bonapartism plays a central role in dissident Marxists' discussions of the Soviet Union in the 1920s and 1930s. Trotsky applied it to Germany immediately before Hitler's victory; then to Hitler and finally to Stalin. See also R. Miliband, *The State in Capitalist Society* (London, 1969), p. 94, and M. Rubel, *Karl Marx devant le bonapartisme* (Paris, 1960), pp. 68 and 157.

[11] See Nicos Poulantzas, *Political Power and Social Classes* (London, 1974), pp. 258–9 and *passim*.

[12] Rubel, p. 149.

had already lost, and the working class had not yet acquired, the faculty of ruling the nation.[13]

While he was not always precise or consistent in specifying the exact relationship between the capitalist state and its ruling class, for Marx, Bonapartism is not, as some modern Marxists hold, 'the very type of capitalist state ... the political form of the modern class struggle in general';[14] it is the political form of a state in crisis and nearing its doom.

Marx's analysis of Bonapartism, however, is central to his political thought in another sense. It is linked with Marx's much greater concern with bureaucracy after 1851 and with his new insistence that the victorious proletariat must not try to enlist the services of existing state organizations and personnel, but must do away with them.

There is no evidence that, before 1851, Marx saw bureaucracy as a profound threat to the revolution. In the *Communist Manifesto*, for example, he advocated a number of measures of centralization for the victorious proletariat to undertake, and he gave no hint that such measures, which appeared to involve taking over and centralizing a large number of existing institutions, might lead to bureaucratization on an unprecedented, or even a worrying, scale. While he may have been naive here, he was not inconsistent. For he did not avoid the problem of bureaucracy only when he came to write of proletarian class rule; he had little to say about it when he wrote of direct bourgeois class rule. In *The 18th Brumaire*, however, Marx suggested that, rather than wrest control of the bureaucracy from its possessors, as previous revolutions had done, the proletariat must smash the institution. In *The Civil War in France* in 1871, Marx's attack on the state is pre-eminently an attack on bureaucracy, and his espousal of the Paris Commune concentrates upon and occasionally invents its anti-bureaucratic measures. In the first draft, Marx claimed that previous revolutions had 'only perfected the state machinery instead of throwing off this deadening incubus';[15] by contrast, 'the true antithesis to the *Empire itself*—that is to the state power, the central-ized executive of which the Second Empire was only the exhausted formula—was the *Commune*' (*ibid.* p. 165). In the other two versions, Marx emphasized that 'the working class cannot simply lay hold on the ready-made state machinery and wield it for their own purpose' (p. 227), and in the second draft this passage continued: 'The political instrument of their enslavement cannot serve as the political instru-ment of their emancipation.' Elsewhere Marx stressed that, in the bureaucratic countries of Europe, the task of the revolution 'will be

[13] *The Civil War in France* (Peking, 1966), p. 66. This edition includes the important first and second drafts.
[14] Poulantzas, pp. 258–9.
[15] *Civil War in France*, p. 164.

no longer, as before, to transfer the bureaucratic military machine from one hand to another, but to *smash* it'.[16] Finally, in the 1872 preface to the German edition of the *Communist Manifesto*, Marx and Engels explained that 'no special stress is laid on the revolutionary measures proposed' in the *Manifesto* and they added that 'one thing especially was proved by the Commune, *viz.*, "the working class cannot simply lay hold of the ready-made state machinery and wield it for its own purposes"' (*SW* I, pp. 21–2).

Bureaucracy and the proletarian revolution

For Marx, as for Saint-Simon, then, there is a sharp break between the bureaucratic arrangements of the old society and the administrative arrangements of the new. But what will these new arrangements be? How will the society born of the proletarian revolution do without the bureaucracy which this revolution smashed? It is not possible to give a precise answer to these questions both because Marx never did so and because his thought displayed an unresolved ambivalence between an extreme *étatisme* and an extreme revulsion against the state. Both tendencies exist in Marx's writings, each has appealed to many of his followers, and it is difficult to conceive of institutional arrangements which could successfully satisfy them together.

In 1883, the Sydney *Liberal* published the following obituary:

> Karl Marx, the ablest of all the Communistic writers is dead. His great work, *On Capital* [sic] is a masterpiece. While, however, agreeing with most of its critical portions, we are not in accord with his remedies. He was a State Socialist and advocated State control of all industries of all kinds whatever.[17]

Though the *Liberal* is not usually cited as an authority in these matters, it helps to show how widespread the belief that Marx was an *étatist* socialist was, even in his own time. There is much in Marx's writings to lend support to this view. The *only* thing for which Marx praised bureaucracy, and the thing for which he consistently praised it, was its role in centralizing nations. In Marx's and Engels's 1850 address to the Communist League, Germans were told that they 'must not only strive for a single and indivisible German republic, but also within this republic for the most determined centralization of power in the hands of the state authority.... As in France in 1793 so today in Germany it is the task of the really revolutionary party to carry through the strictest centralization' (*SW* I, p. 106–7). In *The 18th Brumaire* and *The Civil War in France* the reviled bureaucracy is still

[16] Marx–Engels, *Selected Correspondence* (Moscow, 1955) [henceforth cited in the text as *SC*], p. 262.
[17] *The Liberal*, Sydney, 19 May 1883, p. 4, quoted in Henry Mayer, *Marx, Engels and Australia* (Sydney, 1964) p. 149.

credited with teleological virtue, as it were, by association with that centralization and destruction of feudal 'rubbish' which it was the 'task' of the French Revolution to accomplish.

Marx's endorsement of centralization is not confined to the achievement of bourgeois revolutions. In the *Communist Manifesto*, as we have seen, proletarian centralization was regarded as an unqualified good. In *The 18th Brumaire* Marx wrote, in the context of proletarian revolution, of 'the centralization of the state that modern society requires' (*ibid.*, p. 308). In 1870 Marx commented ironically (to Engels) on the 'Proudhonised Stirnerism' of 'the representatives of "*Young France*" (*non-workers*). . . . Everything is to be dissolved into small "groups" or "communes", which in turn are to form an "association", but no state' (*SC*, p. 179). Even in *The Civil War in France*, Marx emphasized that the communards did not intend to break the unity of the nation and he warned that, though it had been, the Commune should not be 'mistaken for an exaggerated form of the ancient struggle against over-centralization'.[18]

Moreover, as Evans point out,[19] the state in the transition period would have an essentially aggressive role. This arises partly from the specific tasks involved in clearing the way for socialism and partly because, as Marx explained in another context, 'every provisional state set up after a revolution requires a dictatorship, and an energetic dictatorship at that.'[20]

Finally, we have Marx's acknowledgements that, even in the higher stage of socialism, direction and planning will be required, at least in economic production. In *The Civil War in France* Marx refers to a 'national delegation' which was to have been established by the Commune, and 'nowhere does he imply that this new body should ultimately disappear'.[21]

Nevertheless, Marx's vision of the truly human society was a profoundly *anarchist* one.[22] The new society was to eliminate specialization and division of labour, and was to be essentially productive and harmonious, no longer racked by the contradictions which scarred existing societies, nor held in thrall by a massive state machine of oppression. But how, given his *étatisme*, and how, in any case, did Marx imagine that bureaucracy would cease to be a threat to the citizens of the new society? A few clues exist.

[18] *Civil War in France*, p. 70.
[19] Michael Evans, *Karl Marx* (London, 1975), p. 149.
[20] *Werke* v, p. 402.
[21] Shlomo Avineri, *The Social and Political Thought of Karl Marx* (Cambridge, 1970), p. 202, where Avineri comments that 'it is only natural that such statements [by Marx] have caused some consternation.'
[22] cf. M. Rubel, 'Marx théoricien de l'anarchisme', in his *Marx Critique de Marxisme* (Paris, 1974), pp. 42–59.

There is a strongly Saint-Simonian strain in Marx's attitude to existing bureaucracies and to their fate. First of all, like Saint-Simon, Marx frequently suggested that coercion and repression were central to the role of existing bureaucracies. Both thinkers' confidence that the future society would be harmonious and co-operative led them to argue that this central bureaucratic function would become otiose. Neither Saint-Simon nor Marx is concerned to deny the necessity of public affairs but solely that of public coercive power in the new society. And with the end of the state as policeman comes a reduction in the *number* of functions and a complete change in the *nature* of functions carried out by the public power. There will be no need for masses of haughty, brutal, repressive bureaucrats:

> As soon as the goal of the proletarian movement, the abolition of classes, shall have been reached, the power of the state, whose function is to keep the great majority of producers beneath the yoke of a small minority of exploiters, will disappear and governmental functions will be transformed into simple administrative functions.[23]

But since the state's functions are not *all* coercive, will a need remain for bureaucracy to accomplish those that are not? Marx's conviction that there is no such need is again very Saint-Simonian. Both writers shared a second image of bureaucracy, that of a huge and dangerous, but eminently dispensable, parasite. Bureaucracy was parasitic, both for Marx and Saint-Simon, because its historical role had been played and it was inappropriate to the new society. Now it did nothing productive but merely extorted incomes generated by real producers. Therefore:

> The demolition of the state machine will not endanger centralization. Bureaucracy is only the low and brutal form of a centralization that is still afflicted with its opposite, with feudalism [*SW* I, p. 308].

But neither Saint-Simon nor Marx wished to argue that administration *per se* is unproductive; it is legitimate, therefore, to ask them in what ways the organizations of future *administrators* will differ from those of contemporary *bureaucrats*. I have already argued that Saint-Simon has nothing interesting to say about this question, indeed virtually nothing at all. Saint-Simon says a lot about the elites of industrial society and about its need for organization, but almost nothing about its bureaucrats. For most of his life, Marx said even less. There is no evidence that Marx had given the matter close attention, nor that communal decentralization had appealed to him, before 1871, but in the Paris Commune he saw powerful intimations of the way in which a society could be organized without bureaucracy. And in Marx's discussions of the Commune, his thought moves from strongly Saint-Simonian assumptions in a profoundly *un*Saint-Simonian

[23] *Werke* XVIII, p. 50.

direction—not toward a hierarchy of talent but to a free association of equals.

Marx did not regard the Paris Commune as socialist; it was merely 'the political form of the social emancipation'[24] and in its measures there was 'nothing socialist ... except their tendency' (*ibid.*, p. 183). Nevertheless, Marx clearly regarded the anti-bureaucratic measures which he saw as its core as relevant to socialism and not merely to the transitional regime. The Commune was 'the people acting for itself by itself' (p. 141); it was this achievement which the communist society would emulate. In the transitional and the socialist societies the *character* and role of public functionaries would be transformed because they would be really and completely under the control of the producers, that is, at first of the proletariat and then of the whole people. And the institutional means to such control were to be communal. All public functions would be executed by communal agents rather than by agents of a central government, and this would apply even to the 'few, but important functions which still would remain for a central government' (p. 69).

Moreover, the appointment of all functionaries, including magistrates and judges, was to be made revocable at any time, as is done, Marx quaintly notes, by companies and individuals 'in matters of real business' (p. 70). Officials were not to be members of a privileged caste but were to be paid workmen's wages and the appointing and paying body, the commune, would comprise workers or their representatives who would be elected by universal suffrage and be 'responsible and revocable at short terms' (p. 67). This body would combine legislative and executive functions.

Marx was confident that such measures would shatter the bureaucratic mystique, which he had already condemned in his first critique of Hegel. It would destroy

> the delusion as if administration and political governing were mysteries, transcendent functions only to be trusted to the hands of a trained caste— state parasites, richly paid sycophants and sinecurists ... doing away with the state hierarchy altogether and replacing the haughteous masters of the people with always removable servants, a mock responsibility by a real responsibility as they act continuously under public supervision [p. 169].

The *Civil War in France* is Marx's most explicit and detailed account of the institutional arrangements which will replace bureaucracy, and this account can be supplemented to some extent from several of Marx's other writings. The following characteristics emerge:

1 Administrative functions *will* exist and will be important in the new society, but they will be merely 'simple administrative functions';

---

[24] *Civil War in France*, p. 171.

2 The need for administrative *functionaries* will also survive the transition to socialism.[25] However, they will be paid less and their tenure will be less secure;

3 Because functionaries will be paid less and because the standing army and 'state functionarism' will be eliminated, administrative costs will be less than before, and, in particular, 'the general costs of all administration not directly appertaining to production ... will, from the outset, be very significantly limited in comparison with the present society. [They] will diminish commensurately with the development of the new society' (*ibid.*, p. 345);

4 Administrative functions will be divided in an unspecified way between central and communal institutions, though all will be under the communes' control.

Nevertheless, as Marx unconsciously implies in his remarks on Bakunin, all these safeguards may be worthless. Bakunin alleges that the Marxist people's state is simply government of the people by a small number of elected leaders, and Marx retorts:

> *Asine!* This democratic twaddle, political drivel! Election is a political form present in the smallest Russian commune and artel. The character of the election does not depend on this name, but on the economic foundation, the economic situation of the voters, and as soon as the functions have ceased to be political ones, there exists 1) no government function, 2) the distribution of the general functions has become a business matter, that gives no one domination, 3) election has nothing of its present political character [*ibid.* p. 336].

This is quite a tangle. Taken literally, it implies that if the economic foundation is not adequately developed; then the institutional safeguards Marx advocates cannot succeed during the transition period, when functions are still 'political ones'. This version would satisfy the Mensheviks, but not Lenin or Trotsky. But if the economic foundation is adequate, then there is no need for transitional proletarian dictatorship. In this case the Mensheviks, the Bolsheviks, and Marx, were wrong.

The organization of labour

Marx's comments on large-scale capitalist production are studded with political metaphors. He writes, for example, of the 'despotism' and the 'autocracy' of capital; he compares the power of capitalists to that of 'Asiatic or Egyptian kings or of Etruscan theocrats and the like'. So far as I know, he does not describe the factory as a bureaucracy but he does use military metaphors which themselves are frequently used of bureaucracies. In modern industry:

[25] Marx makes this clear in his comments on Bakunin, reprinted in Marx and Engels, *The First International and After* (New York, 1974), pp. 335–56.

> Masses of labourers, crowded into the factory, are organized like soldiers. As privates of the industrial army they are placed under the command of a perfect hierarchy of officers and sergeants [*SW* I, p. 39].

Elsewhere Marx writes of the factory's

> barrack-like discipline, which is elaborated into a complete factory system, involving a full development of the . . . work of supervision—this meaning the division of the workers into operatives and overlookers, into the private soldiers and the non-commissioned officers of an industrial army.[26]

Marx considered this form of productive organization abhorrent and doomed. But what was to replace it? Notwithstanding Marx's occasional flights of Arcadian and pre-industrial imagery, it is clear that he did not envisage any reversion to small-scale production. On the contrary, 'only with large-scale industry does the abolition of private property become possible.'[27] And if part of Marx's *political* vision was anarchist, no part of his *economic* vision was. Modern production required co-operation and co-operation required co-ordination, management and supervision. There must be a 'commanding will' wherever production is a co-operative and not an independent effort, that is, in all capitalist and post-capitalist societies. Engels makes the point with disarming bluntness. In *On Authority*, his reply to anarchist criticisms, Engels argues that:

> Whoever mentions combined action speaks of organization; now, is it possible to have organization without authority? . . . Wanting to abolish authority in large-scale industry is tantamount to wanting to abolish industry itself. . . . Why do the anti-authoritarians not confine themselves to crying out against political authority, the state [*SW* I, pp. 575–7]?

Similarly in a letter attacking Bakunin's views on the future society, Engels writes:

> In this society there will above all be no *authority*, for authority = state = absolute evil. (How these people propose to run a factory, operate a railway or steer a ship without a will that decides in the last resort, without single management, they of course do not tell us) [*SC*, p. 274].

There seems to me to be nothing in these passages with which Marx disagreed, though as was often the case, some of the subtleties of his thought were lost in Engels's translation. For Marx argued that the authority exercised in modern factories was composed of two elements: one was the authority required in all forms of co-operation, the other was only required when the owner of the means of production needed to dominate the producer and extract surplus value from

[26] *Capital* I (London, Everyman edn., 1974), p. 452.
[27] *The German Ideology*, p. 72.

his labour.[28] In communist society there would indeed be planning and co-ordination, and considerably more of it than hitherto; but since it was based on the willing co-operation of the direct producers rather than that *imposed* by capitalists, the 'commanding will' would resemble that of an orchestra conductor rather than that of a field commander. Moreover the specialized cripple who is equipped only to perform one routine function will be replaced by

> the perfect adaptability of the individual human being to the changing demands for different kinds of labour; so that the detail-worker, who has nothing more to perform than a partial social function, shall be super-seded by an individual with an all-round development, one for whom various social functions are alternative modes of activity.[29]

Both Saint-Simon and Marx, then, reveal striking and tantalizing gaps in their accounts of the future society, gaps which occur at similar stages in their argument. Like Saint-Simon, Marx had very little to say about questions of administrative and organizational imperatives which might lead to bureaucratic growth in *any* complex society. Both in his discussions of the administration of the future society and of the organization of factory labour, Marx passes by functional, organiza-tional difficulties and constraints with barely a pause. However, the problems with which administrative theorists have grappled are not all, or at least not obviously, amenable to solutions drawn from the Paris Commune where, as Marx and Engels proudly note, 'the pro-letariat for the first time held political power for two whole months' (*SW* I, p. 22).

These gaps are not simply due to Marx's refusal to draw up blue-prints for the future, for he writes a good deal about future possibili-ties. But repeatedly, when a serious consideration of organizational constraints is required, Marx's solutions and enthusiasms offer little but bathos. When Bakunin suggests that workers who gain representa-tive positions under socialism might '*cease to be workers*', Marx con-siders it enough to reply, 'as little as a factory owner today ceases to be a capitalist if he becomes a municipal councillor'.[30] When he writes warmly of the 'individual with an all-round development' who will replace the crippled specialist in the factory, the only 'factors of this metamorphosis' which he refers to are polytechnic and agri-cultural schools, and schools of craft training.[31] After a lyrical evoca-tion of 'that development of human energy which is an end in itself, the true realm of freedom', Marx concludes: 'The shortening of the working-day is its basic prerequisite.'[32]

[28] See *Capital* I, pp. 348–9; *Capital* III (Moscow, 1974), pp. 382ff.
[29] *Capital* I, p. 527.
[30] *The First International and After*, p. 336.
[31] *Capital* I, p. 527.
[32] *Capital* III, p. 820.

This shrinking from difficulties is quite uncharacteristic of many other areas of Marx's concern, but, given the importance of bureaucracies in the modern—capitalist *and* socialist—world, it is no minor matter.

3

Weber, Lenin and the reality of socialism

Martin Krygier

Neither Saint-Simon nor Marx lived to witness the social revolutions which they predicted; for Max Weber (1864–1920) and above all for Lenin (1870–1924), the nature of organization in the new society became a matter of real and immediate concern. Weber and Lenin both regarded the post-revolutionary fate of bureaucracy as one of the central problems facing revolutionaries; though they are usually considered polar opposites, their thought ultimately came to bear striking and important similarities.

I Max Weber and the bureaucratization of modern society

Domination and the importance of administrative organizations
Weber's most extended and systematic discussion of administration occurs within his sociology of domination, which stands at the centre of his unfinished masterpiece, *Economy and Society*.[1] Unlike Saint-Simon and Marx, Weber insisted that conflict and the struggle for power are ineradicable elements of the human condition, though the forms which they take differ greatly between societies. Moreover, Weber argued that domination, though not important in every case of social action, was one of the 'most important elements' of such action: 'Without exception every sphere of social action is profoundly influenced by structures of dominancy' (*ES* III, p. 941).

The significance of administrative organizations in general arises from the fact that they are integral parts of the kinds of domination with which Weber is concerned. Weber recognizes that, in a broad sense, domination can be said to occur in a wide variety of forms and contexts, but he confines his attention exclusively to a narrower kind of domination, which he defines as authoritarian power of command. For the purposes of sociology, as opposed, he suggests, to those of law,

---

[1] Max Weber, *Economy and Society*, trans. by Guenther Roth and Claus Wittich (New York, 1968) [henceforth cited in the text as *ES*].

for us to say that such power exists it must be actual, that is, it must be 'heeded to a socially relevant degree' (*ES* III, p. 948) and for the power to amount to domination in his sense it must be legitimated in one way or another, it must be obeyed by the ruled as if they 'had made the content of the command the maxim of their conduct for its very own sake' (*ibid.* p. 946). The habit of obedience which is essential to domination, however, cannot be maintained over time without a continually functioning administrative staff which enforces the order. Organized domination therefore is always associated with and vitally dependent upon administration.

Such structures of domination become politically crucial and attain some stability in form and structure as soon as the group in which they exist becomes at all large, and often as a result of increase in size, administration increases in complexity. Thus, for example, Weber explains that 'pure' or 'direct' democracy becomes impossible,

> where the group grows beyond a certain size or where the administrative function becomes too difficult to be satisfactorily taken care of by anyone whom rotation, the lot, or election may happen to designate. The conditions of administration of mass structures are radically different from those obtaining in small associations resting upon neighbourly or personal relationships. . . .
>
> The growing complexity of the administrative tasks and the sheer expansion of their scope increasingly result in the technical superiority of those who have had training and experience, and will thus inevitably favour the continuity of at least some of the functionaries. Hence, there always exists the probability of the rise of a special, perennial structure for administrative purposes, which of necessity means for the exercise of rule [*ES* III, pp. 951–2].

In contrast to Saint-Simon and Marx, then, Weber denies not only that domination of men by men is dispensable, but also that there is an unbridgeable difference in kind, let alone an antithesis, between the imperatives of political and non-political, peaceful and coercive, forms of administration. To be sure, different sorts of administration will possess certain different characteristics. All of them, however, faced with substantial numbers of complex tasks, will require relatively stable administrative staffs to perform them.

On the other hand, Weber would agree with Saint-Simon that the way in which task-oriented institutions are organized results in crucial differences in their manner of operation and that certain modes of organization are better adapted than others for a specific order or range of tasks. It is the mode of *organization* of officials rather than, say, their number, social status or power position, that Weber regards as the fundamental point of distinction between administrative institutions. He would certainly agree with Saint-Simon that forms of administrative organization cannot simply be abstracted from the environment in which they developed and be expected to perform identically in uncongenial environments. But he insisted not only that administrative structures themselves had powerful consequences, allowed certain activities and inhibited others, but also that these forms were not malleable epiphenomena of their environments; often there were basic internal *administrative* reasons for organizational forms, which had little to do with their social, political or economic environments. At one point in his discussion of the city, for example, Weber points to similarities between the development of the *popolo* in medieval Italy and the *plebs* in the Roman Republic, and he observes:

> These similarities between the medieval Italian and the early Roman development are very striking, especially since they appear in spite of fundamental political, social and economic differences.... It is a fact, after all, that only a limited variety of different administrative techniques is available for effecting compromises between the status groups within a city. Similarities in the forms of political administration can therefore not be interpreted as identical superstructures over identical economic foundations. These things obey their own laws [*ES* III, p. 1309].

Bureaucracy as a form of organization

In his scholarly writings Weber used the word 'bureaucracy' not to refer disparagingly to rule by officials, which in his political writings he attacked as *Beamtenherrschaft*, but to designate a quite specific kind of administrative organization. He demonstrated in considerable detail that there were other kinds, which differed in appearance, function and importance, and he insisted that modern bureaucratic organization as a form of apparatus was *sui generis*. He never defined bureaucracy in the explicit way in which, for example, he defined 'class' or 'status group'. But on a number of occasions he outlined in some detail the characteristics of the *ideal type* of bureaucracy, which he had drawn from Prussian administrative theory and European administrative history. These characteristics are generally known. The enterprise is organized on the basis of permanent official agencies, divided into jurisdictional areas and ordered by rules which apply generally and impersonally. Within any area authority is hierarchically arranged, management is based on written documents ('the files') and follows more or less stable general rules which can be learnt and knowledge of which 'represents a special technical expertise which the officials possess' (*ES* III, p. 958). Whereas in many other forms of administrative organization official business is discharged as an avocation, as a secondary activity, the job of the modern bureaucrat demands his full working capacity. Central to his way of working is the separation of his official from his private life, workplace, activity, monies and equipment; 'the more consistently the modern type of business management has been carried through, the more are these separations the case' (*ibid.* p. 957). Only people who qualify under general rules are employed, and, finally, their professional obligations are based not on loyalty to personal superiors in or above the bureaucracy, but rather to the organization's '*impersonal* and *functional* purposes' (p. 959).

Two things should be noted about this conception. First, it must be remembered that this is the ideal type of bureaucracy which is never found in 'pure', 'unmixed', form in reality. When Weber writes of certain actual administrative organizations he calls them bureaucracies, even though none of them possesses all and only these characteristics, and even though some are closer to the pure type than others. They warrant the name to the extent that they, as opposed to non-bureaucratic organizations, share characteristics of this type.

Secondly, since Weber was interested in the form of organization rather than in the uses to which it was put, he was not limited to talking of *government*. He recognized that the state's monopoly of legitimate force put its bureaucracy in a unique position, and in his political writings he usually referred specifically to state bureaucracy when he used the word, but he repeatedly stressed that bureaucracies were found in all kind of enterprise.

From the viewpoint of the sociology of domination, bureaucracy is merely one among several types of administrative structure. Such structures, whatever their form, are likely to be of social and political significance. But Weber does not regard bureaucracy as just another administrative apparatus. It is specifically the most rational form. Again and again, Weber emphasizes the rationality of the pure type of bureaucracy, and the technical superiority over all other forms of administration of the modern Western bureaucracy which most closely approximates to that pure type. He claims, for example, that:

> Experience tends universally to show that the purely bureaucratic type of administrative organization—that is, the monocratic variety of bureaucracy—is, from a purely technical point of view, capable of attaining the highest degree of efficiency and is in this sense formally the most rational known means of exercising authority over human beings. It is superior to any other form in precision, in stability, in the stringency of its discipline and in its reliability. It thus makes possible a particularly high degree of calculability of results for the heads of the organization and for those acting in relation to it. It is finally superior both in intensive efficiency and in the scope of its operations, and is formally capable of application to all kinds of administrative tasks [*ES* I, p. 223].

The indispensability of bureaucratic organization

As a result of its technical superiority to all other forms of organization, rational bureaucracy is indispensable both to the modern state and to modern economic organization. The modern state, itself a unique development, is dependent on bureaucracies, for no other form of organization can cope with the enormous scope and complexity of mass administration:

> If bureaucratic administration is, other things being equal, always the most rational type from a technical point of view, the needs of mass administration make it today completely indispensable. The choice is only that between bureaucracy and dilettantism in the field of administration [*ES* I, p. 223].

The modern economic order, too, can work in no other way. Weber recognizes that bureaucracy is not an 'unmoved mover', and among the many preconditions necessary for it to develop in its purest form is the rational economic base of capitalism. But Weber's social theory allows reciprocal relations to occur between institutions, and the factors explaining the role of bureaucracy in capitalism lie at the core of this theory.

Like Marx, and like Werner Sombart whose work he knew well, Weber regarded the developed capitalist order as a system with imperatives, with rules of action which the individual capitalist had to obey to survive. In this system, the imperatives of mechanized production and incessant competition force enterprises continuously to maximize profit and therefore to operate in the most efficient way possible. For this, bureaucracies are essential in two areas. *Internally*, large scale capitalist enterprises are 'unequalled models of strict bureaucratic organization' (*ES* III, p. 974), simply because bureaucracies get things done better than any other form of organization. For the prisoner of the 'iron cage' of capitalism this consideration is and must be decisive. Externally, the capitalist enterprise is equally dependent on the predictability and calculability provided by a rational legal order and state administration, staffed bureaucratically and working according to strictly formalized rules (*ibid.* p. 1394).

One can argue, as Weber does, that bureaucracy is indispensable to fully developed capitalism without claiming that these phenomena are all parts of the same development, or that bureaucracy developed simply because it was useful to capitalism. Weber recognizes this and points out that:

> Early modern capitalism did not *originate* in the bureaucratic model states where bureaucracy was a product of the state's rationalism. Advanced capitalism, too, was at first not limited to these countries, in fact, not even primarily located in them.... Today, however, capitalism and bureaucracy have found one another and belong intimately together.[2]

[2] 'Parliament and Government in a Reconstructed Germany', appendix II in *ES* III, p. 1465; cf. *ES* I, p. 224.

And bureaucracy was 'found' by modern capitalism for the same reason that it has advanced in all areas of administration—its technical superiority to any other form of organization.

The inescapability of bureaucracy and the power position of bureaucrats

Weber regarded this indispensability of developed bureaucracy, with its expertise born of long and specialized training, as the pivotal political fact of the modern age. The individual bureaucrat is a power-less cog 'in a ceaselessly moving mechanism which prescribes to him an essentially fixed route of march' (*ES* III, p. 988). The ruled in a mass state are increasingly dependent on bureaucracy,

> for it rests upon expert training, a functional specialization of work, and an attitude set on habitual virtuosity in the mastery of single yet methodically integrated functions. If the apparatus stops working, or if its work is interrupted by force, chaos results, which it is difficult to master by improvised replacements from among the governed [*ibid.*]

Finally, whoever gains power is similarly unable to govern without this organization, and he has little incentive to. For the bureaucrat's 'impersonal' attitude to office, unlike the patrimonial functionary's personal loyalty, allows him to work for anyone who gains control of his organization:

> A rationally ordered officialdom continues to function smoothly after the enemy has occupied the territory; he merely needs to change the top officials. It continues to operate because it is to the vital interest of everyone concerned, including above all the enemy [*ibid.* pp. 988–9].

Moreover, not only is bureaucracy indispensable but its influence is inescapable. As an administrative organization found in every kind of enterprise its influence is more pervasive than that of other carriers of the 'rationality' of the modern world, and as the most advanced form of administrative organization it is stronger, more 'escape-proof', than any previous form.

As a result of the attention which has been given to Max Weber's political writings in recent years, it is now well known that he was profoundly uneasy about the social and political consequences of the contemporary, irresistible, spread of bureaucracy. There are two principal foci of Weber's unease. The first is the bureaucratization of the whole of society, in the sense of the permeation of bureaucratic values, ways of thought and of behaviour throughout a population. At the 1909 meeting of the *Verein für Sozialpolitik* Weber and his brother Alfred bitterly opposed older members of the *Verein*, such as Gustav Schmoller and Adolf Wagner, whose 'passion for bureaucratization

... drives one to despair',[3] and Max Weber's interventions passion-ately evoked the danger of bureaucratization in this first sense. In *Economy and Society* Weber pointed to the effect of feudal and patriarchal structures of domination on the ethos and style of life of the societies in which they occurred (*ES* III, p. 1104). Given the far greater pervasiveness which he attributed to bureaucratic domination, one would expect the latter to have even stronger effects of this kind. In *Economy and Society*, Weber also drew attention to the 'socially levelling' effects of bureaucracy on status structure, on the one hand (*ibid.* pp. 983–5), and to the kind of status hierarchy which bureau-cracy itself encouraged, on the other—a hierarchy based on the 'patent of education' and on education of a uniquely important kind, in specialized functional skills (pp. 998–1002). Status in a bureaucratized society, Weber argued in his political writings, went to *Prüfungs-diplommenschen* who valued security and a comfortable, steadily in-creasing salary, based on status rather than performance, before all else.

Weber did not deny that bureaucratic values and *Amtsehre* (the sense of the dignity, calling, and obligations of office) were important elements in proper bureaucratic performance, but he feared greatly that they would come to expel all other kinds of values and all modes of behaviour inconsistent with them. He found it 'frightful' to contem-plate

> that the world might be filled with nothing but these little cogs, with nothing but men clinging to a little job and striving after a slightly bigger one . . . men who need 'order' and nothing but order, who become nervous and cowardly if this order wavers for a moment. . . . That the world should know nothing but these men of order [*Ordnungsmenschen*]—this is the development in which we are already caught up, and the central question is thus not how we can further promote and accelerate it, but what we can oppose to this machinery, in order to keep a portion of mankind free from this parcelling out of the soul, from this total dominance of the bureau-cratic ideal of life.[4]

Weber's second concern was related to but distinct from the one outlined above, and it was more directly political in focus. This was the fear, which the term 'bureaucracy' had originally been used to express, that those who manned bureaucratic organizations might come to be the actual rulers of a state. It was less a fear that we would all become bureaucrats than that we would all come to be *ruled* by bureaucrats. In one sense Weber believed that this was already the case in every modern society because all domination was exercised through

[3] Max Weber, *Gesammelte Aufsätze zur Soziologie und Sozialpolitik* (Tübingen, 1924), p. 414. On the conflicts within the *Verein* see Dieter Lindenlaub, *Richtungskämpfe im Verein für Sozialpolitik* (Wiesbaden, 1967).
[4] *Gesammelte Aufsätze*, p. 414.

bureaucratic agencies rather than 'through parliamentary speeches [or] monarchical enunciations'.[5] But rule, in the sense of ultimate directive power, did not inevitably lie in the hands of officials, for there was a fundamental distinction between the functional *indispensability* of bureaucratic forms of organization and of bodies of trained officials, and the *power* of those officials. In *Economy and Society* Weber explained that:

> It must ... remain an open question whether the *power* of bureaucracy is increasing in the modern states in which it is spreading. The fact that bureaucratic organization is technically the most highly developed power instrument in the hands of its controller does not determine the weight that bureaucracy as such is capable of procuring for its own opinions in a particular social structure. The ever-increasing 'indispensability' of the officialdom, swollen to the millions, is no more decisive on this point than is the economic indispensability of the proletarians for the strength of the social and political power position of that class (a view which some representatives of the proletarian movement hold). If 'indispensability' were decisive, the equally 'indispensable' slaves ought to have held this position of power in any economy where slave labour prevailed and consequently freemen, as is the rule, shunned work as degrading. Whether the power of bureaucracy as such increases cannot be decided *a priori* from such reasons [*ES* III, p. 991].

This analysis, which emphasizes the central importance of bureaucracy but does not claim to pre-determine its specific power position, seems to me to be enormously fruitful and too often ignored. Indeed, Weber himself might well have kept it in mind in some of his last, despairing political writings about Germany, and in his comments on the Bolsheviks' chance of survival in Russia. On the other hand, there was far less of a gulf than is sometimes alleged between the fear of *Beamtenherrschaft* expressed in Weber's political writings and the analysis of bureaucracy in *Economy and Society*. For in the latter work Weber argued that, while the power position of officials could not be predicted in general terms, it was 'always great, under normal conditions overtowering' (*ibid.*). Compared with the trained official, the political 'master' is always a dilettante, and officials are always keen to secure their privileged access to technical and official knowledge against effective supervision, by insisting on the need for official secrecy and by promoting their interests through conveniently ambiguous ideas, such as that of 'reasons of state' (cf. p. 979).

In his sociology, then, as in his politics, Weber argued that, while *Beamtenherrschaft* was not inevitable, bureaucrats had enormous power resources at their disposal which might enable them to rule unless they were kept under political control. In his later political writings he was concerned to show that, in the absence of effective *political* leadership, *Beamtenherrschaft* existed in Germany, that this

[5] 'Parliament and Government', p. 1393.

was politically disastrous and that means of controlling the *Beamtentum* must be devised.

In opposition to the 'conservative' members of the *Verein für Sozialpolitik* who, like Hegel, argued that officialdom represented the general common interests of society, Weber insisted that bureaucrats, far from constituting a 'universal estate', fostered quite particular sectional interests. In Prussia they were recruited predominantly from the one class—the economically declining *Junkers*—and they overemphasized the latters' conservative interests. And in Prussia as elsewhere, officialdom generated its own values and a consciousness of its own special interests, which it was uniquely placed to promote.

But the real problem, for Weber, was not that bureaucrats feathered their own nests. Even if they were determined to serve only the public interest—and Weber believed that many were—they were tragically and inevitably unsuited for the role of political leadership. For politicians and bureaucrats are different types of people; 'the "directing mind", the "moving spirit"—that of the entrepreneur here and of the politician there—differs in substance from the "civil service" mentality of the official.'[6] Bureaucrats cannot be adequate politicians because their training, their ways of working, what they value as professionals, all deny that they should fight for their convictions, that they should act on their personal preferences in the execution of their tasks. Rather, the good bureaucrat prides himself on demonstrating that 'his sense of duty stands above his personal preference. . . . This is the ethos of *office*' (*ibid.* p. 1404). The politician, on the other hand, like the entrepreneur, is forged through struggle. He seeks power, takes risks, and, most importantly, must take personal responsibility for his acts and decisions. Whereas the bureaucrat is to act as an impartial administrator, *sine ira et studio*, 'to take a stand, to be passionate—*ira et studium*—is the politician's element, and above all the element of the political *leader*.'[7]

What Weber feared most was that modern society might come to be dominated by the bureaucrats who controlled an incomparably effective and inescapable administrative machine and that throughout society only those attitudes and values would be generated which were appropriate to this machine. He considered it essential that *nonbureaucratic* leaders be selected who might, as it were, control the controllers. The failure of German politics, he believed, could be attributed essentially to two things—the absence of real politicians since Bismarck and as a result of his initiative-numbing dominance, and the fact that, in default of such leaders, Germany was being governed by bureaucrats. In his last years Weber, in increasing despair, sought to devise means to ensure leadership by men whose

[6] 'Parliament and Government', p. 1403.
[7] H. H. Gerth and C. Wright Mills (eds), *From Max Weber* (London, 1970), p. 95.

'vocation' was politics. Ultimately he argued that only a charismatic leader who appealed directly to the masses could acquire the independence necessary for controlling and setting the goals for German bureaucrats. The changing details of his proposals are less important for our purposes than their fundamental aim—to secure a political leadership able to control the bureaucrats who threatened to extinguish both Germany's chances of greatness and also '*any remnants* of "individualist" freedom in any sense.'[8]

Bureaucracy and socialism

Weber discussed socialism at any length in only one speech, delivered to Austrian army officers in Vienna in 1918;[9] but in a number of other contexts, he developed the points made in that lecture concerning the consequences of bureaucracy for socialist aspirations. In his lecture, Weber explained that development of professional administration is the fate of all modern mass democracies and he traced at some length the movement in this direction of under-bureaucratized America, hitherto administered by 'dilettantes'. Throughout the world:

> Modern democracy is becoming everywhere where it is the democracy of a large state, a bureaucratized democracy. And it must be so, for it replaces the distinguished aristocratic or other honoured officials by a salaried officialdom. That is happening everywhere, it is also happening within parties. It is inescapable, and this fact is the first with which socialism also must reckon: the necessity of a long training in skills, always increasing specialization and management by a skilled officialdom shaped in this way. The modern economy can be managed in no other way [*ibid.* pp. 497–8].

Weber's analysis of capitalism clearly owes much to Marx, but Marx, and socialists generally, he argues, have simply failed to come to terms with the inescapability of bureaucracy. This myopia vitiates both their analysis of contemporary society and what he calls their prophecy. In their analysis, socialists rightly emphasize the separation in capitalism of the worker from the means of production. But they wrongly see it merely as an economic phenomenon and, more wrongly still, attribute it to the existence of private property. In fact, it characterizes *all* bureaucratized enterprises—factories, armies, governmental bodies, universities. The university chemist does not own his laboratory equipment; nor the soldier his gun. In part this separation arises from purely technical considerations having to do with the nature of modern equipment but, quite independently, it flows from the imperatives of bureaucratic organization. Bureaucratic 'discipline', not private property, gives the form to modern relations of administration and of production. Moreover, Weber argues, it makes

[8] 'Parliament and Government', p. 1403.
[9] 'Der Sozialismus', *Gesammelte Aufsätze*, pp. 492–518.

no difference in this regard if the head of an enterprise is changed, if a public functionary replaces a private factory owner:

> The 'separation' from the means of production endures in any case. So long as there are mines, blast furnaces, railways, factories and machines, they will never be the property of a single or more than a single worker in the sense that the means of production of a trade in the middle ages were the property of a single master of a guild or of a local partnership or guild. That is excluded by the nature of present day *Technik* [*ibid*. p. 499].

Weber argues similarly that those socialists who point to the replacement of individual owner-entrepreneurs in public companies by appointed managers are identifying an important development, but he insists that in describing it as 'socialization from within' they are completely misconstruing its significance. This 'socialization' in fact involves an increase in the role of trained officialdom rather than in the role or power of the worker. Thus, here too, 'the dictatorship of the official, not that of the worker is what—at any rate for the time being—is constantly advancing' (*ibid*. p. 508).

And in their predictions, too, socialists are no closer to the mark, nor are their hopes any more likely to be achieved. A socialist revolution *cannot* result in a dictatorship of the proletariat. In modern mass society it can only result in a consolidated dictatorship of the bureaucrats. In economic enterprises bureaucrats would now be in the highest positions, formerly held by private entrepreneurs; strikes would be more difficult than ever before, and the possibility of appeal or support from one enterprise against another would be gone. If private capitalism were destroyed,

> What would be the practical result? The destruction of the steel frame of modern industrial work? No! The abolition of private capitalism would simply mean that also the *top management* of the nationalized or socialized enterprises would become bureaucratic.... There is even less freedom, since every power struggle with a state bureaucracy is hopeless and since there is no appeal to an agency which as a matter of principle would be interested in limiting the employer's power, such as there is in the case of a private enterprise. *That* would be the whole difference.
>
> State bureaucracy would rule *alone* if private capitalism were eliminated. The private and public bureaucracies, which now work next to, and potentially against, each other and hence check one another to a degree, would be merged into a single hierarchy. This would be similar to the situation in ancient Egypt, but it would occur in a much more rational—and hence unbreakable—form.[10]

[10] 'Parliament and Government', pp. 1401–2.

II Lenin and bureaucracy

The simplicity of administration and the dispensability of bureaucracy
Contemporary organization theorists have challenged, refined and
extended Weber's ideal type of bureaucracy in a number of useful
ways, though at times they appear to have ignored Weber's purposes
in developing it and the level of historical and theoretical abstraction
at which he was writing. Since Weber's time, new forms of organization have developed, in response, among other things, to 'post-
industrial' technological developments. Nevertheless, Weber's work
remains an indispensable starting-point for modern investigation of
bureaucracy, both at 'micro' and at 'macro' levels.

In his diagnosis of the dangers faced by twentieth-century Germany
and the West, however, and particularly in the prescription he offered,
Weber seems to me in one respect to have been tragically misguided:
bureaucracies have often been less powerful than he feared and
political leaders catastrophically more powerful than he hoped, in
Germany and elsewhere. For example, Weber's confidence immediately after the October Revolution, that the Bolshevik 'dilettantes' and
intellectuals would lose power within three months was, to say the
least, misplaced. However, as Weber himself emphasized, the cogency
and utility of his social theory does not depend on the accuracy of
his political judgement, though they may, of course, be linked. In
particular, as Weber was careful to remind both his readers and
Michels, the functional indispensability of large, hierarchical organizations of salaried, permanently employed officials neither
ensured nor depended upon the existence of *Beamtenherrschaft*. It is
no refutation of the claim that bureaucracies are indispensable in
modern society to show that political rulers can exercise sway over, and
indeed cut swathes though their administrative staffs. It would,
however, be a refutation to show that bureaucratic organizations and
staffs are readily dispensable in modern societies. It is, in effect, such
a refutation that Lenin attempted in 1917.

Before 1917, European Marxists had not paid conspicuous attention
to the prediction of post-revolutionary institutional arrangements.
Marx had provided epistemological objections to that sort of enterprise and, even where it was attempted, it was a far less central preoccupation than problems associated with bringing the revolution
about. But on one central issue the mainstreams of German and
Russian social democracy converged: most German and Russian
Marxists agreed with Kautsky that the proletariat should take over and
use the existing state apparatus rather than smash it.

Unlike Kautsky, Lenin did not believe that the state could be taken
over peacefully, but he did believe that it should be taken over. In
1916, Lenin's Bolshevik colleague Bukharin challenged this belief,

arguing in an article he sent to Lenin that the socialist movement must '*emphasize strongly its hostility in principle to state power*' and that the proletariat's immediate aim must be to 'destroy the state organization of the bourgeoisie ... *explode it from within*'.[11] In September 1916 Lenin wrote to Bukharin, rejecting the article for publication, describing its conclusion as 'either supremely inexact, or incorrect' and suggesting that Bukharin's reflections 'about the state in general' be left '*to mature*'.[12] Hurt but undeterred, Bukharin defended his views in correspondence, and published another article repeating his earlier characterizations of the state. Lenin's published reply was unambiguously hostile. He explained that Bukharin ('Comrade Nota-Bene') had ignored

> the *main* point of difference between socialists and anarchists in their attitude towards the state. Socialists are in favour of utilizing the present state and its institutions in the struggle for the emancipation of the working class, maintaining also that the state should be used for a specific form of transition from capitalism to socialism. This transitional form is the dictatorship of the proletariat, which is *also* a state.
>
> The anarchists want to 'abolish' the state, 'blow it up' [*sprengen*] as Comrade Nota-Bene expresses it in one place, erroneously ascribing this view to the socialists [*CW* XXIII, p. 165].

Lenin also promised to 'return to this very important subject in a separate article' and in the first two months of 1917 he systematically worked through Marx's and Engels' writings on the state. The result of this research was, in effect, an abandonment of the *Communist Manifesto* for the *Civil War in France* and of the views of Kautsky for those of Bukharin. The views to which Lenin came at this time were systematically elaborated several months later in his famous pamphlet, *State and Revolution*.

Like Marx, Lenin claimed that bureaucracy was objectionable because bureaucrats are 'a privileged group holding "jobs" remunerated on a high, bourgeois scale' (*CW* XXIV, p. 39) and because 'the police ... the bureaucracy ... are unanswerable to the people and placed above the people' (*ibid.* p. 107). Appealing to a strong Russian, rather than simply Marxist tradition,[13] Lenin constantly attacked the existing state machinery as alien, separate, 'above' and not of the people.

But why was it necessary to smash the state machine? Since neither

---

[11] 'K teorii imperialisticheskogo gosudarstva', quoted in Stephen F. Cohen, *Bukharin and the Bolshevik Revolution* (New York, 1975), p. 34; see also Marian Sawer, 'The Genesis of *State and Revolution*', in *The Socialist Register* (London, 1977), pp. 209–27.

[12] V. I. Lenin, *Collected Works* (Moscow, 1964) [henceforth cited in the text as *CW*] XXXV, pp. 230–31.

[13] See Robert C. Tucker, 'The Image of Dual Russia', in *The Soviet Political Mind* (New York, 1972), pp. 121–42.

Marx nor Lenin had ever argued that *communist* society would be administered by 'bureaucrats', Lenin's new position on the proletarian dictatorship cannot follow simply from the inconsistency between 'bureaucracy' and communism. The only reason Lenin seems to give for the necessity to smash the existing machine is the connection between the bureaucrats, police and army and the bourgeoisie. Bureaucrats, he wrote, 'are the most faithful servants of the bourgeoisie' (*CW* XXIV, p. 181), connected to the latter 'by thousands of threads' (*CW* XXV, p. 407). Bureaucrats could not be neutral, let alone amiable to the proletariat; as a result of their social position, connections and conditioning, they would necessarily take the side of the bourgeoisie. They 'would simply be unfit to carry out the orders of the proletarian state' (p. 434).

Lenin was not arguing that the proletarian dictatorship could do without a state; indeed it was precisely on this issue that he distinguished his view from that of the anarchists. A state would be required to suppress counter-revolutionaries, and it would also be required in the first stage of socialism, to administer (cf. *CW* XXV, p. 425). In 1917, however, Lenin rejected all arguments which purported to link the persistence of state *functions* with existing forms of organizing state *functionaries*. Arguments about the complexity of modern society failed to impress him, for he argued that the tasks of the proletarian state had been rendered extraordinarily simple. Since the new 'state' would be, as never before, a state of 'the majority of wage slaves of *yesterday*' and since, again as never before, only a minority of former exploiters would remain to be suppressed, suppression would become a relatively simple task for which special machinery would hardly be required (*ibid.* p. 463). Moreover, drawing on Marx's arguments that the forms of socialist organization are immanent in highly developed capitalism, Lenin claimed that, on the basis of the creations of capitalism,

> Large-scale production, factories, railways, the postal service, telephones, etc. . . . the great majority of the functions of the old 'state power' have become so simplified and can be reduced to such exceedingly simple operations of registration, filing and checking that they can be easily performed by every literate person, can quite easily be performed for ordinary 'workman's wages', and that these functions can (and must) be stripped of every shadow of privilege, of every semblance of 'official grandeur' [*CW* XXV, pp. 420–21; see also p. 473].

Finally, a recurrent refrain in Lenin's writings during 1917 was that workers and peasants would administer better than bureaucrats. Like so many of its critics, Lenin characterized bureaucracy as parasitic, by which he meant both that it was completely dependent on bourgeois society and would fall with it and that bureaucrats played no productive role. Here too, capitalism had, as it were, provided the workers

with on-the-job training—'it was not for nothing that we went to learn
in the school of capitalism' (*CW* XXVI, p. 114)—which, according to
Lenin, would equip them far better than parasitic bureaucrats for
those administrative tasks which would need to be discharged in the
new society.

Lenin, who in 1905 had called the Paris Commune 'a government
such as ours should not be' and who had never before regarded the
Commune's institutional forms as models to be emulated, suddenly
based his 1917 model of the proletarian dictatorship on the Commune;
the Soviets were its heirs. Lenin's scheme was claimed to ensure
popular participation in all public activities and complete popular
control over those functionaries who may be required; the scheme's
central aim was to eliminate 'bureaucracy' from both politics and
economics. Lenin conceded that the new state would require functionaries, but he insisted that these functionaries would not be bureaucrats, that is, people whose '*essence*' is to be 'privileged ... divorced
from the people and standing *above* the people' (*CW* XXV, p. 486). There
would be an apparatus,

> *but* this apparatus will *not* be 'bureaucratic'. The workers, after winning
> political power, will smash the old bureaucratic apparatus, shatter it to
> its very foundations, and raze it to the ground; they will replace it by a new
> one, consisting of the very same workers and other employees, *against*
> whose transformation into bureaucrats the measures will at once be taken
> which were specified in detail by Marx and Engels: (1) not only election,
> but also recall at any time; (2) pay not to exceed that of a workman;
> (3) immediate introduction of control and supervision by *all*, so that *all*
> may become 'bureaucrats' for a time and that, therefore, *nobody* may be
> able to become a 'bureaucrat' [*CW* XXV, p. 481].

It is with these measures, plus the conversion of parliamentary
institutions into 'working bodies, executive and legislative at the same
time', that Lenin turns on Kautsky:

> According to Kautsky, since elected functionaries will remain under
> socialism, so will officials, so will the 'bureaucracy'! This is exactly where
> he is wrong. Marx, referring to the example of the Commune, showed
> that under socialism functionaries will cease to be 'bureaucrats', to be
> 'officials' [*ibid.* p. 487].

Such a solution to the problems of controlling bureaucracies in mass
societies would not have satisfied Weber, or indeed Lenin at any other
time in his life. But while few people suggest that these writings typify
Lenin's life work or that they were the model on which later Soviet
developments were built, they have received a great amount of attention, and many extravagant claims have been made for them.

In fact, as T. H. Rigby has demonstrated, despite 'Lenin's constant
stress on the *non-bureaucratic* character of the new proletarian state,

the task of equipping itself with an effective bureaucracy was in fact
the main preoccupation of the Soviet state during its initial phase,
and predominantly this expressed itself in efforts to "take over" and
"set in motion" the old ministerial machine."[14] And quite apart from
his subsequent practice, it is worth looking in some detail at Lenin's
writings on these matters after 1917, for they are not simply a mass
of *ad hoc* rationalizations designed to cope with individual problems
as they arose. They show sufficient coherence to warrant at least as
much attention as *The State and Revolution* in the search for Lenin's
views on bureaucracy in post-revolutionary society.

The difficulty of administration; the importance of expertise
It had been a fundamental article of faith among Marxists, and another
reason for the shock which Lenin's April Theses caused, that socialism
could only develop out of, and on the basis of, highly developed
capitalism. Lenin played fast and loose with the problems which this
belief created for his resolve to institute an immediate proletarian
revolution, but residues of the belief remained profoundly important
in his thought. Even in *The State and Revolution* itself, there are hints
that the need to build on capitalism might qualify Lenin's wholesale
rejection of the institutions of the *ancien régime*. In that pamphlet
Lenin attributes four categories of tasks to the existing state—suppression of the masses in the interests of the bourgeoisie; keeping
control and account of labour, production and distribution; management within industry; and tasks requiring technical expertise. Under
the proletarian dictatorship, suppression would be carried out in a
totally new way, for the mass of the people, organized in people's
militias, would suppress the emeritus exploiters. Accounting and
control could also be carried out by the people at large, for the tasks
had been so simplified by capitalism. Management within industry
would require functionaries, but their positions would ultimately
become accessible to all, and, in any case the combination of workers'
control and the measures of the Paris Commune would sharply distinguish the new situation from the old.
    In one sphere, however, Lenin emphasized continuity between the
arrangements of the new society and those of the old. He warned
against confusing

> the question of control and accounting ... with the question of the
> scientifically trained staff of engineers, agronomists and so on. These
> gentlemen are working today in obedience to the wishes of the capitalists,
> and will work even better tomorrow in obedience to the wishes of the
> armed workers [*CW* xxv, p. 473].

Certainly, in *The State and Revolution* Lenin pays far less attention

[14] T. H. Rigby, 'Birth of the Central Soviet Bureaucracy', *Politics* VII, no. 2 (1972),
p. 124.

to the technical tasks of the proletarian state than to its other tasks; but his remarks on the former suggest a potentially important point of continuity between the new and the old. The image which emerges is less that of a monolith which must be 'razed to the ground' to be replaced by something totally new and different, than a Saint-Simonian image of a growing and potentially healthy organism afflicted by a harmful parasite. Harsh treatment must be administered to destroy the parasite and certain precautions must be followed to keep it at bay. And at one point, though he mixes his metaphors, Lenin says almost precisely that:

> Imperialism is gradually transforming all trusts into organizations of a similar type, in which standing over the 'common' people, who are overworked and starved, one has the same bourgeois bureaucracy. But the mechanism of social management is here already to hand. Once we have overthrown the capitalists, crushed the resistance of these exploiters with the iron hand of the armed workers, and smashed the bureaucratic machine of the modern state, we shall have a splendidly equipped mechanism, free from the 'parasite', a mechanism which can very well be set going by the united workers themselves, who will hire technicians, foremen and accountants, and pay them *all*, as indeed *all* 'state' officials in general, workmen's wages [*CW* xxv, pp. 426–7].

Shortly before the Revolution, Lenin limited even more clearly the amount of 'smashing' that the state should undergo, and here too, Saint-Simon would have endorsed the terms in which this limitation was cast. In *Can the Bolsheviks Retain State Power?* he made it clear that capitalism had bequeathed far more than the simplification of tasks to the new society. According to Lenin, the existing state rested, in effect, on two separate apparatuses: one—police, bureaucracy and army—was 'chiefly "oppressive" ' and had to be smashed; the other apparatus, however, had

> extremely close connections with the banks and syndicates [it is] an apparatus which performs an enormous amount of accounting and registration work.... This apparatus must not be smashed. It must be wrested from the control of the capitalists; the capitalists and the wires they pull must be *cut off, lopped off, chopped away from* this apparatus; it must be *subordinated* to the proletarian Soviets: it must be expanded, made more comprehensive, and nation-wide. And this *can* be done by utilizing the achievements already made by large-scale capitalism (in the same way as the proletarian revolution can, in general, reach its goal only by utilizing these achievements).

> We shall not invent the organizational form of the work but take it ready-made from capitalism—we shall take over the banks, syndicates, the best factories, experimental stations, academies, and so forth; all that we shall have to do is to borrow the best models furnished by the advanced countries [*CW* xxvi, pp. 106, 110].

Moreover, the proletarian state would not merely preserve and copy existing structures. It would take over the existing employees, 'the majority of whom themselves lead a proletarian or semi-proletarian existence', and deal ' "severely" with capitalists and the higher officials', of whom there are very few, but who gravitate towards the capitalists. But it would not discard them; it would *employ them in the service of the new state*. This applies both to the capitalists and to the upper sections of the bourgeois intellectuals, office employees, etc.' (*ibid.* p. 109).

Though Lenin insisted that the simplification of accounting and control had made possible a vast influx of proletarians into the state service, he cautioned that: 'We are not utopians. We know that an unskilled labourer or a cook cannot immediately get on with the job of state administration' (p. 113). He emphasized the need for 'scientifically trained specialists of every kind', and predicted that 'in all probability we shall introduce complete wage equality only gradually and shall pay these specialists higher salaries during the transition period' (p. 110).

Almost all these propositions have their contradictories in other, more common, statements made by Lenin in 1917; they also contain the seeds of most of what he had to say on these subjects after power had been won. Just as he had distinguished between the oppressive and, in a broad sense, administrative tasks of the old state, so by March 1918 he was distinguishing between suppression of exploiters and administration and organization in the new state, and he was emphasizing that administration had become 'the main and central task' of the state.[15] And the goal of administration was not simply the restoration and maintenance of order. It was a truly Saint-Simonian vision of centrally directed technical and economic advance. It required 'a single state Bank, the biggest of the big' (*CW* XXVI, p. 106); 'the transformation of the whole state economic mechanism into a single huge machine' (*CW* XXVII, pp. 90–91). More prosaically, it required the most efficient possible development of large-scale industry for

> Socialism owes its origin to large-scale machine industry. If the masses of the working people in introducing socialism prove incapable of adjusting their institutions in the way that large-scale machine industry should work, then there can be no question of introducing socialism [*CW* XXVII, p. 210].

Together with these commitments went a real passion for efficiency, for people who could get things done, for practical men, well versed in the tasks they undertook.

The consequences of these commitments and this passion were

[15] *CW* XXVII, p. 242; cf. XXVIII, p. 36, XXXI, p. 371 and XLII, p. 70.

profound. Firstly, they led to an insistence—convenient for the 'hard' elements in the Party—that there were many important tasks which the masses, at least at present, were unable to handle. In 1921, Lenin made the point quite bluntly:

> Does every worker know how to run the state? People working in the practical sphere know that this is not true, that millions of our organized workers are going through what we always said the trade unions were, namely a school of communism and administration. When they have attended this school for a number of years they will have learned to administer, but the going is slow. We have not even abolished illiteracy.... How many of the workers have been engaged in government? A few thousand throughout Russia and no more [*CW* XXXII, p. 61].

That this insistence on the need for administrative competence was not merely a political ploy is clear from Lenin's distinction between the skills of administrators and those of communists. He began relatively politely, stating as early as March 1918 that it was understandable that revolutionaries and agitators know little about large-scale administration and organization; after all, this had not been their *métier* for long. Moreover, some consolation and explanation lay in the fact that there was no precedent for their new activities and no canonical guide to show them the way:

> We know about socialism, but knowledge of organization on a scale of millions, knowledge of organization and distribution of goods—this we do not have. The old Bolshevik leaders did not teach us. The Bolshevik Party cannot boast of this in its history. We have not done a course on this yet [*CW* XXVII, pp. 296–7].

In any event, the Bolsheviks were not only communists but also Russians, and 'so far as . . . [organizing skill] is concerned, the Russian is not in the picture' (*CW* XXXI, p. 424). Lenin's remarks on this issue became increasingly impatient and, toward the end of his life, almost desperate. He exhorted communists to 'frankly admit our complete inability to conduct affairs, to be organizers and administrators' and in 1922 he asked:

> Will the responsible Communists of the RSFSR [Russian Soviet Federated Socialist Republic] and of the Russian Communist Party realize that they cannot administer; that they only imagine they are directing, but are, actually, being directed? If they realize this they will learn, of course: for this business can be learnt. But one must study hard to learn it, and our people are not doing this. They scatter orders and decrees right and left, but the result is quite different from what they want [*CW* XXXIII, p. 289].

As a result of these deficiencies of the masses and of the communists, and as a result of the bourgeoisie's special talents, Lenin insisted that lessons had to be taken from the bourgeoisie. It was they who knew techniques of management, industrial production and trade; they who were scientists, technologists, engineers and agronomists. Lenin insisted that: 'We must take a lesson in socialism from the trust managers ... from capitalism's big organizers' [*CW* XLII, p. 77), he exhorted communists to bear in mind that 'the engineer's way to communism is *different* from that of the underground propagandist and writer' (*CW* XXXII, p. 144). He recognized that the bourgeoisie and petty bourgeoisie might contain traitors and saboteurs, but 'they do know how to run shops', while as he reiterated again and again, no one else did; there were 'no other bricks' with which to build. In direct and conscious contravention of *State and Revolution*, he fought for better treatment and higher wages for 'bourgeois specialists', higher indeed than those of workers and even of Party leaders. Finally, in his most extravagant, but not uncharacteristic, appeal, he argued that:

> Unless our leading bodies ... guard as the apple of their eye every specialist who does his work conscientiously and knows and loves it—even though the ideas of communism are totally alien to him—it will be useless to expect any serious progress in socialist construction. We may not be able to achieve it soon, but we must at all costs achieve a situation in which specialists—as a separate social stratum, which will persist until we have reached the highest stage of development of communist society—can enjoy better conditions of life under socialism than they enjoyed under capitalism [*CW* XXXIII, p. 194].

By 1923, only 23 to 29 per cent of the directors and managers of boards were communists, and according to Azrael, the vast majority of the red communists were bourgeois specialists. By 1921:

> Official sources were able to report that specialists and ex-officials occupied no less than 80 per cent of the 'most responsible posts' in the VSNKh [Supreme Economic Council] and comprised 74 per cent of the membership of the administrative collegia of industrial *glavks* [trusts]. Moreover, the regime saw fit to order those communists who retained high posts 'to command less or, more accurately, not to command'.[16]

Lenin, indeed, was so imbued with Saint-Simonian technocratic zeal that he, of all people, pleaded for the supersession of *politics* by practical control, technical competence and economic reorganization. At the Eighth Congress of Soviets in December 1920 he applauded 'the beginning of that very happy time when politics will recede into the background, when politics will be discussed less often and at shorter length, and engineers and agronomists will do most of the talking. . . . Henceforth, less politics will be the best politics' (*CW* XXXI, pp. 513–14). It is difficult to recognize the Russia of the 1920s, or '30s or '40s, in these remarks, but there is no reason to doubt Lenin's sincerity. At the very least, he was satisfied that his Party was com-

---

[16] J. R. Azrael, *Managerial Power and Soviet Politics* (Cambridge, Mass., 1966), p. 46.

petent to handle political problems and consolidate its power; these were not lessons which a Bolshevik needed to learn in or from Germany or America. The skills required for large-scale economic administration and technological development were. In Russia, they were known only to those who had been involved in these activities; they were, however, best known to those outside. For Lenin was not interested simply in employing the personnel, the administrators, traders and experts of the old regime; he was determined that Russian enterprises be modelled on those enterprises which really worked, those of the West. He sought, as he wrote in 1923, 'a staff of workers really abreast of the times, i.e. not inferior to the best West European standards' (*CW* xxxiii, p. 487). He called for German and American literature to be obtained:

> *Everything* more or less valuable should be collected, especially as regards normalizing *bureaucratic* work (procedure for despatch of business forms, control, typing of copies, inquiries and replies, etc. etc.)

> In my opinion the *most necessary* thing for us now is to learn from Europe and America [*CW* xxxvi, p. 581].

Lenin was fascinated by any technique which promised to increase industrial production—piece-work, adjusting wages to productivity, and, in particular, the Taylor system (cf. *CW* xxxiii, p. 368).

Finally, it was in aid of these same goals that Lenin fought, against great opposition, for single as opposed to collegial authority in industry. Already in March 1918 he called for the separation of 'two categories of democratic functions'; on the one hand the collegiate discussion of questions preliminary to execution and, on the other, 'the establishment of strictest responsibility for executive functions and absolutely businesslike, disciplined, voluntary fulfilment of the assignments and decrees necessary for the economic mechanism to function really like clockwork. . . . The time has come when the achievement of precisely this change is the pivot of all our revolutionary reforms' (*CW* xxvii, p. 211). It was accepted by Lenin and by his opponents on this issue that single authority and, even more, one-man management was 'dictatorial'; Lenin insisted, however, that dictatorship by the competent was often necessary. Though he encountered strong opposition, he managed to win acknowledgement for his position—in January 1920 at the Ninth Party Congress. By the end of 1920, one-man authority was established in 86 per cent of all Soviet enterprises.[17]

These, then, were the essential ingredients of Lenin's programme for post-revolutionary administration and reconstruction. The consequences of this programme for the doctrine of *The State and Revolution* can be easily and chronologically charted. In April 1918, Bukharin

[17] Azrael, p. 46.

was rebuked by Lenin for his laudatory review of *The State and Revolution*, which emphasized the message that the state had to be smashed. This task, Lenin argued, had been accomplished, it was a task of the past. What was now necessary and what Bukharin and the Left Communists ignored, was 'accounting, control and discipline' (*CW* XXVII, pp. 302–3). In July 1919 Lenin wrote an article on *The State* which interpreted the call to smash the state in a somewhat novel manner:

> This machine called the state . . . the proletariat will smash. So far we have deprived the capitalists of this machine and have taken it over. We shall use this machine or bludgeon, to destroy all exploitation. And when the possibility of exploitation no longer exists anywhere in the world, when there are no longer owners of land and owners of factories, and when there is no longer a situation in which some gorge while others starve, only when the possibility of this no longer exists shall we consign this machine to the scrapheap. Then there will be no state and no exploitation. Such is the view of our Communist Party [*CW* XXIX, p. 488].

Lenin claims that he has developed these ideas 'in more detail' in *The State and Revolution*! Finally in January 1923, Lenin called for the *reorganization* of the machinery of state, 'which is utterly useless and which we took over in its entirety from the preceding epoch; during the past five years of struggle we did not, and could not, drastically reorganize it' (*CW* XXXIII, p. 474).

'Bureaucratism', participation and administrative efficiency

It would, however, be quite misleading to end here. For to do so would be to suggest that Lenin's views after 1917 were far more coherent than they were, and that they were *simply* authoritarian and elitist. In fact, his views exhibit many tensions and strains: Lenin emphasized the primacy of politics in a revolutionary state and decried the excessively 'political' orientation of communist administrators; he emphasized the need for bourgeois specialists and continually blamed them for their 'bureaucratism'; he insisted that they be treated well and ordered that they in particular should be harshly scrutinized.[18] Moreover, the utopian and participatory elements of his thought did not simply effloresce and die in 1917, but continued to reappear in his later writings.

After the revolution, Lenin continually attacked 'bureaucracy', 'bureaucratism' and 'bureaucratic methods' in Soviet government. Before 1921 critics of 'bureaucracy' such as Bukharin and Preobazhensky linked their criticism directly to the need to take steps toward the 'withering away of the state'. Lenin no longer made this connection: the weakening or loosening of administrative arrangements was not on his post-revolutionary agenda. When Lenin attacked bureau-

[18] See A. Ulam, *Lenin and the Bolsheviks* (Glasgow, 1975), pp. 685–6.

cracy and bureaucratism after the Revolution, as he so often did, he was referring to 'system-immanent'[19] abuses, excesses, and inefficiencies. An efficient bureaucracy staffed increasingly by workers is what he sought; the 'bureaucratism' he abused was a congeries of flaws in the creaking administrative system that he knew he had.

The flaws which Lenin most often identified with 'bureaucratism' and 'bureaucratic methods' were of three general kinds. The first kind is a predilection for authoritarian dictation from above, for 'bossing' and 'ordering'. Lenin accused Trotsky of this. A second flaw, related to the first, is the making of plans without any kind of test, or realistic assessment of their effects. Thus Lenin warned against 'intellectualist and bureaucratic projecteering' (*CW* XXXII, p. 143), and he confessed in 1921 that: 'The principal mistake we have all been making up to now is too much optimism; as a result, we succumbed to bureaucratic utopias. Only a very small part of our plans has been realized. Life, everyone, in fact has laughed at our plans' (*CW*, XXXII, p. 497). Finally, and most commonly, Lenin vented his fury against inefficiency and red-tape by bracketing them with the sin of 'bureaucratism' or by subsuming them under the category of 'bureaucratic methods'. Again and again, Lenin railed against 'bureaucratism, red-tape and mismanagement', and it would not really be appropriate to try to pin down his meaning too closely; he was clearly writing for audiences who understood with him that: 'Approval from the bureaucratic standpoint means arbitrary acts on the part of the grandees, the red-tape runaround, the commissions of inquiry game, and the strictly bureaucratic foul-up of everything that is going' (*ibid.* p. 142).

How had 'bureaucratism' become so prevalent a malaise of the Soviet state? At various times, Lenin suggested a number of different explanations. One simplistic suggestion of which he was particularly fond was that bureaucratism was simply a legacy of the old regime, and specifically of the need to employ the personnel of the old regime:

> The tsarist bureaucrats began to join the Soviet institutions and practise their bureaucratic methods, they began to assume the colouring of Communists and, to succeed better in their careers, to procure membership cards of the Russian Communist Party. And so, they have been thrown out of the door but they creep back in through the window [*CW* XXIX, p. 183].

Lenin had a substantial temperamental commitment to this sort of explanation, but it is difficult to believe that even he was satisfied with it. It smacks of a particularly vulgar Marxism to suggest that all the problems associated with the attempt centrally to administer a

[19] Daniel Tarschys uses this term to characterize all post-1921 attacks on 'bureaucracy' in the Soviet Union. See his *Beyond the State: the Future Polity in Classical and Soviet Marxism* (Stockholm, 1972), p. 146.

massive state can be explained by the social type of its officeholders. In any case, Lenin gives the lie to this explanation by his constant comparisons between the skills of the old officials and communists' and workers' lack of skills, and since many of the former had never been thrown 'out of the door' there was no need for them to return through the window.

On a number of occasions, particularly towards the end of his life, Lenin acknowledged that the 'bureaucratism' of which he complained afflicted many people besides the old officials. He admitted that the Party was becoming bureaucratized; indeed on one occasion he explained that:

> It is natural that the bureaucratic methods that have reappeared in Soviet institutions were bound to have a pernicious effect even on Party organizations, since the upper ranks of the Party are at the same time the upper ranks of the state apparatus; they are one and the same thing [*CW* XXXI, pp. 421–2].

In this and other passages (*CW* XXXIII, pp. 223–4), bureaucratism appears as a type of disease, which certainly afflicted the tsarist bureaucracy, but was now afflicting the whole range of Soviet official-dom. And this suggests a far more pervasive and deep-seated problem.

Ulam has suggested that the disparate themes of Lenin's last articles and notes, dictated between December 1922 and March 1923, can be linked if one notes how often Lenin uses the word culture; 'culture and its relatives, so to speak, toleration, politeness, the ability to "attach people to oneself" ... are constantly cited by Lenin as neces-sary prerequisites of the art of governing, as both the means and the ends of the achievement of socialism'.[20] It seems to me that this stress on the need for, and the Russian lack of, culture, connects much more than Lenin's last writings. It is the Russian masses' lack of culture and education which for Lenin explains *their* inability to step directly into government and the consequent need to make use of bourgeois leftovers.[21] Russian communists, too, lacked and needed 'a cultured approach to the simplest affairs of state' (*CW* XXXIII, pp. 295–7). Not even the officials of the old regime had much culture; they were all afflicted with the Russian disease (*CW* XXIX, pp. 182–3).

What, then, was to be done? The Mensheviks might, of course, have accepted Lenin's analysis, but he could never accept their solution. In fact, his own answers varied, were not always consistent with each other and only became at all systematic in his very last brooding reflections. One measure which Lenin often encouraged was the punishment, by people's courts or by sacking, of anyone found guilty of red tape. This accorded well enough with Lenin's fury with in-efficiency, his tendency to view 'bureaucratism' as a moral fault, and

---

[20] A. Ulam, 'Lenin's Last Phase', *Survey* XXI, no. 1–2 (1975), pp. 148–9.
[21] See *CW* XXXI, p. 421; XXXIII, p. 389.

his desire to set examples for officials; it would not, however, appear calculated to enhance the level of culture.

But Lenin did not hope to cure bureaucratism simply by throwing people out of the administration; he also wished to bring a new type of person into it. Again and again, he repeated the claim that the only way to cure bureaucratism and red tape was to 'pour as many workers and peasants as possible into this apparatus' (*CW* xxx, p. 351). In 1919 the Workers' and Peasants' Inspection (*Rabkrin*) was set up under Stalin as a means of drawing the masses into supervising the bureaucracy and of training them in state administration. It is in these pleas more than anywhere else in Lenin's post-revolutionary writings that the mystique of class origin survives. Just as Marx had quite failed to take the point of Bakunin's charge, that a communist government would consist 'of former workers, who, however, as soon as they become representatives or governors of the people, *cease to be workers*', so Lenin, at least until 1921, had boundless faith in the consequences of replacing 'hundreds of thousands of bourgeois bureaucrats' (*CW* xxxi, p. 435) by trained workers.

Lenin's pleas are also strikingly reminiscent of the participatory themes of *State and Revolution,* but there is a crucial difference in this respect between his writings of 1917 and those of his period in power. In 1917 popular participation was seen as the antithesis to existing bureaucratic structures and forms of organization; in the later years, it was seen, on the one hand, as a corrective to abuses *within* the existing administrative system and, on the other, as a goal, a good in itself, but only to be approached at a pace and to an extent consistent with centralized and efficient administrative organization. Workers and peasants were to learn from existing specialists: they would 'gradually proceed from the simple duties they are able to carry out—at first only as onlookers—to more important functions of state' (*CW* xxx, p. 415) and would replace the existing, tainted functionaries only when they had learnt 'to administer the state (which was something nobody had taught us)' (*CW* xxxi, p. 435).

In fact, these devices came to nought. *Rabkrin* very quickly grew to some 12,000 officials, very few of whom were workers[22] and it became 'one of the most bureaucracy-ridden agencies in the whole government. Its officials, who had nothing else to do but to snoop around, complain, and censor the work of others, came to be considered the dregs of the Soviet administrative corps.'[23] Nor is it easy to see that *Rabkrin* under Stalin would have lessened bureaucratism even if it *had* introduced more workers into the administration. For in a system such as Lenin's, the Marxist habit of looking to the regime's Indians is often far less apposite than looking to its chiefs. In his last

[22] M. Lewin, *Lenin's Last Struggle* (London, 1973), p. 120.
[23] Ulam, *Lenin and the Bolsheviks,* p. 701.

writings, Lenin seems to have begun dimly to perceive this. At any rate, he gave unprecedented attention to the manners, activities and possibilities of restraining the top leadership of the Communist Party. Here, the proletarian mystique still lingered, and Lenin suggested that the Central Committee be leavened by 50 to 100 workers, whose functions and powers were rather sketchily defined but who were intended to check, restrain and remain independent of the personal intrigues and antagonisms within the Politburo. Lenin also suggested that the Central Control Commission be increased to 75 to 100 in number. But the institution which was to play the big role in curing the administration of bureaucratism was of a quite different sort. *Rabkrin* was to be revamped and reduced to 300 to 400 members, and these members were to be a very select group,

> specially screened for conscientiousness and knowledge of our state apparatus. They must also undergo a special test as regards their knowledge of the principles of scientific organization of labour in general, and of administration work, office work, and so forth, in particular ... they should be highly skilled, specially screened, particularly reliable, and highly paid [*CW* xxxiii, pp. 482–3].

Significantly, the only existing government institution which Lenin singled out for praise at this time was the Commissariat of Foreign Affairs, which itself was staffed with ex-Menshevik experts and experts from the old regime, and which 'by current standards appeared virtually apolitical'.[24] According to Ulam:

> The ministry, in brief, was more efficient, and it worked, not at the behest of some Party bigwig or faction, but for the Party as a whole.
> Thus, in a somewhat roundabout way, Lenin defined his prerequisites for sound administration: efficiency and non-involvement in the personal side of politics.[25]

Lenin was, in other words, trying to replace the 'patrimonial' staffs of 'Party bosses' with an impersonal and efficient bureaucracy. This, I believe, is where we began.

It is extremely doubtful whether Lenin's prescriptions would have been effective even if he had survived. In particular, it is worth noticing how limited his critique is. He never questions the decisive political fact of the regime—one-party dictatorship—nor does he consider the effect that the state's repressive apparatus and activities, the ban on factions, and so on, might have on administrative efficiency, and much besides. No external constraints, checks or balances are proposed, merely internal manoeuvrings among bureaucrats and Party overseers.

In this context, Moshe Lewin is right to complain that:

[24] Ulam, 'Lenin's Last Phase', p. 157.
[25] *ibid.* p. 158.

Lenin, who always claimed to be an orthodox Marxist, who no doubt did use the Marxist method in approaching social phenomena, and who saw the international situation in class terms, approached the problems of government more like a chief executive of a strictly 'elitist' turn of mind. He did not apply methods of social analysis to the government itself and was content to consider it purely in terms of organizational methods.[26]

However, the point is not simply that Lenin 'approached the problems of government more like a chief executive of a strictly "elitist" turn of mind'—that, after all, is almost precisely what he was—but that he had approached these problems like a chief executive who had not expected them to arise and who had no theory for coping with them.

[26] *Lenin's Last Struggle*, pp. 121–2.

4

The revolution betrayed? from Trotsky to the new class

Martin Krygier

Explanations and theories do not develop in a vacuum; they are strongly coloured by the assumptions and presuppositions which a thinker brings to his work. Questions arise, and answers are given, in the context of conscious or unconscious theoretical frameworks, in terms of interests and beliefs that distinguish or seek to distinguish the potentially significant from the non-significant, that lay down what are seen as 'satisfactory' ways of providing explanations. Such frameworks are often very resistant to change; most traditions of thought are held together by agreement on the important problems and the proper ways of solving them rather than by specific solutions. Modern thinkers have called such theoretical frameworks the 'paradigm' or 'problematic' within which a thinker works.

Marxism has operated, for many thinkers, as such a 'paradigm'. It has stipulated what the fundamental activities and actors in society are and where they are carrying men and societies. Individual societies, Marxists have insisted, can only be understood through a proper appreciation of these basic forces: to unravel the nature of a given society, one must grasp its class structure; to discover who rules the society, one must determine which class owns the means of production; to ascertain what the future holds, one must recognize that a new ruling class can only supplant an existing one if it is capable of organizing production at a higher level. More specifically, Marxists have been confident that a *capitalist* society will ultimately fall to a proletarian revolution and that this revolution will pave the way for a society without classes.

Of course, there is much more in Marx that this, and his writings are infinitely subtler, and display many more nuances, than those of most of his followers. 'Orthodox' Marxists, however, were not wrong to believe that these elements stood at the core of Marx's social theory. Moreover, only if one appreciates that these and related beliefs were considered by many Marxists to hold the key to the understanding of social reality, can one understand the rise, nature, and persistence of 'new class' theories and the heat which they have generated. Similarly, without appreciation of the tenacity with which these conceptions have been held, it would be difficult to comprehend why writers who have broken with Marxism on fundamental issues of fact and principle still persist in trying to find new answers to old questions, rather than shift to asking new questions. New class theories are significant Marxist heresies; they stop well short of apostasy.

I Trotsky, Stalinism and bureaucracy

The Revolution betrayed

No Marxist has insisted more strongly on the propositions outlined above than Leon Trotsky (1879–1940). He is of special interest for our purposes because the concept of 'bureaucracy' stands at the core of his post-1923 writings—historical, theoretical, polemical—in a way, and to an extent, that it never did for Marx and that it has rarely done for Marxists.[1] In these writings he grappled persistently with the issues that the existence of powerful bureaucracies posed for Marxists, and his writings had a considerable influence on the reception of the concept of bureaucracy by later Marxists and by many non- or ex-Marxists.

Thoughout the 1930s Trotsky insisted that the October Revolution had been 'betrayed'—betrayed by a stratum of self-seeking bureaucrats who had succeeded in destroying the true 'proletarian vanguard', the Bolshevik Party. This claim was absent from Trotsky's first post-revolutionary criticisms of the Party. In December 1923 he published a number of articles in *Pravda* which were republished as *The New Course* early in 1924. In them he warned the party against the spread of 'bureaucratism', which was 'the result of the transference to the party of the methods and the administrative manners accumulated during these last years'.[2] Linked with this insistence on the *novelty* of Soviet bureaucratism is Trotsky's account of the aetiology of the disease. In 1923 Trotsky was not arguing, as he came

---

[1] I have given a more detailed account and critique of Trotsky's use of the concept in ' "Bureaucracy" in Trotsky's Analysis of Stalinism', in Marian Sawer (ed.), *Socialism and the New Class: towards the Analysis of Structural Inequality within Socialist Societies*, Australian Political Studies Association Monograph no. 19 (Adelaide, 1978), pp. 46–67.

[2] As reprinted and translated in *The Challenge of the Left Opposition (1923–25)* (New York, 1975), p. 70.

later to argue, that leadership had been usurped by a different type of leader. He held rather that a malaise was afflicting the old revolutionary leadership itself as a result of its post-revolutionary involvement in apparatus-work and in its new positions of power. There was, as it were, an *internal* degeneration of the leaders, stemming from the necessity of building and maintaining an effective centralized state and army apparatus (*ibid.* pp. 91–2) rather than from the supplanting of one group of leaders by men of a quite different sort. It was this internal degeneration that threatened the revolution.

Trotsky's analysis, with its emphasis on the role of functional and administrative imperatives and constraints, would not have surprised Max Weber or Robert Michels. But Trotsky was a Marxist, and he insisted that: 'It is unworthy of a Marxist to consider that bureaucratism is only the aggregate of the bad habits of officeholders. Bureaucratism is a social phenomenon in that it is a definite system of administration of people and things' (p. 91). For Trotsky bureaucratism is a 'social phenomenon' in two senses: its *causes* he argues, are ultimately social, 'the heterogeneity of society, the difference between the daily and the fundamental interests of various groups of the population' (p. 91) and its *beneficiaries* and promoters are not randomly or unrelatedly distributed. They are beginning to form 'fairly stable social groupings' (p. 74). It was on that 'social grouping' which he identifies as the bureaucracy that the bulk of Trotsky's explanation was focused. His explanation increasingly moves from a description of a malign tendency that might afflict members of the Party to a way of characterizing the typical ways of behaving, the psychological make-up and working-style of a specific, identifiable stratum, the bureaucracy.

In his later writings, Trotsky insisted that the Soviet tragedy lay in the fact that this stratum had supplanted the political leadership of the Soviet Union, the Bolshevik Party. Trotsky's objection was not at all to dictatorship *per se*; his objection was specifically to *bureaucratic* dictatorship. Late in his life, Trotsky was prepared to concede that the Bolshevik dictatorship 'served as the juridical point of departure'[3] for the Stalinist dictatorship, but he still maintained that it was anarchist—or Stalinist—nonsense to confuse the two. They were totally different kinds of phenomena, and the latter did and could hold sway only after the deliberate and complete emasculation of the Party.

Before the Revolution, Trotsky had consistently and vehemently attacked the Leninist conception of the Party. After 1917, however, Trotsky followed Lenin in insisting unreservedly on the vanguard role of the Bolshevik Party. Moreover, like Max Weber, with whom he shared virtually no other political values, expectations or hopes,

[3] *Stalinism and Bolshevism* (New York, 1937), p. 22.

Trotsky insisted that there was a profound difference between the skills of a political leader and those of a bureaucrat. He was not arguing that bureaucracy could be dispensed with, nor even that it should be diluted: the Maoist slogan 'Better Red than Expert' would have seemed to him nonsense and completely inconsistent with what was required for the building of socialism. Though bureaucracy would disappear after the coming of socialism in respect of the interim period, Trotsky was in effect also a Weberian in another respect, in his conviction that professional, trained bureaucrats manning an apparatus of great power were indispensable. But the bureaucracy had to be controlled and its goals and policies had to be set by people of quite a different stamp, with priorities and goals of a quite different order.

The Soviet tragedy, on Trotsky's view, was not so much that the correct political regime must be superior to a bureaucratic regime in all circumstances and that in the Soviet Union this was not so. After all, when socialism is achieved, the comparison will be empty of reference, for there will be no state or politics at all.[4] But in the Soviet Union, in *transition* to socialism, the quality of the political regime is of unique importance, for 'there is no other government in the world in whose hands the fate of the whole country is concentrated to such a degree'.[5] It was in this country, Trotsky argued, whose future was of fundamental importance for world development and whose own development was uniquely dependent on talented, dedicated and ideologically sound political leadership, that the ranks of far-sighted revolutionaries were being decimated by a bloated, incompetent layer of bureaucrats.

Trotsky's explanation of the rise of this rapacious clique is made up of three partly related elements. The first element appears in occasional, scattered comments on the general fate of revolutions, and suggests a general theory of post-revolutionary development, which the Soviet Union exemplifies. A revolution, Trotsky suggests, is inevitably followed by a 'downswing' in which weariness, apathy and disillusionment set in and reactionary forces have an opportunity to prosper. (Marx took this view of the Thermidorean reaction in the French Revolution, and Trotsky developed it.) In the Soviet Union, then, not Stalin's political skill nor Trotsky's lack of it, but objective concomitants of revolutionary upheaval explain the 'backsliding', the 'downswing' of the revolution. On this view it is not pre-determined that the forces of reaction will be victorious, but it can be expected that they will come strongly into play.

The second element elevated by Trotsky is an amalgam of difficul-

---

[4] *Writings of Leon Trotsky ...* (*1933–4*) (New York, 1972), p. 225, and *The Revolution Betrayed* (reprinted London, 1973), pp. 268, 271.
[5] *The Revolution Betrayed*, p. 43.

ties faced specifically by the Russian revolutionaries—the failure of the revolution to spread through the advanced countries of Europe, the consequent isolation of the Soviet Union in a capitalist world, and the massive 'contradictions' to be overcome in the attempt to establish socialism in a backward country. Even if a healthy leadership did exist, it would have to face these problems; the sin of the bureaucrats was that 'instead of reducing them, the policy of the present leadership aggravates them.'[6]

The third element of Trotsky's explanation deals with the question why the bureaucracy in particular had been strengthened to such a degree. To answer this question, Trotsky considers himself forced to introduce some novelties into Marxism since, he explains, Marx never envisaged a proletarian revolution in a backward country, and Lenin never foresaw so prolonged an isolation of the Soviet state. As a theorist of the laws of proletarian dictatorship in an underdeveloped country, and as a theorist of post-revolutionary bureaucratization, Trotsky has thus *had* to be original. He believed that any workers' regime would require a centralized state to transform society and prepare the way for socialism, and he agreed with Marx and Lenin that ultimately this state structure with its distinct and privileged group of professional bureaucrats would be eliminated. In the period of transition, however, especially in a poor country, Trotsky argues, a distinct bureaucracy must be maintained. It is needed to arbitrate in the struggle for scarce resources, to stimulate maximum production, and to police and regulate distribution as long as contradiction and economic scarcity persist; and while these functions need to be performed, elements of capitalism, such as wage incentives, must survive to encourage the bureaucrats to perform them. Throughout this period, then, bureaucrats have an institutional base for the power and privilege which they seek to protect and enhance.

It is perhaps worth noting that Trotsky, unconsciously following a distinguished Marxist tradition, here manages to stand Tocqueville and Weber, as well as Hegel, on their heads. The growth of bureaucracy on his view varies directly with economic backwardness, scarcity and social dislocation, and inversely with equality and affluence. Trotsky acknowledges that a bureaucracy has a role in promoting economic development, but his view of bureaucracy as a sort of scaffolding which can be dismantled once the building is completed allows him to evade some of the central structural problems of modern society.

Bureaucracy: caste or class?

On Trotsky's argument, there is inevitably a post-revolutionary 'downswing' which threatens to enthrone some reactionary element or

[6] *Writings ... (1930)*, p. 137.

other; there has been such a downswing in the Soviet Union and it has enthroned a contemptible bureaucracy; and this should come as no great surprise (though it did), because such a bureaucracy has considerable sources of power in a transitional, underdeveloped society. Now if all this is true, one might expect that the danger most to be feared in the Soviet Union is the consolidation of this bureaucratic dictatorship. One might also wonder whether it is enough to talk simply of the 'deformation' or 'degeneration' of the revolution: even if the initial promise of the revolution is conceded, has this promise survived or has it been totally destroyed? Trotsky, however, continually denied that the bureaucracy could stabilize its rule. Though bureaucracy came to occupy the centre of Trotsky's immediate focus of attention soon after 1923, it took him much longer —in fact, until a year before his death—to acknowledge it as a potentially major institution in the general course of historical development. The development of an awareness of the importance of bureaucracy, a development which Trotsky did much to create and further within Marxism, is mirrored in microcosm within his own thought. Trotsky's reluctance to acknowledge the long-term significance of bureaucracy and his repeated resistance to those who insisted on it, are interesting not simply as a piece of intellectual biography; they are also of interest as a case study of some of the difficulties faced by a Marxist in dealing with one of the fundamental developments of the modern age.

Trotsky describes the options facing the Soviet Union in terms of a Manichaean struggle between the forces of the proletariat and those of capitalism. The Soviet Union was surrounded by hostile capitalist powers, and internally a similar conflict between bourgeois and proletarian forces was taking place. For most of his life it was inconceivable to Trotsky that a bureaucracy might constitute a rival in its own right to either or both of these great protagonists. Throughout the 1920s, despite his slowly dawning recognition that it was Stalin who was his most significant Party opponent, Trotsky warned that the real danger came not from Stalin or his direct supporters, but from *external* forces pushing on them, 'from the Right, not from the Right wing of our party—the Right wing of our party serves only as a transmitting mechanism—the real, basic, danger comes from the side of the bourgeois classes who are raising their heads.'[7] Indeed in the 1920s Trotsky quickly forsook the insights displayed in his early warnings against the *intrinsic* danger that bureaucratism might affect leaders and insisted that the growth of bureaucratism was purely the result of the pressures exerted by hostile classes. Throughout this period, while Stalin was steadily consolidating his own position, and although, as Lewin has pointed

[7] *The Stalin School of Falsification* (London, 1974), p. 111.

out, 'the Rightist dangers against which they were fighting were phantoms,'[8] Trotsky and the rest of the Left repeatedly warned the party against the threat of a renascent bourgeoisie.

With the crushing of millions of kulaks in the 1930s, this warning became singularly inappropriate, both because they could not now seriously be regarded as an imminent threat to anyone and because the bureaucracy itself appeared more than a little independent of them. Trotsky certainly acknowledged that there had been a significant weakening of the 'bourgeoisie' with Stalin's 'left' turn after 1929. But if many of the native bourgeoisie had been eliminated or crushed, this was no reason for Trotsky to alter his conception of the general course of social development. With one significant exception, Trotsky always insisted that if the proletariat were to be defeated, in the Soviet Union and everywhere else, it could only be at the hands of world capitalism. All that the liquidation of the kulaks meant was that the weapons and means available to the capitalist opponents of communism had been changed and their price since, say, 1927 had been somewhat raised.

But, as Trotsky began increasingly to be asked, why should this be so? Why should a stratum which, as he so often emphasized, had enormous power and resources at its disposal, which was directly responsible for the 'degeneration' of the revolution, be doomed to swing between bourgeois and proletarians? The importance of the answer to this question stemmed from what Trotsky and almost all who debated him took to be its consequences: if the bureaucracy's rule were capable of stable, autonomous development, then the Soviet Union was no longer a workers' state and the Revolution had been in vain, or worse than in vain.

For the notion of the 'workers' state' to make any sense, one must be able to specify the minimum conditions which a state must satisfy to be a 'workers' state'; one must determine, in other words, some boundary within which there is a 'workers' state', however degenerate, and beyond which a 'worker's state' becomes something else. Trotsky recognizes this, and from at least as early as 1928, he attempts to stipulate where the boundary lies. His attempts are not always consistent, but looked at as a whole they do form a pattern of reluctant but steadily growing perception of the potential longevity of the existing regime, a perception which combines uneasily with his determination to affirm that the Soviet Union is a workers' state.

In 1928 and 1929, Trotsky emphasized an essentially political criterion for 'workers' statehood'. One had to determine who had power or at least the possibility of peacefully regaining power. Since,

[8] M. Lewin, *Political Undercurrents in Soviet Economic Debates* (Princeton, 1974), p. 69.

Trotsky insisted, the proletariat could regain power by reform, but the bourgeoisie could not, the Revolution had not been defeated.[9] But by 1933 Trotsky decided that the problem could not be resolved peacefully. In March, after the failure of communist policies in Germany, Trotsky announced that the KPD (the German Communist Party) was 'doomed' and that 'German Communism can be reborn only on a new basis and with a new leadership;'[10] in July he announced that the International as a whole could not be redeemed, and in October he declared that the Soviet bureaucracy could only be defeated by force.[11]

Now, if one were to insist on Trotsky's earlier *political* criterion one would be forced to admit that the Soviet Union was no longer a workers' state. But Trotsky did not admit this. Instead, an *economic* criterion, which he had increasingly emphasized after the latter part of 1929, became for him and for all orthodox Trotskyists the sole and adequate test. Trotsky now repeatedly reminded Marxists that the character of a state is determined by the property relations within it. The achievement of the October Revolution had been to expropriate the possessing classes, to nationalize property and to institute a planned economy under the dictatorship of the proletariat. The result of this was that the proletariat was the ruling class of the Soviet Union. So long as this achievement survived, so long as no other class came to own the means of production, the proletariat would remain the ruling class. It is only if political 'distortions have extended to the economic foundations of the state',[12] that one can properly speak of the defeat or overthrow of the revolution.

These propositions rapidly congealed into part of Trotskyist political dogma, part of a set of assumptions which were unquestioned, indeed unquestionable, and which set the terms within which discussion could proceed. It was the critics who appeared to accept these assumptions but still denied that the Soviet Union was a workers' state whom Trotsky treated most seriously, in particular those who argued that the Soviet Union was ruled by a new class, the bureaucracy. For from Trotsky's premises it is a simple inference that if the bureaucracy dominating the Soviet Union is a new governing *class*, then the proletariat has been expropriated and a new form of exploitative society has come into being. As Trotsky put it: 'If the Bonapartist riffraff is a class this means that it is not an abortion but a viable child of history. If its marauding parasitism is "exploitation" in the scientific sense of the term this means that the

[9] See Trotsky's 1928 replies to the exiled Democratic Centralist, Borodai, reprinted in *The New International* (April 1943), pp. 124 and 125.
[10] *The Struggle against Fascism in Germany* (Harmondsworth, 1975), p. 397.
[11] *Writings ... (1933–4)*, pp. 117 and 118.
[12] *Writings ... (1934–5)*, p. 169.

bureaucracy possesses a historical future as the ruling class indispensable to the given system of economy.'[13] It therefore becomes an issue
of pivotal importance to Trotsky to show that the Soviet Union's
governing 'caste' was not its ruling class.

Trotsky was fully alive to the political power and economic privilege
of the bureaucracy. 'In no other regime', he conceded, 'has a
bureaucracy ever achieved such a degree of independence from the
dominating class.... It is in the full sense of the word the sole
privileged and commanding stratum in the Soviet society.'[14] Nonetheless, this did not make it a class, for 'the *class* has an excep-
tionally important and, moreover, a scientifically restricted meaning to
a Marxist.'[15] A class must have an independent role and independent
roots in the economic structure, that is, an independent role in production and a relationship to productive property that is peculiarly its
own; a ruling class, moreover, has to have a quite special relationship to property in the means of production: it must *own* it. The fact
that bureaucrats own articles of consumption is important enough to
them and to the wretched proletariat, but it is irrelevant to whether
they are a class. The bureaucracy had no independent role in production and no property in the means of production; it 'has neither
stocks nor bonds. It is recruited, supplemented and renewed in the
manner of an administrative hierarchy, independently of any special
property relations of its own. The individual bureaucrat cannot trans-
mit to his heirs his rights in the exploitation of the state apparatus.'[16]
A bureaucracy is an 'instrument', a 'hireling' of class rule which can
be found in every class society. In the Soviet Union it is a
particularly over-weening, incompetent and expensive hireling, but it
is not a class; it is not—since for Trotsky only a class can be—an
independent historical force. It certainly robs the society in which it
exists, but so long as it does this on the basis of the property
relations instituted in October 1917, its theft is social parasitism
like that of the modern clergy, not class exploitation like that of the
bourgeoisie. It has the power to damage the workers' state, to weaken
it in the face of hostile classes and for a time to keep its own head
(even its toes!) above water. As long as it does not have its own
forms of production and property, however, 'it is compelled to defend
state property as the source of its power and its income' (*ibid.*).

Trotsky also seems to be persuaded by a sort of functional
argument that a bureaucracy cannot be a ruling class. This argument
proceeds from identifying the function of an institution to deducing
the roles it must, and the roles it cannot, play. Trotsky does not

[13] *In Defence of Marxism* (Reprinted London, 1971), p. 29.
[14] *The Revolution Betrayed*, pp. 248–9.
[15] *Writings ... (1933–4)*, p. 112.
[16] *The Revolution Betrayed*, p. 249.

employ this sort of argument very often, but it accords with what he believes must be the case in the long term and should be the case at every moment:

> The existence of a bureaucracy, in all its variety of forms and differences in specific weight, characterizes *every* class regime. Its power is of a reflected character. The bureaucracy is indissolubly bound up with a ruling economic class, feeding itself upon the social roots of the latter, maintaining itself and falling together with it.[17]

Soviet bureaucracy, Trotsky concedes, is more independent than any other, but since it *is* a bureaucracy it cannot ultimately prevail against economic classes; there is something intrinsically subaltern about bureaucracy which prevents it from ruling in its own right.

Conversely, a *class* can be identified by its function, its 'historic mission', which is to develop the system of production. If a purported new class does not do this it has simply been wrongly classified, for while 'social excrescences can be the product of an "accidental" (i.e. temporary and extraordinary), enmeshing of historical circumstances, [a] social organ (and such is every class, including an exploiting class) can take shape only as a result of the deeply rooted inner needs of production itself.'[18] Even where Trotsky is not directly concerned with rebutting the new class theorists, his concern with these issues is constantly manifest. The very notion of 'betrayal' suggests the special relationship which Trotsky believes to exist between the bureaucracy and the proletariat—the bureaucracy threatens from within, and not, as a rival class would, from without. The various organic metaphors used by Trotsky have a similar function. Bureaucracy is a 'tumour', an 'ulcer', an 'excrescence'; it is, in other words, a malign growth and not an independent external enemy. Or, when its description as a 'parasite' suggests that it might be external, it also suggests, in common with the other metaphors, that it has no life independent of the workers' state.

Trotsky continued, until his death at the hands of Stalin's assassin in 1940, to resist suggestions that the bureaucracy was a class, just as he continued to reaffirm his revolutionary optimism and confidence in the ultimate victory of the proletariat. But if Trotsky was never prepared to concede that the bureaucracy was a class, what he ultimately did concede was significant enough. In September 1939 Trotsky published 'The USSR in War'[19] in which, though his appraisal of the existing Soviet regime remained what it had been since 1935, he came to entertain seriously a hitherto rejected possibility.

It is crucial in this connection to attend to the context in which

[17] *Writings . . . (1933–4)*, pp. 112–13.
[18] *In Defence of Marxism*, p. 7.
[19] *In Defence of Marxism*, pp. 3–26.

this article appeared, specifically to the effects of the war on
Trotsky's analysis. Fundamental to Trotsky's argument in 'The
USSR in War' is the conviction that capitalism had at last truly
played itself out. Trotsky regarded the war as the latest and most
severe manifestation of the ever sharper contradictions within and
between capitalist states, and its outbreak seemed to him to
confirm that capitalism was not merely moribund but in its 'death
agony'. The war, he wrote, 'attests incontrovertibly to the fact that
society can no longer live on the basis of capitalism' (*ibid* p. 10).
Given what he elsewhere had called 'the progressive tendencies of
the objective historical process itself'[20] and given that the disorganizing
core of capitalism was the anarchy of production, the societies to
emerge from the crisis would have to have been purged of this
anarchy; their 'productive forces must be organized in accordance
with a plan' (p. 9). The future course of human development will
depend on 'who will accomplish this task—the proletariat or a new
ruling class of "Commissars"—politicians, administrators and technicians?' (p. 9). It is in terms of this assessment of the effects of the
war on capitalism that Trotsky's predictions regarding the Soviet
Union must be understood.

Trotsky's most important remarks on the future of the Soviet Union
occur in his discussion of a book published in 1939, *La Bureaucratisation du monde*,[21] by Bruno Rizzi.[22] Rizzi argued that the
bourgeoisie was an exhausted social force and that a new form of
society which he called 'bureaucratic collectivism', was expropriating
the bourgeoisie and capitalism throughout the world—it had emerged
in the Soviet Union, was partially achieved in Nazi Germany,
fascist Italy and Japan and was developing via the New Deal in the
United States. Rizzi regarded bureaucratic collectivism as a
historically progressive social order between capitalism and socialism,
and he argued that there was, therefore, no danger of a capitalist
restoration, for this would be a historically retrograde step, and
history does not move backwards. Rizzi insisted that in developed
bureaucratic collectivism the bureaucracy formed a class which
collectively exploited the mass of the population and drew surplus
value from it.

[20] *Writings ... (1937–8)*, p. 68.
[21] This book was apparently destroyed during the Second World War and the original
edition is extremely difficult to obtain. It has been reissued in an Italian edition,
Il collettivismo burocratico (Imola, 1967). The book's first and best section, which
deals with the Soviet Union, was republished in Paris in 1976, as *L'URSS:
collectivisme bureaucratique*.
[22] For the remarkable story of the identification and discovery of Bruno Rizzi, some
twenty years after Trotsky had mentioned him, see Daniel Bell, 'The Strange Case
of Bruno R.', *New Leader*, 28 September 1959, and Bell, 'The Post-Industrial Society:
the Evolution of an Idea', *Survey* XVII, no. 2 (1971), pp. 143–4.

We have seen the dismissive way in which Trotsky had hitherto treated writers who claimed that the Soviet bureaucracy was a class. Rizzi, on the other hand, was not dismissed in the same way. 'Bruno R.', Trotsky wrote, had 'the merit of seeking to transfer the question from the charmed circle of terminological copybook exercises to the plane of major historical generalizations'.[23] Trotsky nonetheless rejects this analysis too, especially on the ground that, despite the considerable *political* similarities between Stalinism and fascism, there is an unbridgeable gulf between the partial statism of the fascist regimes and the nationalization of the means of production achieved in the Soviet Union. But the effect of Rizzi's analysis on Trotsky is obvious, and the way in which he deals with it is an index of the distance his views have moved under the pressure of recent events, and particularly of the war. In a letter to James P. Cannon written while 'The USSR in War' was being composed, Trotsky wrote: 'The USSR question cannot be isolated as unique from the whole historic process of our times. Either the Stalin state is a transitory formation, it is a deformation of a worker state in a backward and isolated country, or "bureaucratic collectivism" (Bruno R., *La Bureaucratisation du monde*) is a new social formation which is replacing capitalism throughout the world (Stalinism, Fascism, New Deals etc.). The terminological experiments (workers' state, not workers' state, class, not class, etc.) receive a sense only under this historic aspect' (*ibid.* p. 1). Again, in the most frequently quoted passage from 'The USSR in War' Trotsky writes:

> The historic alternative, carried to the end, is as follows: either the Stalin regime is an abhorrent relapse in the process of transforming bourgeois society into a socialist society, or the Stalin regime is the first stage of a new exploiting society. If the second prognosis proves to be correct, then, of course, the bureaucracy will become a new exploiting class. However onerous the second perspective may be, if the world proletariat should actually prove incapable of fulfilling the mission placed upon it by the course of development, nothing else would remain except only to recognize that the socialist programme, based on the internal contradictions of capitalist society, ended as a Utopia. It is self-evident that a new 'minimum' programme would be required—for the defence of the interests of the slaves of the totalitarian bureaucratic society [p. 11].

These passages represent much more than an alteration of mood or of tone. As the dissident American Trotskyists were quick to point out, they betray a completely new direction in the movement of Trotsky's thought. The 'historic' alternatives have been completely redrawn. As we have seen, Trotsky had insisted throughout his previous writings that the real threat to socialism in the Soviet Union

[23] *In Defence of Marxism*, p. 12.

and in the world, the phenomenon constantly to be struggled against, was a restoration of capitalism: the bureaucracy was to be opposed for what it might clear the way to, rather than simply, or even primarily, for what it was.

On the rare occasions when Trotsky had considered the theoretical possibility of the stabilization of bureaucratic rule,[24] he was heavily sceptical, and even on these occasions the possibility of a third form was little more than raised by Trotsky. It was always overshadowed in his mind by a far more daunting and probable alternative, a capitalist restoration.

In 'The USSR in War', however, 'bureaucratic collectivism' is portrayed not merely as a possible successor to socialism, which itself would be fairly new for Trotsky, but as the only possible successor. It is true, as Trotsky says in attempting to deny that his views had changed, that 'Marxists have formulated an incalculable number of times the alternatives: either socialism or return to barbarism,'[25] but in 'The USSR in War' the specific nature of the barbarous alternative has completely changed, and even on Trotsky's account, let alone Rizzi's, the alternative is in no way a return. If bureaucratic collectivism triumphs, it will be, according to Trotsky, a totally new kind of social formation, the successor to both capitalism and socialism: it may be a step downward, but it is not a step backward. On this view, it will be a modern, post-capitalist phenomenon in which, for the first time, bureaucracy will have come into its own.

II Theorists of 'the new class'

Until the postwar disputes between Yugoslavia and the Soviet Union, Trotskyism, as John Plamenatz wrote at the time, was 'the only major heresy since the seat of Marxism was shifted to Moscow' and Trotsky himself was 'the arch-heretic, more evil and more dangerous than all the others together'.[26] The doctrinal core of Trotsky's heresy was expressed in his claim that the Soviet bureaucracy had betrayed the Revolution. As we have seen, precisely because of his role as heresiarch, it was crucial for Trotsky on the one hand to determine whether Soviet bureaucracy could be a class, and on the other to deny that it was one. 'New class' theorists have been prepared to go a good deal further than Trotsky; *not* in disputing the importance of the questions which he asked, but in rejecting his answers to them.

'New class' theories have appeared in a variety of forms. Already in

---

[24] *Writings ...* (*1935–6*), pp. 121–2; *The Revolution Betrayed*, pp. 253–4; *Writings ...* (*1937–8*), pp. 61–71.

[25] *In Defence of Marxism*, p. 37.

[26] John Plamenatz, 'Deviations from Marxism', *Political Quarterly* XXI (1950), p. 48.

1872, the anarchist Bakunin directly accused Marx and his followers of seeking to install

> the reign of *scientific intelligence,* the most aristocratic, despotic, arrogant, and elitist of all regimes. There will be a new class, a new hierarchy of real and counterfeit scientists and scholars, and the work will be divided into a minority ruling in the name of knowledge, and an immense ignorant majority. And then, woe unto the mass of ignorant ones![27]

The writings of the Polish revolutionary, Jan Wacław Machajski (especially his *The Intellectual Worker*) were animated by a similar belief that Marxists sought a state in which the 'intellectual capital' monopolized by their class, the intelligentsia, would be pre-eminent. These themes were taken up in anarchist and 'Left-communist' critiques of Bolshevism in the 1920s and 1930s.

In 1939 and 1940 there appeared a number of new class theories of a special sort—global theories which suggested that a new class, unforeseen by Marx, was coming into power throughout the developed world. Like Trotsky's reflections in 'The USSR in War', these writings were stimulated by a combination of Stalin's success in the Soviet Union and the extraordinary breakdowns, changes and fascist successes in capitalist states of the 1930s. The most famous of these books, James Burnham's *The Managerial Revolution*,[28] was the culmination of the author's split with the American Trotskyist movement. Well before this book appeared, Trotsky had accused Burnham of apostasy, and Burnham himself had confessed that: 'By no stretching of terminology can I any longer regard myself or permit others to regard me as a Marxist.'[29] Yet, as *The Managerial Revolution* makes abundantly clear in its relentless determination to answer the questions which Trotsky posed, both Trotsky and Burnham were mistaken on this point. Burnham's journey to apostasy took much longer than he seems to have anticipated: his most famous work, and the earlier theses of Bruno Rizzi and the non-Bolshevik, democratic Marxist, Lucien Laurat,[30] were merely heresies.

The most striking feature of these theories, and the one which distinguishes them from more recent theories emanating from within the 'socialist' states, is that none of them is simply concerned with socialist states. The belief that socialism would be a successor to

[27] Reprinted in Sam Dolgoff (ed.), *Bakunin on Anarchy* (New York, 1972), p. 319.
[28] First published 1941; here cited from the Penguin edition (Harmondsworth, 1962).
[29] 'Letter of Resignation from the Workers' Party', in Trotsky, *In Defence of Marxism*, p. 257.
[30] Lucien Laurat, *Marxism and Democracy* (London, 1940), first published as *Le Marxisme en faillite?* (Paris, 1939).

capitalism on a world scale, rather than a mere international competitor, was, after all, basic in classical Marxism. Laurat, Rizzi and Burnham retained the scope of the original drama but inserted a new character. Laurat identified the new class as 'pluto-technocratic' in the West and 'bureau-technocratic' in the Soviet Union; Rizzi was content with Trotsky's 'bureaucracy'; Burnham believed that 'managers' were introducing 'managerial society' throughout the world.

These authors all considered the growth of the state and of state functions as the most important vehicle for the rise of the new class. Indeed Rizzi concentrated on this factor and on developments associated with, or contributing to, it. But to minds willing to dismiss distinctions between the nature of state intervention and control in the Soviet Union, Germany, Italy and America, there were also other distinctions to be blurred. The most important of these was that between state and non-state functionaries, and both Laurat and Burnham insisted that capitalists had been virtually expropriated by members of the ascending class and that the new expropriators were part of the same group as those who were coming to run the state. There was, then, an omnipotent state in the Soviet Union and, in the West, an unprecedentedly active one linked to a completely new group of corporate controllers. The latter were also members of the new class.

This crucial but scarcely argued-for connection between state and non-state functionaries is made plausible largely because of the definitional vagueness so characteristic of 'new class' discussion. Thus Laurat simply points to the rise of technicians in all fields and assumes that their interests, at least vis-à-vis anyone else, will converge. Burnham relies on modern developments to encourage the rise of a new type of man—not ex-seminarians or postcard painters, but technically competent administrators—in both government and private industry.[31]

It is their determination, not to say obsession, to identify and demarcate a new ruling class which indicates the profoundly Marxist nature of these theories. Trotsky had insisted that to a Marxist the birth of a new class was not a haphazard affair but signalled profound economic developments and indicated that the new class was economically more progressive than the former ruling class. So Laurat, Rizzi and Burnham emphasize that the coming economic system is a great economic advance on the capitalism which it replaces. So, too, its progressive elements are familiar to most Marxists:

1.   The increasing organic fusion between the State and the economic

[31] Burnham, pp. 105, 141.

system; the development ... of 'control levers'; the rapidly increasing centralization of all economic activity; the development of decentralized control lacking co-ordination in the direction of centralized and co-ordinated control.

2. The development of property towards more and more collectivist forms (increase in the numbers of the shareholding public, the decline of the private sector of the economic system before the advance of the public sector); the broadening of social legislation; the development of increasingly collectivist legal forms.[32]

Laurat, it is true, believes that such a system will be less progressive than it might be unless the proletariat can win control over it, but he also has no doubt that the new ruling class is economically superior to the old.

Again, Trotsky insisted that a ruling class must own the means of production, and an enormous amount of ink, and some blood, has been spilt as a result of a new class theorists' attempts to show that what the new class has amounts to ownership. Rizzi was one of the first to sound an oft-repeated note by arguing that the bureaucracy *owned* property as much as the capitalists had, but that it owned it—as it exploited the proletariat and drew off the surplus value which the latter produced—not individually but collectively, *en bloc*. True, Rizzi concedes, this is a different manner of ownership from bourgeois ownership, but, he insists repeatedly, it is ownership nonetheless. Burnham, too, is determined to show that his managers 'own' the means of production. He agrees with Rizzi as to the collective nature of managerial ownership; he goes on to claim that there is no distinction between ownership and control and that since the managers are in control of the means of production, they therefore own them. Laurat is less obsessed with the term 'ownership' than are those who argue with Trotsky: he dismisses the importance of legal property, but he too gives primacy to the new class's economic exploitation and total economic control.

Finally, what in other circles might pass for arid terminological disputes gains substance here from what orthodox and heretics agree are the consequences of identifying the class which owns the means of production. As Burnham explains:

> In most types of society that we know about, and in all complex societies so far, there is a particular, and relatively small group of men that *controls* [for the orthodox read '*owns*'] the chief instruments of production.... Where there is such a controlling group in society ... we may speak of this group as the socially dominant or ruling class in that society. It is hard, indeed, to see what else could be meant by 'dominant' or 'ruling' class. Such a group has the power and privilege and wealth in the society, as against the remainder of society.[33]

[32] Laurat, p. 211.
[33] Burnham, p. 63.

And Rizzi also reveals what must have been, in the case of Russia,
an extraordinarily powerful argument for many Marxists:

> The 'clerk' who, following Trotsky, is only the transmission mechanism
> of imperialism, has ruled in Russia for over twenty years and rules a
> country which takes up a sixth of the continents, with a population of
> 180 millions. Obviously, the clerk has alarming proportions, much
> greater than those of his masters themselves. Such domination requires
> a 'staff' which on the national scale, represents for us a class. To reinforce
> it, this class pushes its domination into all domains of society, and
> where it encounters resistance, bypasses it by climbing over mountains
> of corpses. The bureaucratic regime of the USSR has, first, sacrificed
> the Communist Party and the Third International, then the Red Army
> itself. Tasks of this magnitude cannot be done by 'cliques' or 'staffs' or
> 'clerks' but only by classes.[34]

The Second World War, the collapse of fascist regimes in Germany
and Italy, and the distinctly unMarxist postwar concern with contrasts
between democracy and totalitarianism, laid global new class theories
to rest for a time; the more fashionable theories of 'convergence'
between communist and noncommunist states that followed them in
some quarters in the West owe much to ideas such as Burnham's,
however. With the establishment of communist rule in Eastern
Europe another form of new class theory has been developed,
primarily by dissidents within communist states, meant to explain the,
to them, disillusioning nature and development of those states.
There are fundamental differences between the 'global' new class
theorists discussed earlier and these 'socialist' new class theorists. The
former claimed to be identifying and explaining a worldwide phenomenon; the latter have more restrained and realistic ambitions. The
former, especially Burnham, claimed that industrial managers and
analogous functionaries were inheriting the earth; the latter believe
that the new class is based on the *political* bureaucracy which
forms around the Communist Party. The former saw the new class as
a phenomenon of the developed world, as a successor to advanced
capitalism; the latter see it as a means of bringing rapid industrialization to the less-developed areas of the world. And there are
many other differences between these two groups of writers and within
each group. What is therefore striking is the similarity between the
moulds into which their different analyses were poured.

The most famous and politically prominent of the latter writers is
Milovan Djilas, a one-time leader and ideologist of the Yugoslav
Communist Party. Anyone familiar with Trotsky's post-1923 writings
will experience an extraordinary sense of *déja vu* in tracing Djilas's
road through heresy to ultimate apostasy. Djilas's reflections on
'bureaucracy' and 'bureaucratism' began as part of the Yugoslav

[34] *L'URSS*, p. 48.

critique of the Soviet Union after the Cominform split of 1948 and the Rajk trial of 1949. By 1950 Djilas had become the most outspoken public critic of the Soviet Union, and in a speech to Belgrade students in March of that year he became the first Party leader to ask publicly whether the Soviet Union was still a socialist state. Djilas explained that the dictatorship of the proletariat could develop in one of two ways —either toward its own disappearance or 'in the direction of strengthening and transformation of bureaucracy into a privileged caste which lives at the expense of society as a whole'.[35] The latter development, he argued, had occurred in the Soviet Union. Like Trotsky, Djilas was careful to distinguish this claim from a far more dangerous one:

> In the Soviet Union, there are no economic bases for the creation of a new class. What is happening there, the outward manifestations of which we see, does not mean and cannot mean a return to capitalism. This is actually a matter of new phenomena which arose on the ground and within the framework of socialism itself. . . . There we see the creation of a privileged bureaucratic stratum, bureaucratic centralism, temporary transformation of the state into 'a force above society'. (Some of the reasons for this are the fact that the USSR was for a long time the only socialist country, that it was backward, surrounded by capitalism, that the masses had a relatively weak conscious role in the struggle for socialist building and that there were relatively weak foreign and internal revolutionary forces) [*ibid.* pp. 12–13].

As Trotsky's writings have already made plain, a communist leader, even a heretical one, has the greatest difficulty in referring to post-revolutionary bureaucracy as a class. In an article entitled 'Class or Caste?,' published in April 1952, Djilas explained the difficulty. He recognized, as Trotsky had, that the Soviet bureaucracy had accumulated many of the advantages of the traditional ruling classes: it had exclusive control over production and distribution; it grabbed 'the lion's share of the surplus for itself' and it lived at the expense of the 'direct producers [who] have no rights'. However, the bureaucracy was not a class, for 'it does not own the means of production in the traditional sense'; Djilas concluded that it was a 'caste'. Like Trotsky, Djilas had no doubts about the importance of the characterization one chose:

> It is very important, both for us in Yugoslavia and for socialism in general, to be sure of the answer. If the bureaucracy were a new class, its victory could not be prevented; it would be inevitable because it is brought about by objective social processes. Thus, if we were dealing here with a class, a new class, and not a caste, the struggle against the bureaucracy would be futile and utopian, and we who fought

[35] Milovan Djilas, 'On New Roads to Socialism', address delivered at the pre-election rally of Belgrade students, 18 March 1950 (Belgrade, 1950), p. 10.

against it would be comical, reactionary figures. But since the bureaucracy is not a class, but a reactionary anti-socialist tendency that appears in the transition from capitalism to Communism, the struggle against it is revolutionary and progressive. And it can succeed.[36]

Hitherto, Djilas had been a rather outspoken exponent of the corporate Yugoslav attack on Moscow. In 1953 he took the unprecedented step of shifting his attack from the Soviet Union to Yugoslavia, and in a series of articles which led to his expulsion from the Party, he bitterly attacked the attitudes, behaviour and mores of the communist leadership and insisted that the main danger was not the bourgeoisie or capitalism but bureaucratic despotism of the Soviet type. His attack was replete with bitter characterizations of bureaucratic behaviour, snobbishness and social exclusiveness, but while Djilas proposed a number of measures to allow greater democracy, he still contented himself with pointing to the danger of bureaucratic perversion of the revolution rather than suggesting that a new class had emerged.

In *The New Class*,[37] Djilas took this final step, a step Trotsky never took. In other ways, too, he went further in repudiating the movement to which he had given his life than any other comparable Party leader, including Trotsky. An index of how much further than Trotsky he chose to go, can be found by comparing what the two writers were referring to as 'bureaucracy'. When Trotsky attacked the 'bureaucrats' who had betrayed the revolution, he always distinguished between them and the political leaders, such as himself, whose power had been usurped. For Djilas, on the other hand, the ruling bureaucracy *was* the political leadership, and all other strata, including Burnham's managers, were subordinate to it (*ibid.* pp. 42–3). In other respects, however, Djilas was quite orthodox. He was well aware that a class must be shown to own the means of production before it can be said to rule, and so he explained that:

> As defined by Roman law, property constitutes the use, enjoyment, and disposition of material goods. The Communist political bureaucracy uses, enjoys, and disposes of nationalized property....
> The new class obtains its power, privileges, ideology, and its customs from one specific form of ownership—collective ownership in which the class administers and distributes in the name of the nation and society....
> To divest Communists of their ownership rights would be to abolish them as a class [pp. 44–5].

Lest anyone still doubt that the bureaucracy is a ruling class, Djilas shares Rizzi's confidence that the very excesses for which communist

[36] Milovan Djilas, *Parts of a Lifetime*, ed. M. D. Milenkovitch (New York, 1975), p. 176.
[37] (New York, 1957).

rulers have been responsible decide the issue (pp. 76–7). Indeed, while the class had exercised dreadful tyranny over those whom it ruled, it, too, had a historic 'task', though hardly the one predicted by Marx. It had to introduce modern industry to the less developed East. And Djilas occasionally cuts across the outrage he feels by insisting that: 'One reason for total tyranny is historical; the people were forced to undergo the loss of freedom in the irresistible drive toward economic change' (p. 98).

Djilas is particularly interesting because he ran the whole course from orthodoxy to heresy and, after *The New Class*, to apostasy.[38] One need not, however, be as politically eminent, nor move as far, as Djilas, to adopt a new class analysis. For dissidents within communist states, and for Marxists elsewhere who are disillusioned with the progress of such states, a new class analysis requires an initial doctrinal heresy, but thereafter it can be readily combined with the categories and intellectual baggage which lie to hand. It is thus not surprising, 'no accident', that writers as diverse as the dissident American Trotskyist Max Shachtman, the Poles Jacek Kuron and Karol Modzelewski and the Yugoslav philosopher Svetozar Stojanović should exhibit striking similarities not merely in the form but also in the substance of their analyses.[39] Like Trotsky, these authors insist that the October Revolution was a workers' revolution, but they go on to argue that bureaucratic degeneration led to the installation of a new ruling class; Stojanović, for example, explains that the October Revolution was a 'socialist revolution par excellence, although a new form of class, statist society was born with Stalinism' (p. 38). Shachtman, constantly wrestling with Trotsky's ghost, developed an ingenious argument to solve the problem of ownership. The capitalist, he explained, has individual property rights in the means of production, from which his power derives, and he therefore does not

---

[38] In his *The Unperfect Society: beyond the New Class* (London, 1969), Djilas argues that the communist system constitutes a refutation of historical materialism; see pp. 101 102 and 125.

[39] Shachtman was leader, initially with Burnham, of a group of American Trotskyists who broke with Trotsky and the majority wing of American Trotskyists in 1940. He took with him the Party journal, *The New International*, and his articles on the Soviet Union appeared there until the close of the magazine in 1958. These articles have been collected in Max Shachtman, *The Bureaucratic Revolution: the Rise of the Stalinist State* (New York, 1962). Kuron and Modzelewski published their 'Open Letter to Communist Party Members' in 1965 after having been expelled from the Party in November of the previous year. They were brought to trial in July 1965, and sentenced to several years' imprisonment. Their Open Letter is included in George Lavan Weissman (ed.), *Revolutionary Marxist Students in Poland Speak Out (1964–8)* (New York, 1972). Kuron is again active politically and is a prominent member of the Committee for Workers' Defence (KOR). Stojanović was later a member of the 'Belgrade Eight'. His analysis is contained in 'The Statist Myth of Socialism', *Between Ideals and Reality* (New York, 1973), pp. 37–75.

always need immediate control over the political apparatus. The proletarian, on the other hand, since he has no property rights, only comes to own the means of production through his control of the state; deprive him of that and he has nothing. Kuron and Modzelewski and Stojanović are less bothered by the problem of bureaucratic ownership than Shachtman; like Rizzi they stress that it is collective rather than individual, and that such ownership is not unprecedented.

Shachtman makes another distinction which is very often echoed by those new class theorists who remain socialists—that between property relations and property forms. Trotsky, Shachtman argued, was beguiled by the property forms in the Soviet Union—state ownership—but ignored the real relationships between groups, which had changed completely, notwithstanding these forms, since 1918. Kuron and Modzelewski made a similar distinction between state and what they called 'social' ownership, and Stojanović also distinguishes between early Soviet 'state socialism' and its present 'statism'. All of these writers insisted that the system they criticized was no longer 'genuine' socialism, and had outlived its 'historical' purpose—to force industrialization. It was now an exploitative system which was destined to fall and be replaced by genuine socialist relations of production.

III

The analyses which I have discussed clearly differ from each other in many ways. In particular, there are sharp differences over the nature of the groups which make up the new class. One line of such theories, deriving originally from Bakunin and Machajski, suggests that the source of the new class's distinctiveness is its education and training; this strongly Saint-Simonian claim lies at the heart of 'technocratic' new class theories and is a strong element in the 'managerial' thesis. Within this line, however, one would have to distinguish sharply between two sub-strands. On the one hand, Saint-Simon, many 'new-skilled class' Marxists and, for that matter, convergence theorists in general, tend to argue that the skilled owe their positions to industrial and technological developments in modern society which have occurred independently of their will or their plans. In Bakunin and Machajski, on the other hand, the story is altogether more voluntarist: Marxists *intend* to make over the state to serve their interests, and they must be opposed.

A second line of new class theory, of which Trotsky is an important precursor, suggests a new class which has little in common with the intellectuals attacked by Bakunin and Machajski; the last accusation which Trotsky would have made against Stalin is that he led a despotism of the intellectuals! This line draws on the rich and almost wholly bad associations of the word 'bureaucrat': pervasive, parasitic, thugs, power-wielders, administrators of a brutal and wholly unimaginative kind. This line usually stresses the power and control position of the new class vis-à-vis the masses rather than their intrinsic sources of distinctiveness. Again this line has its voluntarists and those who, like Djilas and Kuron and Modzelewski, believed that this class originally had a historic task to perform. Among the voluntarists there are some who believe that establishing the new class was the *aim* of Lenin and his followers, though this accusation comes usually and more readily from outside the tradition altogether. New class theorists more usually argue that there was an unforeseen degeneration, that the revolution had been betrayed by a rising class of power-hungry bureaucrats.

These two lines—the 'technocratic' and the 'bureaucratic'—can also be interwoven, as they are in Laurat's suggestions, which Stojanović repeats, that 'bureaucrats' form the first stage of the rise of the new class, and then give way to 'technocrats'.

Given these and other differences between new class theorists, the amount they have in common is all the more striking. They all pick out a group of power- or skill-wielders and all insist that, although Marx did not predict the importance of this group, it has now become dominant. They all claim that the group with which they are concerned has displaced either or both of the protagonists in Marx's historical drama: all agree that it has displaced the proletariat in the socialist states, and those who claim to detect the convergence of capitalism and communism argue that it has dispossessed or is dispossessing capitalists in the capitalist states. Finally, and most important of all, they are all convinced that the group on which they focus is a *class* which owns or threatens to own the means of production, and that this matters; that only classes can rule a society, and that the group they discuss is a ruling class.

It is not surprising that concepts such as 'bureaucracy' and 'technocracy' should have been prominent in new class theories. The massive twentieth century growth of bureaucratic personnel, on the one hand, and the increasing importance of those with training and technical skills, on the other, are crucially important developments in modern societies. Orthodox Marxists frequently underplay the significance of such developments, by comparison with the alleged importance of capitalists and proletarians; disenchanted Marxists, used to emphasizing the importance of large-scale social groupings, are well placed to notice and draw attention to such developments.

It is not obvious, however, that analysis is aided by a determination to identify a society's ruling class, old or new. Where analysis requires careful distinctions between power-wielders and executors, leaders and led, power and indispensability, new class analysis tends to blur these crucial distinctions. It can also serve to over-emphasize the importance and power of the designated group, at the expense of forces which fit such theories less well, such as individuals or small groups of political power-holders. Vis-à-vis the Russian population in the 1930s, for example, the Russian 'bureaucracy' had awesome power; vis-à-vis Stalin, millions of 'bureaucrats' discovered after 1937, it had distinctly less. Within the bureaucracy itself, Burnham's technical managers were far less powerful than their political masters.[40]

In the face of the diversity of 'new class' theories, and the difficulties they face, what, then, accounts for their persistence and the vocabulary and preoccupations which they so manifestly share? Rizzi's often repeated charge of plagiarism against Burnham can be quickly dismissed. It is unlikely to be true of Burnham—Rizzi, for example, had very little to say about changes *within* the modern corporation—and it certainly cannot be generalized to other new class theorists. Very few people have been able to obtain, let alone read, Rizzi's book, and, with the exception of his discussion of the Soviet Union, they have missed little. Another suggestion which has been pressed strongly in the case of the early Yugoslav critique of Stalinism, is that the Yugoslavs, and one might argue, *mutatis mutandis*, later heretics such as the Chinese, have taken up Trotsky's arguments, for as Plamenatz puts it well:

> He has forged weapons that no liberal could use effectively, but they are ready to hand for every communist who quarrels with Moscow. The Yugoslavs are already using them; and they won't use them the less freely because they denounce their maker.[41]

This seems to me to catch a good deal of the truth, but it does not explain 'new class' analyses which preceded Trotsky's arguments or the special importance that Trotsky himself and those who argued with him attached to those arguments. Moreover, in the Yugoslav case itself, it is not clear that the protagonists had read or were influenced by Trotsky's writings.[42]

More recently, it has been argued that new class theories are adopted in an attempt to influence revolutionary action, that

> these theories should be assessed primarily in terms of their expressive and mobilizing functions, and as a protest against patterns of social

[40] I have discussed these points more fully in my ' "Bureaucracy" in Trotsky's Analysis of Stalinism' (see note 1, p. 89, *supra*), especially at pp. 62–5.
[41] Plamenatz, p. 55; see also Roy Macridis, 'Stalinism and the Meaning of Titoism', *World Politics* IV (1951–2), pp. 235–7.
[42] Djilas, *Parts of a Lifetime*, p. 19, and A. Ross Johnson, *The Transformation of Communist Ideology: the Yugoslav Case (1945–1953)* (Cambridge, Mass., 1972), p. 237.

organization which are *assumed* in other theories of industrial society. In terms of the Marxist theory of history it obviously makes more sense to symbolize relations of dominance as class relations than to attempt to mobilize the masses against abstractions such as 'bureaucratic deformations'.[43]

This 'expressive' element certainly has been important in many new class theories, but it seems to me that it is only one use among several to which such theories can be put, rather than an explanation for them. Trotsky and, for some years, Djilas *resisted* calling the bureaucracy a class precisely because they believe that classes are borne by objective historical forces, that they have historical 'tasks' to perform, and that resistance to a 'new class' would be futile. Again, except for the penultimate chapter, which contradicts the arguments of the whole of the book, Rizzi used his 'new class' analysis to argue that 'bureaucratic collectivism' was inevitable and should not be resisted by workers, even in Italy and Germany; workers should resist only capitalists because they were obsolete, and Jews because they were capitalists. Nor did Burnham draw revolutionary lessons from his analysis.

New class theories can be used for a variety of purposes, though often, and within communist countries almost necessarily, they will be used by opponents of the existing rulers. But their common features do not stem from the uses to which they are put. Rather they share what they do because they are a natural, though not the only possible, way in which a Marxist heretic can analyse a society, especially one with growing numbers of 'bureaucrats' and 'technocrats', from within a tradition which provides a restricted range of fundamental categories.

---

[43] Marian Sawer, 'Theories of the New Class from Bakunin to Kuron and Modzelewski: the Morphology of Permanent Protest', in Sawer (ed.), *Socialism and the New Class*, p. 13.

5

Freedom, law and the bureaucratic state

Eugene Kamenka and Alice Erh-Soon Tay

The fear of bureaucracy, as Martin Krygier stressed in the first chapter of this volume, creates strange bedfellows; bureaucrats have been resented and the state has been attacked both by radical socialists and by the strong upholders of private enterprise and middle-class liberties. Yet both sides have recognized, in all practical situations in the modern world, their need of the state, both have sought to use public power for private or sectional or political interest. The more we talk of 'community', of the rights of the underprivileged, of multi-cultural societies and regional and ethnic self-development, the more we demand that the state create or expand another department to further these worthwhile 'human' causes.

The dependence of much contemporary industry on the state is now widely recognized; it is a development accelerated by the physical destruction of Europe in the Second World War, the enormous funds now required for research and development and modernization of plant, and the susceptibility of production and trade, in modern conditions, to state policies at home and abroad. The social welfare functions of the state have undergone even more rapid expansion. The view that the state in Western Europe and the United States is simply the executive committee of the bourgeoisie is not yet dead; but it is certainly less appealing, even to socialists, than it used to be. At the same time, the millowners and sweatshop proprietors who were the paradigm capitalists of *Das Kapital* and of countless socialist tracts of the late nineteenth and early twentieth centuries have been replaced, at the minimum, by faceless corporations, military-industrial complexes, holding companies, banks and pension funds, statutory bodies and boards of nationalized industries. Private property that really matters has become corporate property; who controls it is now, at least, a matter of argument and the claims of property owners to autonomy have once again grown weaker and weaker. It is not surprising, in these circumstances, that much of what used to be the ever-present resentment of the rich, first of landlords, aristocrats and merchants, then of capitalists as employers of labour, has become resentment of the state, of the 'system' and of private and public 'experts', managers and 'bureaucrats'. There is a widespread fear today, by no means confined to those who would regard themselves as socialists, of a new despotism, even if the descriptions of its causes, its character and its agents vary enormously. For many, as a result, the term 'bureaucracy' has become a general (and confused) way of expressing these fears. Let us first consider some of them.

I The despotism of the intellectuals

Socialism, one of its most intelligent critics, Joseph Schumpeter, believed, was inevitable: it would arise out of the very logic of capitalism. It would not be brought about, however, as Marx had thought, by the *economic* logic of capitalism, by the collapse of its economic system, by class war, the revolt of the proletariat. It would arise out of the original entrepreneurial values and procedures of capitalism giving way to routinized planning and research within the 'trustified' capitalist firm and the consequent growth and increasing social prestige of values and attitudes that are those of socialist planners. Not the working class, but the Saint-Simonian engineers, scientists and administrators would usher in the new society. 'Research and Development', as it were, would be written over its portals; 'bureaucracy' would be its password.

This nightmare—for many socialists—has haunted socialism since its very inception as a movement of the working class and as a fundamental critique of bourgeois society in the 1830s. Socialism, from its beginnings, was a movement that sought to combine the yearnings of the deprived and oppressed, the traditions of popular revolution, popular participation, community and spontaneity and identification with the interests of those who labour with the acceptance of industrialization and the consequent need for social planning —the need for placing society, as the socialist Saint-Simonians put it, under the rule of a great central bank, for which property would become a social and not a private function and by which all wealth and productive activity would be rationally assessed and administered. The great attempt to synthesize these competing socialist trends lay in the work of Karl Marx; it was not successful—as the vacillations in his own thought and the subsequent history of the movement or movements created in his name show. The tension between workers and intellectuals or technocrats, between freedom and necessity, spontaneity and planning, breaks out again and again in the history of socialism and Marxism, both before and after the assumption of power, in one form and another. Perhaps no literate attack on the intelligentsia and its role in working-class and revolutionary movements is as vicious, thorough-going and uncompromising as that launched, in 1898, by the Polish revolutionary Jan Wacław Machajski[1]—though it was only one of a long line of attacks that began with Weitling, was given publicity and invective by Bakunin and reached its most interesting culmination, intellectually, in the work of Georges Sorel.

Socialism, Machajski argued in his chief work, *The Intellectual Worker*, published in 1905, was threatening to become the rule of a new class, the *intelligenty*, formerly hirelings of capitalism, and before that of feudalism, but now increasingly hostile to aristocratic and bourgeois rule. That new class's monopoly of education constituted, in modern conditions, a most powerful form of property or capital and its interests lay entirely in a self-seeking attempt to use workers and the socialist revolution to gain power, to assure its members of better jobs and higher salaries. The threat of this eventuality lay deep in socialist theory itself, even in the *Communist Manifesto*. 'Scientific socialism', indeed, was not a theory of the *workers'* revolution at all, but an attempt to capture it on behalf of the intellectuals who were now seeking to make a revolution in their own interests and providing it with an ideology for that and no other purpose. It is no wonder that Mensheviks and Bolsheviks alike united to denounce—in similarly vulgar style, incidentally—the heresy of 'Makhaevshchina' ('Makhaevism'—a term produced by Russifying Machajski's name), the heresy of relying upon and promoting for revolutionary purposes spontaneous, 'economic' working-class action not guided or illuminated by Marxist theory and the help and theoretical leadership of the revolutionary intelligentsia. For Machajski was not denouncing a particular revolutionary theory, but the role of revolutionary theorists in general, not particular tactics or forms of party organization and struggle, but the entire participation of the intelligentsia in that struggle. He proclaimed that the conflict of interests between workers and the educated was fundamental and irreconcilable—in no case would the *intelligenty*, the possessors of higher education, surrender their 'capital' for the common good. The workers would have to act by themselves, bring the government to its knees through strikes and economic demands and then dictate to the state laws created by the workers in their own interests—laws that would universalize education on the

[1] For an outline of the career of this interesting thinker, see the appendix to this chapter, pp. 131ff.

basis of a general increase in living standards and thus end its function as 'capital', while at the same time removing the possibility for envy and conflict between those who have and those who have not.

'In every country, in every state', Machajski wrote in his *The Bourgeois Revolution and the Workers' Cause* published within a year of *The Intellectual Worker*:

> There exists a huge class of people who have neither industrial nor commercial capital and yet live like real masters. They own neither land nor factories nor workshops, but they enjoy a robber's income no smaller than that of the middling and large capitalists. They do not have their own enterprises, but they are white-hands just like the middling and large capitalists. They too spend their whole lives free from manual labour, and if they do participate in production, then it is only as managers, directors, engineers. That is, they are commanders and masters just like the capitalist proprietors.[2]

It was to combat the rise and domination of this class, within socialism and through it, that Machajski devoted his life and theoretical work. The argument of *The Intellectual Worker*, though set in the concrete context of Eastern European revolutionary activities and arguments and written as a polemic that begins from within Marxism and what was then the Marxist Social Democratic Movement, was basically simple. The lesson of the development of Polish socialism was that Social Democrats put patriotism, the achievement of national independence, first and saw the working class as a tool for achieving those ends. Patriotism and nationalism, by the 1890s, could not be given new life in Poland without socialism but the total unpreparedness of the movement for the Lodz general strike of 1892 showed how far even this socialist nationalism or nationalist socialism was from grassroots worker demands. The Polish Socialist Party, it is true, attempting to link more patriotic and more cosmopolitan elements, now saw the Polish revolution in a wider context as part of a general revolutionary movement in the Russian Empire and as an outpost of European socialism. But in all this, in its many variations and computations, the workers are always being subordinated to something else, the demands of a general interest, of history, of wider concerns. And whose concerns were these wider concerns? They were the concerns of the new class of the *intelligenty*, of the 'white-handed ones', of the intellectual workers, who were setting before the worker the goals of economic progress, capitalist industrial development, democratic and parliamentary support and who in Poland, in their anxiety to appro-

---

[2] Jan Wacław Machajski, *Burzhuaznaya revoliutsiya i rabochee delo* (St Petersburg, 1906), p. 86, as translated in Marshall Shatz, 'Jan Wacław Machajski: the "Conspiracy of the Intellectuals"', *Survey* (1967), no. 62, pp. 50–51.

priate the national surplus currently held by Russians, were making common cause with aristocratic *szlachta* elements.

The lessons of Polish socialism, then, were that the East European socialist movement was infected by the betrayal of Marxism by European social democracy—the drawing back from militancy and direct working-class action, the elevation of parliamentary socialism, the call to the worker to defer direct struggle while he 'educated' himself in trade unions and political movements—that is, subjected himself to the tutelage of the intelligentsia, of the white-handed ones. By the time that he was writing his conclusion to the first part of *The Intellectual Worker*, 'The Evolution of Social Democracy', it was clear to Machajski that Marxist criticisms of social democratic 'opportunism' were inadequate. These criticisms treated opportunism as the product of petty bourgeois elements, elements that according to Marx would be swept away with growing economic development— elements such as rural smallholders and lower middle-class shop- keepers, and so on. But in fact, especially in Eastern European socialism, there was a new socialist intelligentsia drawn from the professions, journalists, would-be managers and officials, and this class could only spread and become more important with the spread of education. Scientific socialism was *its* ideology in its elevation of a general social interest, of progress, technical planning and economic management, in its desire to control and direct revolutionary action.

Once we saw this clearly, Machajski insisted, we could see that the rot began with the great founders and teachers of scientific socialism themselves, with Karl Marx and Friedrich Engels. And it began not only in their later works, in the clearly opportunistic positions taken by Engels in the 1890s in regard to an evolutionary path to socialism through the ballot box, but in the very model of Marxist revolutionism, *The Communist Manifesto*. The *Manifesto* had elevated the correct revolutionary strategy of despotic inroads into the right of property, but it accompanied this with the elevation of democracy, both as a strategy to make the revolution and as a basis for the workers' state after the revolution. It thus foreshadowed the democratic strategy of the (Second) International, the false reliance on represen- tation and class collaboration. It was thus that Marx in the *18th Brumaire* had failed to appreciate the antagonism of the June Days of 1848, the fact that the workers were opposed, not only by the Party of Order as Marx called it, by the whole of *bourgeois* society, but by all *educated* society. There was an enormous gulf between the democratic cause and the proletarian cause. The intellectual worker stood with the democratic cause, he had to attack the 'narrow' class horizons in order to prevent the worker from making major inroads into the national surplus value, surplus value that the *intelligent* wanted for himself, surplus value that was already and under socialism would be even more the source of the intellectual worker's privileged position.

The second part of *The Intellectual Worker*, therefore, not surprisingly, is an attack on the second volume of Marx's *Capital*— a claim that it justified the intellectual worker's theft of the national surplus value and showed that Marx in essence stood with the state socialism of Rodbertus, concerned for the perpetual existence of national capital, for a centralized industrial order managed by those who had the requisite technical skill. This is why Marx had such respect for the growth of constant capital. This constant capital would be the foundation of the socialist profitless organization of society which Marx envisaged. Marx's insistence that exploitation, the capitalist drawing off of surplus value from the worker, was based on variable capital, on wages rather than investment in machinery, was an obfuscation. Marx's doctrine has as its god the establishment of perpetual national capital, of a perpetual incommensurability of social product with social income.[3]

For Marx, too, the product will never pass into the hands of the worker and Marx's distinction between labour of greater and lesser utility was the basis for wage differentials that talk about skilled labour but favour completely the maintenance of a parasitic upper layer of intellectual workers supported by the unpaid product of other people's labour.

In reality, Machajski insisted, Marx's socialism was not science but a religion, the old utopian religion of one society, one humanity —an ideology of modern progressive, positivist, what we would today call technocratic, society. History and Marxism combine to work against the proletariat because a new class was taking over productive forces. The salvation of the worker lay in not relying on history, in not turning his eyes, as the Marxists would have him do, to the laws of the system, but in recognizing the power of the worker's will as opposed to the so-called laws of human society. The guarantee of the worker's freeing himself from the religious illusion of scientific socialism, from the ideology and would-be domination of the new class of the *intelligenty*, was his direct pursuit and elevation of his material interests, appropriating more and more of the national product and through that appropriating also the new capital in modern society, education.

[3] The relationship of socialism to human needs, and the political degeneration that results from a 'dictatorship over needs' in the interests of industrial development, were raised more sharply by Rosa Luxemburg and have recently been taken up again by Marxist critics of aspects of contemporary Soviet-style socialism, who are being driven out of Poland, Hungary, the German Democratic Republic and even Yugoslavia.

Martin Krygier has already referred to the importance of Machajski as an originator or precursor of 'new class' theories and the resultant revival of interest in him. The themes Machajski raises, or exemplifies, have long caused basic tensions in socialist and revolutionary thought. These themes are the insistence on direct action and direct participation; the feeling of hostility for the educated and better-off and for those who have 'white hands'; the rejection of the executive planning and service functions as not 'real' work (which long had, and perhaps still has, such deleterious effect on Soviet economic life); the demand for *immediate* improvement with its direct appeal to the very, very poor, the outcast and the unemployed, as well as a consequent hostility to 'objective conditions', a pitting of the will, even of violence, against necessity, reason and rationality. Bureaucracy as commonly understood, even in its broadest meaning, and socialism as the belief in social and economic planning, stand *for* everything that Machajski is *against*. Of course, like virtually all the socialist thinkers discussed by Krygier, Machajski is in the end himself inconsistent; he fails to think things through. He sees the revolutionary workers, in the hour of triumph, dictating to the state rather than abolishing it; he wants expropriation and redistribution of surplus value at the workers' command but through the use of state authority and centralized state decrees; he 'universalizes' education, in principle, with the greatest ease. But in his insistence that the 'clerk' was now capable of breaking loose from feudal and capitalist patronage to seek power in his own right, that education was in modern conditions a form of 'capital', he was both recognizing an important social change and expressing an increasing anxiety of post-industrial, welfare-state men and women, who find themselves confronted more and more by managers rather than owners, experts rather than policemen, bureaucrats rather than the fear of hunger. Increasingly, the resentment is of the well-off salariat, much more numerous than the rich.[4] All this is often reflected in the popular dislike of bureaucrats, now confused and conflated, for these purposes, with the educated generally, of whom they are a sub-class. Krygier's discussion of new class theories has shown that this extension of the term bureaucracy may capture a certain popular mood, and may constitute an attempt to explain, on the basis of function and the administrative imperatives of large-scale production and mass society, the comparative power and privileges of what began

[4] In a comparatively egalitarian society like Australia, with its lack of traditional class structures and no very great extremes of wealth and poverty, this expresses itself in a deeply rooted dislike of 'fat cats', almost always seen as public servants. It is a sentiment naturally accompanied by an equally strong dislike of tall poppies and by a firm conviction that push-pin is as good as poetry and much more democratic. None of these sentiments, of course, is confined to Australia.

as a subordinate group of functionaries. But for social analysis and clear thinking it raises more problems than it solves, it dilutes the conception of bureaucracy still further and ultimately brings out the difficulty of dealing with modern developments in terms of a Marxist or neo-Marxist conception of class.

The radical Maoism of the Great Proletarian Cultural Revolution in 1966–9, as exemplified by the behaviour of the Red Guards and at least some of the subsequent doings of the Gang of Four, betrays and draws on a similar deep-seated hostility to education and technical competence as socially divisive, as producing the expectation or fact of power and privilege. The traditional association of education with state service in the Mandarins of Imperial China, the political weakness of Chinese landlords as landlords in traditional Chinese society and the virtual absence of a native capitalist class no doubt helped to make concern with the phenomenon of bureaucracy a more central theoretical issue for Chinese communism than for that of the Soviet Union and the West. It is thus that Mao and the public ideologists of his regime for a period preferred Marx's *Civil War in France* to the *Communist Manifesto*, and the somewhat more anarchist drafts of the *Civil War* to the final version. In practice, the worst period of the Cultural Revolution came very close to Machajski's total rejection of the role of the educated; in theory, Marxism made even Mao stop short of regarding the bureaucracy or the educated as a class. The attack was on the 'bureaucratic working style' and on the separation of mental from physical labour. The educated had to change their habits by learning from the peasants and working with them. Bureaucrats, in theory if not actually in practice, were to be kept in place on the principles established by the Paris Commune of 1871— no salary differentials, no special privileges, no security of tenure, frequent rotation between administrative and manual work and constant criticism and self-criticism in 'struggle' sessions.

Machajski thought in terms of antagonistic classes, desperately fighting for shares of the national wealth for themselves. The Red Guards and the ageing Mao were radical egalitarians, objecting to all social distinctions. Harold J. Laski, *enfant terrible* that he may have been to 'respectable' British society in the 1930s and later, stood in a different position in the socialist spectrum and had a better and more realistic appreciation of history and government in politically civilized countries than they did. To him it seemed clear that the emancipation of the bureaucracy in Western Europe from being a mere appendage of the aristocracy was by and large a good thing, as were the values and procedures ascribed to the bureaucracy by Weber. The advent of democratic government in the nineteenth century, he believed, overthrew in the Western world the chance of maintaining a system—burgeoning in eighteenth-century France—

whereby officials could constitute a permanent and hereditary caste, a new aristocracy. 'In modern times', Laski wrote around 1930, 'bureaucracies have, outside of Russia under the czarist regime, rarely been corrupt in a crude sense. Most of the advantages they obtain for themselves (security of tenure, superannuation, incremental salaries, annual vacation) are recognized as the necessary accompaniments of sound work. Nor has there been the tendency to nepotism which distinguished earlier types. Of course there have been scandals; in France notably there have been some sordid exposures worthy of the *ancien régime*. But it is in a broad sense just to say that in its political context the economic morality of the modern civil service, where it has had the advantage of permanence, has been far higher than that of private enterprise.'[5] The values and selection procedures of Western public bureaucracies might put undue emphasis on caution, on the 'safe' man, but they did not breed self-seeking and corruption. That, it seems to us, is still true, not only in comparing the bureaucracy with private enterprise but also with politicians and the populace at large. Hence the notion of 'bureaucratic collectivism' is extended, in popular thought, from the neo-Marxist conception of bureaucrats now being the real 'owning class', at least in communist societies, but owning only as a class, to the notion that bureaucrats, or the educated more generally, seek and defend their group interests even more firmly than their individual interests, and do not, like capitalists, live at each other's expense. The movement from concern with profit to concern with security is, in this context, a movement from individual to social or group concerns and postures; it produces the white-collar trades unions and *not* an oligarchy.

The Soviet Union, whether we like it or not, is *the* socialist superpower—the one socialist/communist society organized on the basis of state or public ownership of the means of production, distribution and exchange and a Marxist ideology that has a huge population and an advanced and complex system of production, administration and politically effective control on a mass scale. Its official view on the need for and function of a bureaucracy—that is, of a staff of experts and professional administrators functioning in the context of political direction and 'popular' control—comes surprisingly close, in recent years, to that of Laski and indeed of classical political philosophy based on the Westminster system, if we exclude the question of 'apolitical' service, of 'impartiality'. Current Soviet writing emphasizes more and more the need for a framework of constitutions, codes and systematic decrees and directives, the need for specialization and

---

[5] H. J. Laski, 'Bureaucracy', in E. R. A. Seligman and A. Johnson (eds), *Encyclopaedia of the Social Sciences* (15 vols, New York, 1930–35) III, pp. 70–74 at p. 72.

participatory and expert functions.[6] The enormous, and for many horrifying, differences between Soviet government and the Westminster model—totalitarianism, political oppression and the stifling of all criticism, the ubiquity of the secret police and the total lack of genuine elections or of independent institutions— are not to be explained by words like 'bureaucratic socialism' or 'state capitalism', by the rule of a functionally based administrative bureaucracy, the need for which Soviet thinkers now recognize so clearly, or even by the usurpation of the new class that Machajski feared. The evils of the Soviet Union are political and more easily and convincingly explained in terms of the history of Russia, the logic of revolutions, the elevation of Leninism and of a single, tightly controlled but highly politicized Party and set of allied political instruments, the brutalizing effect of the Civil War and a long tradition of state-centredness and state domination to be discussed below. A class analysis of the Soviet tragedy, it seems to us, is particularly unconvincing and the treatment of the 'bureaucracy' as an independent and ruling class not defined as a *political* elite has no plausibility whatever. Those of the intelligentsia, the 'bureaucrats' or the educated who are time-servers benefit and in recent years have done so increasingly, but that only helps to bring out their dependence, their lack of independent or class power. Even their apparently 'interest-group' organizations, from the Union of Soviet Writers to the recently mooted Union of Motorists, exist or are brought into being to control them, to supervise their work and their lives, to prevent their independent opinion, power and organiza- tion. The ubiquitous popular belief in the Soviet Union that there is a distinction between 'us' and 'them' contains a very strong element of Makhaevist hatred of those who are better off and know how to work the system, but as a class analysis it mistakes the superficial for the essential and blinds itself to the fact that the same distinction exists, on a political and character basis, within the educated class which is as much or as little in opposition as the worker. Only those who are forced, as Krygier puts it, to draw their concepts from a tradition with a restricted range of fundamental categories would want to treat Soviet totalitarianism as based on class rule or, in a newer fashion, derive the murder of 20 million people from the habits, the attitudes or the self-interest of the modern bureaucrat. It is not the transmission belt that drives the engine. The greatest evils of modern society have been firmly rooted in politics, not bureaucracy. Eichmann may have been a bureaucrat; Hitler was not. Neither, despite the skills that brought him to power, was Stalin.

[6] See, on this question, our 'Socialism, Anarchism and Law' in E. Kamenka, R. Brown and A. E. S. Tay (eds), *Law and Society: the Crisis in Legal Ideals* (this series, London, Melbourne, New York, 1978), pp. 48–80, esp. at pp. 76–7.

II The despotism of the state

Tyranny was not unknown among the Greeks, any more than dictator-ship was unknown among the Romans of the Republic. But both saw these despotic breaks in their own societies as exceptions, rather than the norm, as born of unusual circumstances and either properly and legally controlled or necessarily meeting with resistance and producing instability. Politics as the dialogue and public dealing between free citizens, politics as the science of freedom, many Greeks believed, was a Greek invention. The Asiatic 'barbarians' that made up the Persian Empire lived, on the contrary, in a system of public and universal slavery, ruled by monarchs who were despots and whose despotism was stable because their people were not citizens but servants.

Behind the welter of prejudices that we find from Herodotus to Aristotle, lay a striking if complex truth—the extraordinary power of the oriental despot and the almost total absence of any comparable degree of state centralization, state power and total dependence on the ruler in Western societies. It was from these seeds that the concept of oriental despotism was born, adopted from Aristotle by thirteenth-, fourteenth- and fifteenth-century thinkers in their struggle against Papal claims to unlimited power, and blossoming in the sixteenth, seventeenth and eighteenth centuries as Europeans once more became directly acquainted with the absolute power of Eastern potentates and began to fear or support the absolutist pretensions of their own kings at home. In Burma, Siam and Cambodia, they heard, land was entirely in the royal domain and those who tilled the soil were royal chattels; in Turkey, lands were distributed as non-heritable service lands; in China, an emperor ruled with and through a highly educated and organized bureaucracy selected on the basis of merit by examination. This was 'seigneurial monarchy' or 'oriental despotism'.

European attitudes to Asia generally and to oriental despotism in particular varied, notoriously, with internal European problems and preoccupations.[7] With the rise of political economy and the assump-tion of colonial responsibilities in India, serious studies of the pheno-menon began—studies that now concentrated on the weakness of private property in land in Asia and on the fundamental role of the state in organizing agriculture and public works. The nationalization of the land or a high land tax or rent were for them the foundations of oriental despotism; its virtue was competent organization and

[7] These attitudes have been traced for us by Donald Lach in *Asia in the Making of Europe* (1, Chicago, 1965), and are summarized in the context of a full discussion of the concept of the 'Asiatic mode of production' up to the present time in Marian Sawer, *Marxism and the Question of the Asiatic Mode of Production* (The Hague, 1977).

control; its weakness was the intrinsic lack of dynamism Hegel saw as characteristic of China and which nineteenth-century thinkers inevitably ascribed to any form of state domination, to weakness of private property and the resultant weakness of economic classes. Marx, to the scandal of many of his more recent followers, took over these views, seeing oriental despotism as based on an Asiatic mode of production, or public slavery, in which the state, because of arid climatic conditions and a dispersed population, very early on became the organizer of the material foundation of agriculture in Asian conditions (requiring irrigation, corvée labour, developed communication, roads, and so on) and the appropriator of surplus value. Internally, for Marx, such a society was doomed to stagnation—without cities, without real classes or class struggle, without steadily developing productive forces and consequent conceptions of human power and of human dignity. Historically, however, oriental despotism was nearing its end; free trade would batter down Chinese walls and Indian superstitions; colonial penetration, the district officer and the foreign comprador, cheap cottons and the power of trade and of private property, would bring Asia into the history of Europe and radically revolutionize her economy, her politics and her view or views of life.

History betrayed us all—not because traditional societies were proving more resistant to capitalist transformation than the *Communist Manifesto* had predicted or many imperialists believed, but because in the heart of civilized Europe in the 1920s and 1930s there arose the new and then fearful despotisms of Mussolini and Hitler, while on the fringes of civilized Europe the last word in social revolution was turning into another, in some respects strikingly similar, despotism. It was from these seeds that not only Burnham's managerial society was born, but also the concept of totalitarianism— the belief that we were witnessing the emergence of new and powerful states that sought to control and subordinate all significant social, political and economic activity to their direction, to make men subject to one ideology, to destroy classes and all independent institutions, to dichotomize society into a powerful and structured state on the one hand, and on the other a mass of atomized individuals that could find structure, purpose and connection—character and a sense of mission—only in and through the state.

Nazism and fascism proved to be more temporary and less stable phenomena than many had feared; it was only the Soviet Union that marched from strength to strength. But at the same time, communism captured China and it was not long before, in the work of Karl A. Wittfogel, the concepts of totalitarianism and of oriental despotism became linked in a quasi-Marxist, quasi-Weberian theory of the impact and basis of totalitarianism in history. In his *Oriental*

Despotism (1956), Wittfogel argued that Marx and those who had earlier spoken of oriental despotism had correctly perceived (even if Marx had then proceeded largely to ignore) a major historic social formation not based on private property but on the despotic potential of political managerial functions arising on a geopolitical basis. This formation, which Wittfogel prefers to call hydraulic or agro-managerial because it is neither confined to Asia nor universal in it, differs fundamentally from the non-hydraulic civilizations of the West in the utter political unimportance of private property. It arises in conditions where irrigation and above all flood control need to be performed on a vast scale, but it also depends on favourable institutional and ideological settings which are absent, for example, in the Netherlands and Italy, areas that are part of a wider, non-hydraulic civilization. The state that arises from these hydraulic foundations is managerial in a political way, attaining a level of public organization, organization of labour, communication and engineering skills undreamt of by non-hydraulic societies of the time. Such states arose early in human history, in Egypt, Mesopotamia, India and China, but also in the higher agrarian civilizations of pre-Spanish America, and their political system spread by contact and imitation—to Russia, for instance, through the Mongol conquest. It is a political system in which the state is always stronger than the rest of society and in which everything outside the control of the state is kept politically powerless and irrelevant. It goes beyond tyranny and dictatorship to total, 'totalitarian', control, even though its rulers recognize a 'law of diminishing administrative returns' that allows some communal organization to continue as 'sub-political'.

Wittfogel's theses, often put in highly emotionally charged language and with a certain readiness to dismiss difficulties of historical detail, have aroused a great deal of controversy, as have the various formulations and applications of the concept of totalitarianism. There are those who agree with Wittfogel in seeing an enormous contrast between oriental despotism, satrapy or 'bureaucratic' (Islamic and Asian) 'feudalism', where power outside the ruler is derived from and continually dependent on service to him, and the genuine plurality of power centres, the elevation of reciprocally contractual rights and duties and legally maintainable 'liberties' of European feudalism, but who believe that the totalitarianism he fears is to be found in many non-hydraulic settings, in Byzantium, for example. For them, it might well be derived from the nature and internal requirements of empires, or from special ideological factors, or from consistent military danger combined with poverty of resources, as in Russia, rather than from contact with and imitation of classical oriental despotisms. But be that as it may, there is general agreement among serious scholars that the history of Russia, for instance, and the victory and character of communism there cannot be understood without recognizing that the Russian state, based on the dominance of Muscovy from the fourteenth century onward, was a political system founded on the utter centrality and pervasiveness of the state. The land, the property and the persons of Russia's citizens for crucial centuries belonged in principle to the state. What rights and possessions men and women had were granted by the state, social categories or classes were determined by the state and determined according to their varying but always severe obligations to it. The same was true of China. Whether we call this an oriental despotism or a patrimonial state with a highly developed bureaucracy, it is a command society in which the state had long been, and now is again, the only social force, the innovator and carrier of all significant social reform—reform that is always dictated from above, and in which all social power is, in one sense of the word 'bureaucratic', bureaucratic power, power based on state position and state service.

The concepts of totalitarianism, of hydraulic society, of oriental despotism, do not now appeal to most Marxists. They smack of the Cold War and are a constant reminder of the abstract possibility of despotism based on economic managerial functions, on state planning and pervasive dictatorships of the proletariat, although some Marxists, as Dr Sawer argues, have attempted to use various versions of the concept of the Asiatic mode of production, shorn of the emphasis on despotism, as ways of overcoming the alleged Euro-centrism of the unilinear model of human historical development set out in the *Communist Manifesto*. But in a more general context, the widely perceived fact that there *are* totalitarian regimes and that these regimes have been immeasurably strengthened by the potentialities of modern technology for almost instant communication, control and surveillance has led to very real fears of the despotism of the state exercised through its bureaucracy becoming stronger and stronger. An increasing number of people today, including radicals in the more affluent and organized societies, are no longer concerned only to wrest control of the state from the present wielders of power, but also to build barriers against it, to avert what seems to many the real possibility of Orwell's *1984*. The renewed interest in decentralization, devolution, municipal bills of rights, 'community' as opposed to departmental action, is part of this development; the appeal above the head or heads of the nation-state to a wider international or human community, to international declarations of human rights, international organizations and so on, is another part. People still want from the state as much as they ever did—in fact, far more—but its moral authority, its claim to obedience and respect, have been greatly undermined and the respect for its servants— the bureaucracy—has suffered the same fate.

III The despotism of the 'system'

Totalitarianism in the 'homeland of the toilers', the increasing
power of state structures and nationalized industries everywhere, the
emergence of bureaucratic and political elites whose 'class' origins
and base were at best confused, have helped, as we have seen, to make
Marxist class analyses of contemporary society, with their central
emphasis on the struggle of bourgeois and proletarian, seem cruder
and cruder, if not entirely irrelevant, as our century progresses.
Under the impact, or with the aid, of the newly fashionable
writings of the young Marx, first made fully available in the late
1920s and early 1930s, and under the conscious or unconscious
influence of sociological trends that owe as much to Ferdinand
Tönnies and Max Weber as to Karl Marx, a new social category
was fashioned to explain oppression and dehumanization in both East
and West—the category of *alienation*. Marx, it was now remembered
and increasingly emphasized, had never seen the proletarian as
enslaved by the capitalist. Both, for Marx, were slaves of the capitalist
system; both had to play out the roles allotted to them; both were,
in that sense, unfree and dehumanized—even if the bourgeois found
comfort and profit in his objective enslavement, a feeling of subjective
freedom, while the worker found in it misery and degradation,
both objective and subjective unfreedom.

As a critique of modern capitalism, the concept of alienation can be
integrated without great difficulty into classical Marxism as it had
indeed been integrated into Marx's own increasing concern with
the economic logic of the capitalist order.[8] The worker was alienated
under capitalism in that the product of his work and his very
capacity to work, his labour time, were severed from him and sold
to another; his fellow men confronted him as competitors or as
exploiters; the whole system of production, meant to satisfy *human*
needs, had become, through money and the fetishism of commodities,
an alien monster determining man instead of being determined by
him. Alienation in human society, according to Marx, had existed
from the introduction of private property and the division of
labour, but it had reached its most subtle and pervasive stage under
capitalism. In the 1950s and 1960s, however, those Marxists who took
up the concept of alienation most enthusiastically and called
themselves 'socialist humanists' had in mind not only the evils of
capitalism. They believed that the concept of alienation could also be
applied to socialist/communist economies and societies, where the

---

[8] For a fuller discussion of the role that the concept of alienation has played in Marx's
work and subsequently, see Eugene Kamenka, *The Ethical Foundations of Marxism*
(London and Boston, 1972), and his *Marxism and Ethics* (London and New York, 1969).

worker was still not in control of his life and work, where a dogmatic ideology and a forced labour confronted him as external necessities, where society was still divided and both political life and the system of production were still inhuman. In the work of the more metaphysical followers of this trend, originating with the Frankfurt School, in the writings of such men as Adorno, Marcuse and Habermas, the category of 'alienation' was indeed taken beyond the critique of contemporary capitalism and contemporary Soviet-dominated socialism to a more radical critique of the whole of industrial society and the Enlightenment trends that gave it birth. The evil lay, for these thinkers, in the development of *Technik*, of instrumental reason which treats man as an object or component in the industrial process, and not as a self-determined subject becoming one, through self-conscious *Praxis*, with other men and the environment, finding in dialectical interaction with them his dignity, potentiality and freedom.[9]

All this, metaphysical as it may be, confused and open to objection as it is, captured to an extraordinary extent an ever-growing component in the contemporary mood—a revulsion from external necessity, economic growth and technological progress, a fear of science, a retreat from the organized, the goal-directed, the urban, to what Professor John Passmore has called the 'new mysticism'.[10] Rationality itself, as instrumental rationality at the very least, was attacked and rejected; the values of the bureaucracy as described by Weber were seen as precisely the values that made the despotism of the system possible, that introduced depersonalization, dehumanization, into every aspect of human life. The task, it was said, was to repersonalize society—in government, in law, in administration, in work and in education. New, non-bureaucratic attitudes and a rejection of hierarchies and fixed structures were the voice of the future and of man as he rediscovered himself and his community with other men. The call, for some, has become to reject everything that is heteronomous in relation to man instead of autonomous, that seeks to subject human beings to transcendent rules, impersonal, external ends or social 'necessities', or to convert them into statistics, files or instances of a general principle.

[9] For a more detailed examination of such contemporary discussions, emphasizing, *inter alia*, the differences between Marcuse and Habermas in their respective critiques of Weber and the role of instrumental reason and bureaucratization in modern industrial society, see Wolfgang Schluchter, *Aspekte bürokratischer Herrschaft* (Munich, 1972).

[10] John Passmore, *The Perfectibility of Man* (London, 1970), final chapter, 'The New Mysticism: Paradise Now', pp. 304–27. See also his recent Mason Welch Gross lectures at Rutgers University, published as *Science and Its Critics* (New Brunswick, N.J., 1978).

IV The coming of post-industrial society

The resentment of the power and privilege that seem to come easily, even if at comparatively subordinate levels, to those who are educated and professional, the fear of the state and, above all, the fear of depersonalization and helplessness within mass society, mass administration and mass production provide the basis and constitute the content of the evergrowing use of 'bureaucracy' as a pejorative word to describe almost anything that stands in our way. The rage of Caliban at not seeing his face in a glass, at finding that he is not the centre of the universe and that it does not simply bend to his will, is more widespread in affluent and developed societies than it is in other places or has been in other times. The desire for *autonomy*, or at the least for a world in which our actions and opinions really count, has led to or been accompanied by a desire for *recognition*, for emotional *rapport*, for a world of human beings instead of files or computer cards. Much of this, as we have written elsewhere,[11] resolves itself into the flight from New York to Marlboro country, from industrialized mass society to the village or neighbourhood community, from the *Gesellschaft* and its successor, the bureaucratized state, to the *Gemeinschaft* and its intensely local, personal, human ties. The effects of this movement—some expressing themselves in romantic fantasies and mystical nonsense, others in practical and sensible shifts of interest and method—can be felt on all sides, in education, relations in the work place, administrative reforms. They constitute something of a revolt, or at least of a countervailing trend, against the forecast bureaucratization of the world.

The emphasis on personalization, on not being a cog in the system, has also led to what is perhaps an excessive readiness to blur the boundaries between the administrative and the political, between those who carry out the orders and those who give them. Eichmann, many of us want to say, is as guilty as Hitler and when we find that Eichmann's insensitivity is part of his 'bureaucratic' mentality, we draw the false conclusion that 'bureaucracy'—which made possible the holocaust—therefore produced it. Coupled with a widespread but exaggerated belief that bureaucracies do everything possible to maintain and increase their power at whatever cost to others and society generally, this has led to a surprisingly prevalent belief that the evils of the modern world can be traced to the existence, the ways of working and mental attitudes of members of bureaucra-

[11] 'Beyond Bourgeois Individualism: the Contemporary Crisis in Law and Legal Ideals', in E. Kamenka and R. S. Neale (eds), *Feudalism, Capitalism and Beyond* (Canberra and London, 1975) pp. 126–44, and 'Socialism, Anarchism and Law', in *Law and Society*; see also A. E. S. Tay, 'Law, the Citizen and the State', in *Law and Society*, pp. 1–17.

cies. The contemporary trend is to elevate moral and political commitment over technical and administrative expertise, personalization over rule-bound behaviour, 'concern' over impartiality, to forget that ideology kills more people than bureaucracy.

Politics, social administration and intellectual life have their changing fashions no less than the garment industry. Popular discussion of these matters tends to proceed by elevating one thing at a time—objectivity in one decade, commitment in another, sympathy and receptivity in a third—obscuring our reliance on the fact that, whatever the media say, none of these will be completely wiped out. The instability of social thought and social attitudes today, the glaring inconsistencies and contradictions in much that has been said, do reflect not only a general increase in the *rate* of change and a fear of it continuing, but a major technological revolution ushering in what the sociologist Daniel Bell has called 'post-industrial' society.[12] In economics, he argues, there has been a shift from manufacturing to services. In technology, we have the centrality of a new science-based intellectual technology in which information and knowledge replace capital and labour as major structural features, in which data banks play a greater role than the discrete, identifiable and readily commercially exchangeable manufactured commodity. In social structure, new technical elites and types of 'class' stratification have arisen, with a technical and professional class, as Machajski had foreseen, growing faster than any other and with managers making up, in the United States in 1975, 25 per cent of a labour-force of 80 million. In the face of these major revolutions, the comparatively confident ethos of traditional nineteenth-century liberalism and its view of society have collapsed and its attempted harmonizing of its socio-economic, political and cultural systems on the basis of an ethos of individualism and the work ethic has lost both plausibility and appeal. As men and women, faced by data banks, statistical analyses, production schedules and market surveys, long more and more for their lost individuality (as distinct from individualism), they are confronted by the fact that the basic ingredient of modern production—knowledge—is social and that even research has become bureaucratized, that is, organized on a rational, routine, planned basis with hierarchical authority, demarcated functions and the setting of specific tasks. It is thus that we arrive at Daniel Bell's description of society today as one in which the socio-economic system, the political system and the cultural system are no longer in step and in which society has no shared ethos holding these systems together. It is thus, too, that bureaucratization and

[12] See Daniel Bell, *The Coming of Post-Industrial Society* (paperback edn with a new introduction, New York, 1976), as well as his *The Cultural Contradictions of Capitalism* (New York, 1973).

the rejection of bureaucracy and bureaucratic values can emerge as equally notable features of our time. Perhaps the most striking 'contradictions'—or tension—of our time are the simultaneous pursuit and limited elevation of three classical paradigms of social life— the organic, personalized community (*Gemeinschaft*), the individualistic, commercial-contractual society (*Gesellschaft*) and the bureaucratic-administrative welfare state. We seek and fear all three. We strive for and will have to learn to live with an optimal mix. Abusing bureaucracy as a substitute for thinking will not speed us on the way, even if it has special appeal to, and connection with, a fourth underlying trend of our time, connected above all with affluence and the prolongation of a work-free youth—the elevation of the 'free' individual and his 'right' to instant and constant gratification.

V Freedom, bureaucratization and the law

Gemeinschaft structures, as the sociologist Ferdinand Tönnies argued, rest on kinship, shared locality and religion or ideology, on 'natural' and traditional leadership, on the sense of an organic community or social family in which every member is recognized as a specific person, carrying with him all his social relations, his context, status and ties. The *Gesellschaft* is Hobbes's society of atomic individuals, standing in relation to each other as abstract right- and duty-bearing individuals, held together by contracts and commercial exchange under the rule of an abstract, depersonalized, impartial and impersonal legal system. Bureaucratic-administrative structures elevate social policy and social plan as complex and developing technical and rational exercises, requiring the organization of knowledge, the allocation of resources, the planning and supervision of activities. In law, the movement from status to contract was a movement from the centrality of the *Gemeinschaft* paradigm to the centrality of the *Gesellschaft* paradigm and the current movement from private law to public administration, to ever-increasingly specialized regulations and bodies of law, is a further movement to the growing centrality of the bureaucratic-administrative paradigm. All three paradigms, of course, have always been part of the legal system of any complex society; it is their relative weight, the strength of their claim to centrality or overriding validity, that vary. It is the shift, glaring in communist countries, but steadily mounting in post-industrial societies, from *Gemeinschaft* and *Gesellschaft* paradigms to the bureaucratic-administrative paradigm that constitutes the equally desired and feared bureaucratization of the world. The atomic individual and his rights and duties as against the rights and duties of other individuals no longer occupy the centre of the stage; laws are no longer comparatively simple and universal, seeing all citizens as equal, and bearing responsibility for individual action; laws become increasingly regulations distinguishing between citizens and between their activities in terms of social policies and social consequences, substituting specific status for abstract right, providing concrete security in place of abstract autonomy.

This is one side of the picture—a growing bureaucratization of work, law and social life that does justify the phrase 'bureaucratization of the world' and that confirms, though not quite in the way he meant it, Karl Marx's belief in the growing power of socialism and the socialization of capitalism from within. On the other side, the socialist belief that the increasing 'mechanization' (now read computerization and automation) of labour and the accompanying increase in standards of living and of education would result in a certain democratization of labour and social life, in a decrease in the use of force and hierarchical authority in the organization of work and the distribution of resources, was not entirely misplaced. The extent to which that is so and the bearing of this on the more careful and limited use of the word 'bureaucracy' to describe specific structures and ways of working in society is discussed by Robert Brown in the next and final chapter. Our own much broader, and no doubt less exact, conception of the bureaucratic-administrative as a historically active ideology and social paradigm we explore further in the next volume in this series, *Law and Social Control*.

Appendix

Jan Wacław Machajski, whose life and work are still not well known, was born in Russian Poland in December 1866 or January 1867 (New Style), the son of an indigent clerk who died early in Machajski's childhood. At high school, he met and became a close friend of the young Stefan Żeromski, who was to become one of Poland's leading novelists and short-story writers. (In Żeromski's novel, *The Labours of Sisyphus*, which described the patriotism and illegal radical activity of their high school days, Machajski appears as the character Andrzej Radek, the young *intelligent* who is a leading protagonist in the story and probably combines features of the young Machajski and the young Żeromski. The young Polish Marxist Sobelsohn was sufficiently impressed with the character when he read the novel to adopt the name as a *nom de guerre* and become the ill-fated Bolshevik Karl Radek.) Żeromski and Machajski were to maintain some friendship through most of Machajski's life, even when their political views had diverged quite strongly.

Graduating from the high school of Kielce, Machajski entered the University of Warsaw, first to study natural sciences and then transferring to medicine. He began, like Żeromski, as a radical nationalist with an interest in social questions, becoming involved at the university in conspiratorial activity connected with the Union of the Youth of Poland.

This was associated with the patriotic *Liga Polska*, which believed that working-class support would be important in the struggle for Polish independence and conducted propaganda and educational activities among Polish workers. By 1888, Machajski was moving strongly to the left, attracted by the newly formed *National-Socialist Commune*, whose leader Boleslaw Limanowski, in exile in Paris, insisted that a free Polish nation would be possible only under socialism. Machajski himself, in the Union's organ *Pobudka (The Clarion)*, reported in 1892 that Polish revolutionary students wanted to build bridges to the workers but lacked revolutionary socialist literature or clear ideas on the subject. Before that, in 1891, Machajski had been arrested by the Austrian police while trying to smuggle forbidden radical literature from Austria into Russian Poland. He was imprisoned for four months in Cracow and allowed to emigrate to Zurich. He enrolled in the university there, but did not complete a degree. By this time, according to his widow, he had become a zealous Marxist and an out-and-out internationalist, flatly opposed to nationalism and the use of the workers as a tool for nationalist purposes. In 1892 he penned a revolutionary leaflet calling on the striking Lodz textile workers to fight on and awaken the Russian workers as well. He endeavoured to bring the leaflet into Russian Poland, was arrested by the Russian police and spent the next three years in Tsarist prisons, followed by five years in exile in north eastern Siberia.

In Siberia, in 1898, he wrote and hectographed the first of the three pamphlets that he later entitled, collectively, *The Intellectual Worker*. More copies were run off the following year. It is not clear whether the second part also appeared in Siberia in 1899, as Russian sources say, or whether it was mimeographed in Zurich in 1904, as Max Nomad says, but by the time he had completed the work and summed up his conclusions, Machajski was no longer a Marxist, but had developed the distinctive doctrines thenceforth associated with his name. These doctrines unquestionably reflect a suspicion, going back to his Polish illegal activity, of nationalist intellectuals using the workers for their own ends, and owe more than Machajski ever admitted to the anarchist Bakunin. But according to his own testimony in the subsequent 1905 preface, he began writing the first part of *The Intellectual Worker* as a Marxist criticizing from within, and clarified for himself his new position only when he came to summing up the argument. Released from his Siberian exile in 1900, Machajski was rearrested, apparently in error, while *en route* for European Russia; he was found to be carrying revolutionary pamphlets. Involved in a variety of legal troubles as a result, he was alternately kept in gaol or under surveillance in Irkutsk until his escape in 1903, but during that period he attracted around him in Siberia a small number of followers, some of them revolutionary exiles, others local workers (artisans). After his escape, in autumn 1903, he settled in Geneva. By then small groups of Makhaevists were forming, probably as a result of the circulation of his hectographed pamphlet, in Odessa, Yekaterinoslav, Vilna, Byalostok and finally St Petersburg and Warsaw—'Makhaevtsy' being especially active in the two latter centres in 1905–6 and 1906 respectively. In Geneva, meanwhile, Machajski converted, and formed a close relationship with, the young anarchist Max Nomad who remained a disciple for some ten years; he received financial support for his cause from Janina Berson, the young daughter, living in Germany, of a wealthy St Petersburg banker. He paid a year's visit to Russia in 1906—too late, for the 1905 Revolution had already been suppressed—but remained chiefly in Western Europe until the Revolution in 1917. In Geneva, in 1904, he had adopted the pen-name 'A. Vol'sky' and there he revised and expanded his *The Intellectual Worker*. It was published in Russian, as a book, in Zurich in 1905. It consisted of a preface, dated Geneva, April 1905, three parts—'Part I: The Evolution of Social Democracy'; 'Part II: Scientific Socialism'; 'Part III, section I: Socialism and the Workers' Movement'; 'Part III, section 2: Socialist Science as a New Religion'—and an appendix, 'The Workers' Revolution'. In the same year in Geneva, he published pamphlets in Russian on the bankruptcy of nineteenth-century socialism and in Polish on bourgeois revolution or workers' rights. He went on setting out his views in a periodical published from Geneva, *Rabochii Zagovor* (*The Workers' Conspiracy*). His *Intellectual Worker* was published in St Petersburg in 1906. In the same year he published, also in Petersburg, a two-volume Russian translation of Marx's and Engels's *Holy Family*; his notes to that attack Marx's still philosophically Feuerbachian materialism—a materialism that was not the class standpoint of the proletariat, but which concealed an elevation of the social whole and of general national needs as well as a utopian reliance on the 'logic' of history.

When the February (March) Revolution broke out in Russia in 1917, Machajski was living in Paris and working in a bank. He returned to Russia, accepted the Bolshevik take-over and published, in the summer of 1918, a single issue of a small magazine *Rabochaya revolutsiya* (*The Workers' Revolution*). In it, he welcomed the Bolshevik *coup* as 'true to the Marxist form of seizing power in its rejection of social democratic parliamentarianism' and recognized that the Bolsheviks were closer to his views, more genuinely proletarian, than any other socialist party of the time. But he was unhappy with the then slow pace of nationalization and expropriation and argued that 'the task of the working masses is not to overthrow the Soviet Government to the delight of all conciliators and counter-revolutionists, but to push it forward through their economic working-class demands which, after the seizure of power by the Soviets, should not have ceased, but, on the contrary, should have risen to the point of demanding the expropriation of the bourgeoisie in the interests of the working class.' Thereafter, so far as we know, Machajski was silent. He worked as a minor copy editor and researcher for the journal of the Supreme Economic Council and died on 19 February 1926, of angina pectoris, at the age of 59. Obituaries, largely denunciatory but grudgingly respectful of his revolutionism, were published in *Izvestiya* of 24 February 1926, and *Pravda* of 2 March. The anarchist paper *Delo truda* (*The Cause of Labour*), published in Paris, noted his death with somewhat more sorrow and respect in its issue no. 11 of April 1926.

Żeromski's diaries, as well as his novels, are one of our sources for Machajski's views and character. There are other references by contemporaries, Polish nationalists writing about him in Warsaw and Russian revolutionaries recalling him as a fellow exile in Siberia. Trotsky refers to him in *My Life*; we have Machajski's newspaper articles, some of his pamphlets and books, the recollections of his former disciple Max Nomad and a memoir of Machajski left by his widow in Nomad's keeping. In the large Menshevik history *The Social Movement in Russia in the Beginning of the Century* (St Petersburg, 1909–14), B. I. Gorev discussed anti-parliamentary groups, the anarchists, the maximalists and the Makhaevists as a sort of anti-intellectual grassroots, half-anarchist half-syndicalist strain in Russian revolutionary activity from 1905 on. Marxist attitudes to him were uniformly hostile; contemporaries saw his views as representing the class ideology of the *Lumpenproletariat*. The 'new class' theories described by Martin Krygier in the preceding chapter have led to a revival of interest in Machajski's work among socialists and those concerned with the analysis of Soviet and East European society. His chief work, *The Intellectual Worker*, was republished in Russian by the Inter-Language Library Associates in 1968 with disappointing introductions (by different people) in English and Russian. Articles had appeared earlier in *Soviet Studies* and *Survey*; the best article in English, from which we have drawn some of the material above, is that by Anthony D'Agostino, 'Intelligentsia, Socialism and the "Workers' Revolution": the Views of J. W. Machajski', *International Review of Social History* (1969) XIV, pp. 54–89.

6

Bureaucracy: the utility of a concept

Robert Brown

The present utility of the concept *bureaucracy* depends almost entirely upon there being both bureaucratic and non-bureaucratic organizations in the societies which concern us. For the concept of bureaucracy, whether applied to a form of government or to the administrative instrument of a government, or to a private organization, would have virtually no work to do if all these organizations were thoroughly bureaucratized. Not only would there be no important contrasts to be drawn between the bureaucratic and non-bureaucratic organizations known to us, but there would be no practical considerations which would impel us to distinguish between degrees of bureaucratization. Only our interest in pre-bureaucratic history or in post-bureaucratic utopias would keep the concept *bureaucracy* alive.

Similarly, if modern societies were completely innocent of bureaucratization we should have little use for that concept unless we either foresaw a future change or were dealing with bureaucracies of the past. Thus the absence of the concept of bureaucracy at a particular period of time would be a *prima facie* indication either of the complete success of bureaucratization or its total failure to develop. Which of these situations actually held would have to be discovered by investigation. On the other hand, the absence of the concept *bureaucracy* could be no more than *prima facie* evidence that one of these situations existed. For partial bureaucratization might exist in the absence of any explicit concept of bureaucracy. It is not an essential feature of the concept *bureaucracy* that its practitioners, or anyone else, possess the concept. But in practice a great many of them do, and it is simply a point of fact that absence of the concept is likely to be a good sign that partial bureaucratization is absent also.

Of course it is undisputed that the mere existence of the concept *bureaucracy*, and the use of the term, however widespread, cannot ensure the existence of actual bureaucracies, whether past, present, or future. Our conceptual usage in this case may apply accurately to our existing social organizations, but it neither creates them nor presupposes their existence. If conceptual usage could do either of these things, then the existence of the concept *witchcraft* would ensure that sorcery was practised, and the existence of the concept of a creature from outer space would be sufficient for that creature to exist. Nevertheless, the fact that both the concept *bureaucracy* and the corresponding term are much used to characterize contemporary organizations is excellent evidence that some people believe, rightly or wrongly, that their employment of the concept does useful work now. They may share Max Weber's fear of 'the irresistibly expanding bureaucratization of all public and private relations of authority', but their continued employment of the concept *bureaucracy* is a strong indication that they are committed to believing that the process, whether irresistible or not, remains unfinished today.

Because the present utility of this concept is heavily dependent on the actual state of our social organizations, to ask about the continuing usefulness of the concept is, in large part, an indirect way of asking about the future role of bureaucratic organizations in our societies. It is usual to ask, for example, whether Weber's fear is likely to be realized—whether it is true, as he thought, that bureaucratic organizations are indispensable to the full development of bourgeois capitalism because bureaucracies provide reliable, continuous, precise, and therefore predictable, administration. But when we consider this claim do we find that bureaucratic organization is both indispensable to bourgeois capitalism and indispensable because of the superiority of its procedures for applying and interpreting formal rules as they bear on individual cases? Can rational capitalist enterprise not develop under non-bureaucratic forms of administration? What would such forms be like? These and many related questions have been much discussed under the heading 'the future of bureaucracy'. It is worthwhile, however, to examine several of them yet again, but this time under a somewhat different heading, that of 'the future of hierarchical authority'. Although the two headings refer to closely related topics, we shall see that there are advantages in emphasizing certain differences between them.

I The features of bureaucratization

Let us begin by trying to become clearer about the supposed features of bureaucratic organization. A simple way of doing this is to recall some basic points made by earlier sociological writers on the subject. In a paper entitled 'The Concept of Bureaucracy: An Empirical Assessment', R. H. Hall[1] reported on his measurements of the six

[1] *American Journal of Sociology* LXIX (1963–4), pp. 32–40.

important features of bureaucracy which were most frequently cited in the literature by 'major authors'. These six features were: 1 a functionally specialized division of labour; 2 an explicit hierarchy of authority; 3 rules which describe the duties and rights of officials; 4 a set of standard operating procedures; 5 impersonal relations between officials; 6 employment and promotion based on technical merit. The degree to which these features were present in an organization served as a measure of the extent of its bureaucratization. Hall then asked: 'To what extent do actual organizations show these features?' He determined their presence by administering a scaled questionnaire to a sample of the staff of ten organizations of varying size. While mean scores for each feature were calculated for each organization, and these scores varied significantly, they did not reflect the possible differences between official policy and actual behaviour within the organizations. This difficulty aside, both the raw scores and the intercorrelation coefficients among the six features justified Hall in drawing some conclusions of considerable interest for our purposes here.

The first conclusion, as we might reasonably expect, was that each feature was present in significantly different degrees in the various organizations tested: they were bureaucratized to varying degrees rather than being either bureaucratic or non-bureaucratic. The second conclusion was that the six features were not highly intercorrelated, that is, the degree to which each feature was present in an organization was relatively independent of the degree to which the other features were present. There was some suggestion, however, that hierarchy of authority might be the central feature in determining the total degree of bureaucratization. A third conclusion was that neither the age nor the size of any of the organizations was significantly correlated with the degree to which any of the six features was present; in particular, the increased size of an organization did not in itself seem to produce a higher degree of bureaucratization in it.

Finally, Hall drew attention to the fact that one of the features, that of technical merit or competence, was negatively associated with the presence of the other features. This strongly suggested that technical merit was not one of the characteristics of bureaucratization. For as Hall put it: 'In a highly bureaucratized situation (along all dimensions) the highly competent person might not be able to exercise the full range of his competence due to specific procedural limitations, limited sphere of activity, limited authority due to hierarchical demands, etc.'[2] Unfortunately, it is not clear whether Hall had in mind the use of technical competence (successful performance) as a basis for selection and promotion or had slipped into discussing the rather different feature of the staff's level of technical qualifications. The negative

[2] *Ibid.* p. 39.

association, and Hall's explanation of it, might well hold of both features.

We are left, then, with a set of five apparent characteristics of bureaucratization—job specialization, hierarchical authority, personnel rules, standard operating procedures, and impersonal relations. These characteristics seem to vary independently of each other and of the age and size of the organization. It is a plausible suggestion that hierarchical authority is the feature with the most important influence in determining the degree of total bureaucratization. If this is so, then the question of the future employment of hierarchical authority in organizations bears directly on the question of the future bureaucratization of technically advanced societies.

It is of interest, therefore, that in a still earlier investigation by Stanley Udy[3] of 150 organizations engaged in 'the production of material goods in 150 different non-industrial societies' he found that three organizational features were everywhere present and strongly correlated. They were differential rewards based on office, specialized staff administrators, and hierarchical authority. Clearly, this cluster of features is closely related to those which Hall investigated. For much of what staff administrators are concerned with is the operation of personnel rules and the maintenance of standard operating procedures; and the presence of such rules and procedures tends strongly to ensure the presence of staff to administer them. Similarly, the presence of these three features is a good guarantee that operational continuity will be present. Thus the apparently distinctive features of each list are derivable from the features of the other list. The chief conflict between the two lists is that Udy's list is a set of interrelated characteristics. But however this conflict is to be accounted for, the similarity in 'bureaucratic' features of so many organizations drawn from both industrial and non-industrial societies is impressive, and especially interesting is the presence, yet again, of hierarchical authority.

Udy went on to suggest that 'the technological nature of the task being performed'[4] determines an organization's minimum degree of bureaucratization. Hall agreed 'that the type of organizational activity may be highly related to the degree of bureaucratization'.[5] Both these remarks are generalizations of Weber's view that bureaucratization is encouraged by the need to deal with large continuous flows of administrative jobs. All three of these claims were given an empirical foundation and a much enlarged content in a paper written by

---

[3] Stanley Udy, Jr. ' "Bureaucracy" and "Rationality" in Weber's Theory', *American Sociological Review* XXIV (1959), pp. 791–5.
[4] *ibid.* p. 794.
[5] Hall, p. 39.

Arthur Stinchcombe.[6] He began by drawing a useful distinction, that between the administrative features of a craft-based industry such as building construction, and those of a mass production manufacturing industry such as the producers of motor vehicles or chemicals. In the latter, both the product and the production process (the job location, the arrangement of tools, materials, and workers, the time schedules, the task operations and their standards) 'are planned in advance by persons not on the work crew'.[7] In the former—the craft-based industry—all these aspects of the work process are controlled by the craftsmen and foremen themselves rather than by the staff of specialized departments such as production, engineering, cost accounting, and operations-inspection. In consequence, said Stinchcombe, the proportion of communication-processors (clerks) in the two sorts of administration is very different. He found that the building construction industry employed less than half the proportion of clerks found in the motor vehicle, iron and steel, or chemical industries. The significance of this difference, he thought, is that a strong clerical staff permits the concentration of decisions in the higher echelons, lessens the need for 'self-discipline at the work level', and allows that discipline to be replaced by hierarchical and centralized control. This difference lends some support to Weber's view that administration based on files is a characteristic feature of bureaucracy. In short, Stinchcombe wrote, craft administration 'differs from bureaucratic administration by substituting professional training of manual workers for detailed centralized planning of work. This is reflected in the lack of clerical workers processing communications to administrative centres and less complex staffs of professionals planning work. It is also reflected in the simplification of authoritative communications from administrative centres.'[8]

But what conditions are favourable to one kind of administration rather than the other? Stinchcombe pointed out that the building construction industry was subject to considerable seasonal variation in both the volume and types of work. This variation made it uneconomical for the industry to carry the constant high overhead expenses produced by a bureaucratic administration; the variation in work flow also made such an administration relatively inefficient, since its staff and organization could not be altered in sympathy with the work flow. When clerical employment was used as 'an index of bureaucratization, a close relation was found between seasonality in branches of

[6] 'Bureaucratic and Craft Administration of Production: A Comparative Study', *Administrative Science Quarterly* IV (1959), pp. 168–87.
[7] *ibid.* p. 170.
[8] *ibid.* pp. 175–6. On the inverse correlation between professionalization and centralized authority, see P. M. Blau, W. V. Heydebrand and R. E. Stauffer, 'The Structure of Small Bureaucracies', *American Sociological Review* XXXI (1966), pp. 179–91.

construction and bureaucratization'.[9] Moreover, the seasonal variation in work-flow had produced both a labour market which was
adjusted to variable demand and a subcontracting system which
organized that labour only when and where it was needed. Neither
requirement could be met as cheaply and effectively by bureaucratic
administrations which depend, of necessity, on continuous work
flows and on permanent appointments that have continuity of
status.

Stinchcombe concluded that three of the features which make up
Weber's ideal bureaucracy are interrelated. They are career continuity
within the organization, hierarchical authority, and a fixed communication system (administration based on files).[10] All of them are
characteristic of the centralized bureaucratic administration found in
the mass production industries; none of them is found in the administration of the craft-based industries; each of them is found to be
related to features listed by Weber, Hall and Udy. Thus career
continuity is connected with Udy's differential rewards based on office
and Hall's job rules for officials. Administration based on files is a
consequence of all three factors on Udy's list—differential rewards,
specialized administrators, hierarchical authority—as it is of three of
the factors listed by Hall—specialized division of labour, hierarchical
authority, and job rules for officials. But more important than this
agreement is Stinchcombe's suggestion that one of the conditions
which is favourable to the development of these features is 'continuity
of work load'. Given such continuity in sufficient volume, it becomes
possible to lower costs and increase output by standardizing tasks; and
this is one of the important operations which is performed by
centralized administration. In the absence of the required volume of
continuous work-flow, the standardization of tasks is uneconomic.
Obviously, there is no advantage in having an elaborate assembly line
when its product is both occasional and one of a kind. This is
another reason for believing that a generally high level of technical
qualifications on the part of the staff is not a characteristic
feature of centralized bureaucratic administration. It standardizes
tasks where possible, and substitutes central planning and supervision
for the craft skills of a decentralized work force—or for the expertise
of highly educated professionals. Far from being an organization of
highly qualified experts, a typical bureaucracy is, for the most part, an
organization in which relatively unskilled workers become adept at
performing routine tasks.[11] It is only because of such routinization
that a centralized bureaucracy provides the predictable outcomes

[9] Stinchcombe, p. 180.
[10] For the differences introduced by professionalization see Blau, Heydebrand
and Stauffer.
[11] Blau, Heydebrand & Stauffer.

which Weber thought were so essential to the growth and maintenance of 'bourgeois capitalism'.

II The indispensability of bureaucratic administration

In a well known passage Weber wrote:

> The development of the modern form of the organization of corporate groups in all fields is nothing less than identical with the development and continual spread of bureaucratic administration. This is true of church and state, of armies, political parties, economic enterprises, organizations to promote all kinds of causes, private associations, clubs and many others. Its development is, to take the most striking case, the most crucial phenomenon of the modern state.[12]

A few sentences later, Weber went on to say of bureaucratic administration that, 'for the needs of mass administration today, it is completely indispensable.' The use of the phrase 'mass administration' is worth noticing since what is 'identical with the development and continual spread of bureaucratic administration' is the development of *mass* corporate groups. It is not that centralized bureaucratic administration for a small corporate group must somehow fail to function, but that the economic and technical advantages of centralized bureaucracy are not realized in small work-flows. Because the advantages are not realizable under such conditions, there has been, in European history, a powerful incentive for clear headed administrators either to avoid the establishment of small-flow bureaucracies or to ensure that the volume of work was sufficient for the economies of scale produced by larger ones. Less clear-headed administrators have found that their small scale bureaucracies either created their own sufficient, and expensive, work-flow or disintegrated vertically into more suitable sub-groups.

Now various historians have argued that the growth of modern bureaucratic administration has gone hand in hand, and causally interacted with, the growth of the modern nation-state. It is this view which Martin Krygier refers to when he writes: 'Such developments were especially marked in the European absolute monarchies of the seventeenth and eighteenth centuries. What particularly distinguished these monarchies from their forebears was the increasing concentration of military and administrative power in centrally directed institutions.'[13] To explain this, Marc Raeff has suggested that once the Protestant Reformation had swept away the regulatory powers and moral guidance previously exercised by the

---

[12] *The Theory of Social and Economic Organizations*, translated by A. M. Henderson and Talcott Parsons (Glencoe, Illinois, 1947), p. 337.

[13] See above, p. 3.

Catholic church and its associated feudal institutions, these tasks fell
to the civil rulers:

> As the Divine Maker has put into motion the well-regulated mechanism
> of nature and has kept it in operation by means of rational laws, so
> should the ruler enact the laws and regulations that shape society and
> keep it on the right path. This is the conception that is at the root of
> the drive for centralization and uniformity, as well as of the excessive
> mania for regulation that we observe in the absolute monarchies of the
> later seventeenth century. . . . The detailed and petty regulations were but
> means for the realization of the essential purpose: the maximizing
> of all the creative energies and potential resources of a stable and
> harmonious society so as to further the spiritual and political ends set
> by God through natural law.[14]

But although the princes may have been set those tasks, the administrative instruments were yet to be developed. When they were
developed by the French and Prussians, in the ways which Krygier
summarizes, those administrative instruments of centralized power
found a natural employment in the training, supervision, and
supplying of large military forces. From such logistical operations
it was simple for the same administrative procedures to be extended
from the barracks to the other institutions left open to state control—
schools, asylums, hospitals, and factories. All these institutions served
large numbers of people on a national scale, and they grew in scope
as they came under the direction of an expanding bureaucratic
administration. They thus became mass corporate groups for whose
administration a bureaucracy, in turn, seemed to be indispensable:
but indispensable in what way?

There is a problem embedded here in Weber's use of 'indispensable'
(or 'essential'), for it is not obvious exactly what is supposed to be
indispensable (or essential) to what. Weber said that bureaucratic
administration is indispensable 'for the needs of mass administration
today'; for the development of rational enterprise; and for the full
development of bourgeois capitalism. He also said that the modern
bureaucrat is indispensable because when he 'comes to predomin-
ate, his power proves practically indestructible since the whole organization of even the most elementary want satisfaction has been
tailored to his mode of operation.'[15] However, the development of
capitalism, or rational enterprise, is something quite different from the
needs of mass administration, even though each has strongly
influenced the other two. Again, the irremovability of the bureaucrat

---

[14] 'The Well-Ordered Police State and the Development of Modernity in Seventeenth
and Eighteenth-Century Europe: an Attempt at a Comparative Approach', *American
Historical Review* LXXX (1975), pp. 1226–7.

[15] *Economy and Society*, edited by G. Roth and C. Wittich (New York, 1968),
p. 1401.

and his organization, while associated in various ways with capitalism, rational enterprise, and mass administration, is a question of its own. When all these factors are taken together with Weber's remark that the development of the modern organization or corporate groups—including the church and state—is identical with the development of bureaucracy, there is, in this view, little to which bureaucratic administration is not essential.

In brief, the indispensability of bureaucracy, as conceived by Weber, runs the grave danger of being trivialized through over-expansion. Every kind of modern rational administration is called 'bureaucratic', and is then identified with the organization of all forms of contemporary corporate groups. Yet if the bureaucratization of the modern world were actually so pervasive, we should rapidly be approaching the time when the concept *bureaucracy* had little work left to do. The truth, however, is that since bureaucracy is only one form of rational administration, the indispensability of the former cannot be identical with the indispensability of the latter. The conscious and deliberate maximization of resources by rational means —modernization—is not the same as the bureaucratization of the modern world, whether by private capitalism or state socialism.

Krygier reminds us that as early as 1765 Baron de Grimm was complaining that in France the bureaucracy, or government by officials, was constantly increasing the scope of its operations. 'Here the bureaux, clerks, secretaries, inspectors, *intendants* are not established to benefit the public interest, indeed the public interest appears to have been established so that there might be bureaux.'[16] This complaint can be re-cast so as to enlarge on a point which was made earlier, namely, that the advantages of centralized bureaucratic administration are dependent upon the presence of large work-flows. In other words, the existence of mass corporate groups is indispensable to the growth and maintenance of centralized bureaucratic administration—always assuming that it is subject to some kind of cost-benefit control. If a bureaucracy were indispensable, under certain conditions, for the administration of mass corporate groups, then, under those conditions, they would be equally indispensable to the maintenance of the bureaucracy. Because it is adapted to large-scale flows, because its design encourages further growth by excluding outside interferences, a genuinely centralized bureaucracy is not only self-maintaining but self-developing. Its organizational design rewards bureaucrats who extend the scope of their power by maximizing their organization's size or wealth or budget. They are rewarded in prestige, influence, money, and in other ways, for exploring and establishing new areas of public interest which then

[16] See above, p. 22.

produce new 'bureaux'. De Grimm was partly correct in this matter: the public interest *is* often established in such a way that bureaucrats can deal with it—a process which in itself becomes self-perpetuating.[17]

There is a further question raised by Weber's view that bureaucratic administration was, and is, indispensable for the growth and maintenance of modern corporate enterprise. It is the question, 'How are we to interpret the term "indispensable" here?' If we interpret it as meaning 'necessary in the circumstances', then once we have specified the circumstances—if we can—the claim at issue is not obviously true. To assert that bureaucratic administration is a necessary condition, in the circumstances, for the development of modern rational enterprise and capitalism is to claim that in the specified circumstances the latter cannot proceed in the absence of centralized bureaucracy. But we have already seen in the case of craft-administration and shall see in other cases later, that there are apparent counter-examples to this claim, and that they seem to give us good reasons for believing it to be false. Of course, the circumstances can be chosen in such a way as to rule out our counter-examples, for example, by characterizing the beliefs of seventeenth-century administrators, the technology of the period, and the requirements of seventeenth-century national development so specifically that only bureaucracy will meet the description which is given. However, if this defence is used, then bureaucracy will turn out to be indispensable only under conditions so narrowly drawn as to be unrepeatable in principle; under all others the general relationship will not hold. A claim thus restricted is tautological and of no interest to us in our attempt to account for the rise of mass administration, rational enterprise, or bourgeois capitalism.

Again, if the term 'indispensable' is merely used to mean 'necessary to produce in all their details the consequences which were actually produced', no other form of administration is admissible in place of bureaucracy. For no other form would have produced exactly the same consequences; and no other consequences will be counted as being proper instances of bourgeois capitalism or rational enterprise or mass administration, as the case may be. This kind of verbal manoeuvre will not help the thesis, however, since it makes tautological the claim that bureaucracy is indispensable for those consequences which only it can produce. Yet once we abandon defence of the thesis by tautologies, and ask such empirical questions as 'Why are the modern bureaucrat and his organization indestructible in capitalism?', we can consider a more serious answer. This answer is that leaving aside the efficiency, continuity, reliability, and precision of centralized bureaucracy, its indestructibility is due less to these

[17] See, for example, J. A. Stockfisch, *The Political Economy of Bureaucracy* (New York, 1972), pp. 21–2.

desirable features—which have to be recognized and valued as such by those in authority—than to another property of its structure. This familiar property is self-maintenance (or self-persistence) by means of negative feedback. Large, complex, centralized bureaucracies are so organized as to defend themselves—maintain certain of their properties in a steady state—by various adminstrative devices against both external and internal disruptive forces. The volume and character of the work-flow, the pattern of life within the organization, tend to be maintained at a point of stable equilibrium; movements from this point activate counter-forces which have a strong tendency to return the organization to its previous position of stable equilibrium. This ability of a self-maintaining system produces the continuity, efficiency, reliability, and predictability of centralized bureaucratic administration by which Weber was so impressed. It also produces its indestructibility and indispensability whose nature and source we are considering now.[18]

For the reason why centralized bureaucracies appear to be 'indispensable' to capitalism, rational enterprise, mass administration—to so much of the corporate life of modern societies—is not that they are, or were, causally necessary (or essential) in the particular circumstances. It is that centralized bureaucracies are examples of self-maintaining systems which, once established, become enmeshed with the other institutions—their political sponsors, their clients, their suppliers—that provide them with their work-flows, their rewards, and their fields of operation. The relationship between bureaucratic administrations, the economic structure of the state, and its political apparatus is straightforwardly symbiotic. They come to be indispensable to each other in the sense that they become inseparable in everyday operation because of their social, political and economic interchange. They can be forcibly separated or eliminated, of course, but when this happens to bureaucratic administrations their clients and partners usually want the same services to continue, even if they have to be supplied by other means. What tend to be indispensable are the services which they provide; but what are inseparable over particular periods of time are the bureaucracy and associated institutions which provide those services. However, as long as the services supplied by these symbiotic complexes continue unchanged, there is a strong tendency for each of the institutional members to remain internally stable. Not only do some portions of the economic and political systems have self-persisting properties of their own, but these systems and the bureaucracy interact, under certain conditions, in such a way as to strengthen the self-maintaining

[18] The organizational features which produce self-maintenance are discussed in Michel Crozier, *The Bureaucratic Phenomenon* (Chicago, 1964), pp. 175–98 and throughout Anthony Downs, *Inside Bureaucracy* (Boston, 1967).

ability of each member of the complex. The self-maintenance of the bureaucratic members is most directly threatened by changes in the character and quantity of their work-flow—their output. When this type of threat is absent, they are capable of adjusting to a wide variety of other external forces, including such changes in their symbiotic partners as are produced by political and economic revolution.[19]

The practical inseparability—the symbiotic relationship—of bureaucratic administration and the regulatory nation-state in modern history has misled many critics. Some of them, as Krygier points out, have not been clear about the difference between the growth of state power and the growth of bureaucratic administration as one of its institutional partners; the critics have gone on to blame the administrative partner for carrying out the interventionist policies of its political masters or sponsors, and have not distinguished the power of the state's political apparatus from the power of the state's bureaucracy. Still other critics, John Stuart Mill among them, have argued for the restriction of governmental power as though this can occur independently of alterations in the character of the administrative system which is its symbiotic partner. To restrict political power is quite different from restricting bureaucratic power, yet to do the former is usually to produce consequential changes in the other members of the institutional complex, the bureaucracy included. However, the bureaucratic official operates within an organization to which many external social arrangements have been adjusted. So altering the official's role may produce, in turn, many consequential changes outside the bureaucracy. The length of this sequence of changes creates considerable resistance to the initial variation. In general, because a self-maintaining system is organized so as either to exclude or soften the impact of interfering factors it has what Weber called 'indestructibility'.

On the other hand, it is important to keep in mind the differences between the partners in an institutional complex. Thus we need to distinguish between the value of the routine which Mill said was 'the disease which afflicts bureaucratic governments, and which they usually die of', and the value of the routine which results from the standardization of tasks in a centralized bureaucracy, and which is one of its chief advantages. Political initiatory power may suffer when routinized, but administrative-bureaucratic power requires it. We should remember also that routinization is only one of such useful bureaucratic features as reliability, impartiality, efficiency, and continuity. Taken together, they offer a highly desirable alternative to earlier administrative practices, many of which were unreliable,

[19] For detailed discussion of these institutional interactions see Crozier, Downs, and W. A. Niskanen, *Bureaucracy: Servant or Master?* (London, 1973), pp. 13–26.

haphazard, filled with partiality, humiliating, and cruel. The elimination of these practices by the growth of bureaucratization helps us to understand why its benefits have become incorporated into the structure of a self-persisting system.[20]

III The depersonalization of bureaucratic administration

Let us return now to the set of questions which have commonly been grouped under the heading 'the future of bureaucracy'. What are we to make of the popular claim that modern advanced societies are becoming increasingly bureaucratized—that the constantly increasing size and scope both of business firms and governmental administrations have been closely accompanied by their use of bureaucratic methods of organization, and that the large masses of clients served by these methods rely on them because of their technical superiority to all other means? Are we to believe that bureaucratic administration, whether public or private, is so stable in its self-maintenance that it is not subject to the ordinary processes of social change? To ask these questions is to doubt their affirmative answers.

Modern centralized bureaucratic administration, as we have seen, is usually taken to be one whose work-flow is dealt with in terms of a system of rules which prescribes the tasks, duties, and privileges of specialized employees within a pyramidal chain of command. To this type of organization, W. G. Bennis has declared,[21] there are four threats—1 'rapid and unexpected change'—for bureaucracies deal best with 'the routine and predictable in human affairs'; 2 an increase in size beyond sustainable growth—the organization becomes too large for its tasks since the rules, procedures, and structure do not permit satisfactory processing of the work-flow; 3 an increasing variety of specialized skills which replaces the previous mass of simple repetitive jobs; 4 a demand from the work force that the tasks themselves should be made more satisfying.[22] Bennis suggested that at present these factors are beginning to combine with certain other social changes—such as closer relations between industries and governments, an increase in large-scale multinational enterprises, an increase in job mobility, a rise in educational level, and a greater demand for worker participation—and that the effect of this combination will be to produce major alterations in bureaucracy as it now exists.

These remarks of Bennis form a brief introduction to a large literature. For our purposes here we need draw from it only

[20] On these benefits see Crozier, especially pp. 203–8.

[21] W. G. Bennis, 'The Coming Death of Bureaucracy', in *Behaviour Organizations: a multidimensional Approach*, edited by A. C. Athos and R. F. Coffey (Englewood Cliffs, New Jersey, 1968), pp. 256–66.

[22] *ibid.* p. 259.

enough to present an outline of the argument at issue. We can begin by recalling that two common features of bureaucracy are centrally planned decisions and multiple tiers of authority. It has been found from various case studies[23] that these two features work against each other: the highly placed decision-makers lack the necessary data which only the lower echelons of data-gatherers possess. The resulting inefficiency can be avoided by delegating authority down the chain of command, and this is the solution which has been widely resorted to by many organizations. But the senior managers also require information about the extent to which the organization is achieving its goals, information which they can obtain only if they make the goals explicit and set standards by which progress towards them can be determined. If this is done and made known, and if decentralized control has encouraged the development of self-servicing and self-directing units, there is an increased flow of information up the chain of authority; for the subordinates are then in a position to assess and monitor their own performance more adequately than they could when directed only by commands from a higher echelon. So the increased efficiency of the organization in achieving its goals is obtained by removing some of the powers of the higher tiers and strengthening those of the lower ones, that is, by making the chain of command authority less hierarchical.

One consequence of this change—so the argument continues—is that sub-units become increasingly specialized in their work and it slips beyond the understanding, and hence the direct control, of the responsible managers. Since they cannot afford to make expensive mistakes based on ignorance, they have to rely on the knowledge and judgement of their subordinate specialists. The effect of this is that the managers are forced to administer and lead their subordinates in a way which does not depend chiefly on issuing orders and supervising their execution. One way which managers can, and do, employ is that of explicit codes and standard operating procedures. However, these codes and procedures can be criticized by the staff. In the words of P. M. Blau and M. W. Meyer, the codes and procedures 'are subject to challenge, review, and change. The bureaucratic hierarchy becomes a network for channeling information and appeals for review. Thus, managerial authority still exists in the organization, but it is depersonalized, being exercised not so much through issuing commands and close supervision as through designing effective impersonal control systems.'[24]

Blau and Meyer have remarked that the spread of automation en-courages the 'depersonalization of authority' since automated

[23] See, for example, Crozier, pp. 40–51, 187–90, and Downs, pp. 112–58.
[24] P. M. Blau and M. W. Meyer, *Bureaucracy in Modern Society* (2nd edn, New York, 1971), p. 143.

machines are an example of effective but impersonal methods of control: 'It is the information supplied by the machines themselves, not the foreman, that determines what work must be done. In emergencies, of course, the foreman retains the authority of his office, but otherwise he has no legitimate reason for ordering people about.'[25] He has less need to do so, however, for as Blau and Meyer put it: 'Competent specialists tend to be consulted by colleagues and superiors, and the resulting greater frequency of social interaction concerning the work contributes to co-ordination, further reducing the need for commands.'[26] All these features hold equally well of computerization, especially since computerized office management has affected the administrative bureaucracies so directly and power-fully. Once they commit their operations to computerization their chains of authority must run through the programmers, the technically qualified operators, and the research directors. But what more can this authority amount to than the right to ask the computer staff whether the desired results are technically feasible? Those results may be requested—and the request may be rejected on technical grounds—but the results cannot sensibly be ordered unless the administrative managers are themselves technically qualified. If they are, they do not require the full services of expensive computer staff; if they are not, they are simply favoured clients of their staff. Here again, both the desirability of, and the oppor-tunities for, maintaining a pyramidal hierarchy of command authority are much diminished.

IV The future of bureaucratic traits

It is clear that according to this sketch—a sketch of what such well informed people as Blau and Meyer have believed to be the present state of bureaucratic administration in the technologically advanced countries—centralized bureaucracies are now being exposed to at least three of the four conditions which Bennis thought were the chief threats to their stability. They are undergoing 'rapid and unexpected change' in their methods of information processing, in the sources of their decision-making, and in the organization of their work-units. Because of automation, computerization, and other radical changes in equipment, the bureaucracies are absorbing a large variety of new technicians with highly specialized skills while ridding themselves of officials who lack them. Finally, bureaucratic organizations are having to satisfy the demand from their staff for tasks which are intrinsically more satisfying. In addition, all these threats have to be met at roughly the same time.

[25] *ibid.* p. 142.
[26] *ibid.* p. 144.

Bennis concluded, therefore, that the work force of the post-bureaucratic organizations would consist of temporary teams of specialists with diverse skills; each specialist would have divided loyalties, much as members of academic staffs do now. On the one hand, the specialist would pursue his professional goals, and on the other hand, he would pursue those of his organization. The administrators would co-ordinate the teams of specialists, would arrange support for them, and would evaluate their contribution. Since the teams would be temporary, they could not be the object of prolonged loyalty. Nor could their members be given a permanent rank other than by the skill and training each member brought to each temporary team.[27] Under these conditions the bureaucracies' pyramidal hierarchies of authority would largely disappear. They would be replaced, we might say, by 'extended families' of inter-connected and self-programming computers under whose direction automated machines would carry out all the routine tasks created by large work-flows. The teams of specialists, and their associated administrators, would deal with the remaining tasks. Because there is evidence that such changes are already under way—as in the USSR's plan for a national 'automated system of control'[28]—and are likely to be spurred on by the relative costliness of semi-skilled labour, it is worth raising the question 'How would these changes affect the other features of bureaucratic administration?'

The answer to this question, clearly, must be divided into two parts since the changes produced by automation of large work-flows are different from those produced by the employment of specialist teams. Now there is no doubt that automation of work increases both the standardization of tasks in particular, and routinization in general. Automation is introduced for that very purpose and there is no reason to believe that the outcome, in such cases, is uncertain. There is also no doubt that explicit codes and standard operating procedures not only remain in use but take on increased importance with the decline of the direct control exercised by hierarchical authority. For example, a large portion of these codes and procedures act as the 'enabling legislation' for the use of automated machinery and computers; without the fomer there could not be the latter. Again, such other features of traditional bureaucracy as the existence of job specialization (including staff administrators), personnel rules, rewards based on position, and a fixed communication system might well remain unchanged.

In the case of specialist teams, however, some extensive alterations

[27] Bennis, pp. 263–5.
[28] Described by R. F. Miller in 'Organizing for the Technical and Scientific Revolution', in *Political and Administrative Aspects of the Scientific and Technical Revolution in the USSR*; Occasional Paper no. 11, Department of Political Science, Research School of Social Sciences, Australian National University (Canberra, 1976), pp. 61–115.

could be expected. The personnel rules applying to teams, and especially the rewards and career continuity of their members, the communication networks among teams, computers, and their administrative staffs, and the types of personal relationships within the teams—all these would be new factors. Their combined effect might well be to eliminate completely the characteristic of 'impersonal work relations'. For the teams might ensure for their members the intrinsic satisfaction, the consensus on goals, and the participation in settling issues which other types of organization have traditionally provided. If this were to occur, then not only would impersonal work relations disappear, but the distinctions drawn by Blau and Meyer between three types of organization would become somewhat blurred. They distinguished organizations with specific objectives —such as profit-making or tax-collecting—both from those such as political parties, which create opportunities 'for establishing consensus on common objectives', and from those such as tennis clubs which provide 'intrinsic satisfactions'.[29] If all three types of objective were to be pursued, in a serious way, within one organization, we should need to examine carefully the usefulness of these distinctions. In doing that we should also have to examine the conflicts which would arise between the appropriate means required for fulfilling such different purposes. Would dedication to the efficient pursuit of profits be compatible with similar dedication to the critical pursuit of common objectives and to the search for intrinsically satisfying activities?

If one organization could embrace such different purposes, it would become a political and social community in miniature. The organization would no longer maintain that sharp distinction between work life and domestic life which was taken by Weber to be an important feature of modern bureaucracies. (It might, of course, develop into a total institution—enclosed, rule-bound, authoritarian, and isolated from the outside society—but then its members would not be freely pursuing common objectives and intrinsically satisfying activities.) The earlier contractual obligation to perform only a certain sort of task would widen into the obligation to participate full time in an organizational community. In such a situation the term 'bureaucracy' would no longer apply.

If, on the other hand, one organization could not fully embrace these different purposes, then such bureaucratic features as impersonal work relations might well remain; and participation, consensus, and satisfaction would be constrained, of course. But in the absence of a pyramidal hierarchy of authority could the organization properly be called a 'bureaucracy'? To answer 'yes' is to judge that 'depersonalization of authority', decentralization of control, the presence of semi-

[29] Blau and Meyer, p. 155.

independent groups and of computerized automation are outweighed by other, purely bureaucratic, features. But which could these be? Of the ones which we have discussed in connection with specialist teams, only three might remain unchanged—the presence of specialized staff administrators, job specialization, and impersonal relations. While these are characteristics of most large modern organizations, they are not peculiar to them; the three features are also present in craft administration and in some small and transient enterprises. Moreover, these three features do not encapsulate what historically has been fundamental to bureaucratization—1 detailed planning and decision-making concentrated in a central office of senior officials; 2 personal, authoritarian, but rule-bound supervision of the work of the member of each grade by officials of the next higher grade. It is this hierarchical arrangement of work supervision— the close surveillance by more senior officials of the execution of tasks by more junior officials—which both betrays the military influence on the growth of European bureaucracies and gives them reliable discipline. Surveillance of this type would be absent from specialist teams; and in the large-scale automated work flows it would be carried out by machinery. There might be an hierarchy of reliable and efficient supervisory machines but their surveillance could be neither personal nor authoritarian. The result would be a form of organization whose structure of authority was quite different from that of the bureaucracies which we have been describing. The fact that the new form might be even more reliable, efficient, predictable, impartial, and continuous in its operation than the bureaucratic form would not obliterate the important differences between them.

V Bureaucratic change and the utility of 'bureaucracy'

If this account of likely changes in bureaucracy turns out to be correct, how would these changes affect our present concept of bureaucracy— and its future utility? The answer is that both our classificatory and explanatory uses of the concept would undoubtedly alter. It could no longer perform quite the same work which we now value. For at present we employ the term 'bureaucracy' to refer to a form of organization whose characteristics are distinctive enough to make us distinguish it from other forms. We fasten upon these characteristics because they are useful indicators of certain properties typical of bureaucratic organizations and not of other kinds. The chief of these properties is that of being a self-persisting system which by negative feedback maintains some of its other properties in a steady state, a state which is maintained throughout the variations in strength (within certain limits) of the causal factors which operate upon the system. The maintenance of these steady states depends upon the system's possession of self-compensating devices which both monitor variations from the norm and compensate for them by reducing the forces responsible. In the case of bureaucracies, all the characteristics which we have been considering do act, separately or jointly, as self-compensating devices. Thus labour specialization, job rules, standard operating procedures, impersonal relations, and especially hierarchical authority, all limit variation, both of input and output. The freedom of action given to officials in dealing with cases is limited to the application of certain rules; anomalous cases must be referred to higher officials who are constrained by different, and more general, rules. The standardization of tasks and procedures has the double effect of screening the flow of work in such a way as to direct tasks to officials supposedly equipped to deal with them and of ensuring that they do so appropriately; impersonal relations prevent 'cross-overs' of tasks and aid in preserving the chain of command authority. Hence the phrase 'routinization of the entire system' is simply another way of referring to the system's general ability to cope with variations of input and output—to maintain the work-flow in a steady state and, consequent upon that, to maintain the jobs and entitlements of the officials in a steady pyramidal arrangement of supervision, responsibility, and rewards.

Thus to learn that an organization is bureaucratically organized —to a particular degree—is to learn that it is likely to have certain properties which will ensure that the organization operates and responds in specific ways. For example, one of the more important consequences of a system having the property of self-maintenance is that a particular kind of causal relationship holds within it, namely functional relationships between some of the traits of the system. Just as we can say of the human body that one of the functions of a self-adjusting device like the sweat glands is to regulate the body temperature, so we can say of a bureaucracy that one of the functions of standard operating procedures and hierarchical authority is to regulate both the character and volume of the internal work-flow. Because irregular cases must be decided by higher officials, the clients are given slow and unsatisfactory service which deters them. Clients with conventional requirements are given faster and better service, and so are encouraged. If, however, too many conventional cases are presented, the resistance offered by the standard procedures ensures that the service deteriorates towards the level of that given to the irregular cases, and potential clients are discouraged. When the volume decreases to a manageable level the service improves and clients again find it worthwhile to apply.

Now functional relationships like this one obviously require a self-maintaining system, for it is only in such a system that the necessary self-adjusting devices are found; and it is they, with their negative feedback, which maintain certain of the system's properties in a steady regulated state. To say that the trait x is the function of trait y within system S is to say, in part, that y causally maintains or regulates x within S; it is to say that an effect x is not only produced but is maintained in a steady state—maintained, that is, within a range of certain values. It is also to imply that x's steady state helps the system to persist. Functional statements, then, and the explanations which make use of them, presuppose self-maintaining systems, and of these bureaucracy is one example. The chief value of our present concept of centralized bureaucracy, then, is that it authorizes us to use such functional explanations in accounting for the behaviour of bureaucracies and the people who work in them.

If bureaucratic organizations continue to change in the way which has been described, pyramidal command authority may well disappear from them. If so, we are left with the question whether the new form of organization will be self-maintaining. Suppose that, as in the USSR plan,[30] it divides into two sections—one a task force of temporary teams with minimum supporting staff, rather like Stinchcombe's craft-administration; the other an 'extended family' of interconnected computers and automated machinery which deals with large routine flows of work and requires only a skeleton staff of overseers. The first section, by hypothesis, will not be self-maintaining, but what about the other section? The answer, surely, is that substantially fewer traits will be maintained in a steady state, and that in consequence the new system as a whole will not be as strongly self-persisting as the old one. In other words, the new organization will have fewer self-compensating devices. The presence of standard operating procedures, for example, will have a regulatory influence on the character and volume of the work flow. But the decentralization of control, the absence of a long chain of authority, and the ability of the machines to adapt automatically to variations in the volume of work is likely to decrease the system's resistance both to irregular cases and to operation at constant full capacity. With increased machine tolerance for variations in work-flow, the new organization should need fewer self-adjusting devices developed within its social structure; their jobs will be taken over by the interactions among the mechanical components. Moreover, the elimination of pyramidal authority, and the computerization of some types of decisions, ought to reduce considerably the devices devoted to maintaining the stability of the authority pyramid itself. No doubt the organization will retain some self-maintaining traits from the past and will develop some new ones also. Yet all these will have to be discovered anew. This means that the full extent of the system's ability to maintain itself

[30] See Miller, pp. 94ff.

against various external forces will also have to be discovered as the system develops.

Under conditions so changed as these, we shall still find the concepts of functional explanation and self-maintaining system of much use. But it will not be in connection with functioning centralized bureaucracies as we have known them in modern European history. Their high overhead cost, rigidity, and eventual inefficiency are likely to relegate the purely administrative ones to the role of make-work organizations in economically undeveloped countries, useful for disciplining members of a newly emergent labour force in the rule-bound authoritarian procedures of the recent past.

Contributors

Robert Brown is Professorial Fellow in the History of Ideas in the Institute of Advanced Studies of the Australian National University, a former editor of the *Australasian Journal of Philosophy*, and a Fellow and Executive Member of the Academy of the Social Sciences in Australia. Born in New York in 1920, he was educated in anthropology, sociology and philosophy at the University of New Mexico, the University of Chicago, and University College, London, where he took his doctorate in 1952. He has lectured at universities in California, Wisconsin, and Massachusetts. He is the author of *Explanation in Social Science* (1963) and *Rules and Laws in Sociology* (1973), the editor of *Between Hume and Mill* (1970), and the co-editor of *Contemporary Philosophy in Australia* (1969) and, in this series, of *Law and Society: the Crisis in Legal Ideals* (1978). Besides publishing extensively in philosophical journals in North America, Britain and Australia, he has contributed to *Explanation in the Behavioural Sciences* (1970), edited by Borger and Cioffi, and to *Rationality in the Social Sciences* (1976), edited by Benn and Mortimore. At present he is working on a history of the idea of social laws.

Eugene Kamenka is Foundation Professor of the History of Ideas in the Institute of Advanced Studies of the Australian National University and in 1978/9 Visiting Fellow in Trinity College, Oxford, and Visiting Professor in the Max-Planck-Institut für ausländisches und internationales Privatrecht in Hamburg. He is a Fellow of the Academy of the Social Sciences in Australia and Fellow and Secretary of the Australian Academy of the Humanities. Born in Cologne in 1928, Professor Kamenka was educated in Australia in the Sydney Technical High School, the University of Sydney and the Australian National University. He has also worked and taught in

Israel, England, Germany, the United States, Canada, the USSR and Singapore. His books include *The Ethical Foundations of Marxism* (1962), *Marxism and Ethics* (1969) and *The Philosophy of Ludwig Feuerbach* (1970); he has edited *A World in Revolution?* (1970), *Paradigm for Revolution? The Paris Commune 1871–1971* (1972), *Nationalism: the Nature and Evolution of an Idea* (1973), with R. S. Neale *Feudalism, Capitalism and Beyond* (1975), and *The Portable Karl Marx* (1979). He is general editor of this series, 'Ideas and Ideologies', in which he has co-edited and contributed to *Law and Society* (1978), *Human Rights* (1978) and *Intellectuals and Revolution* (1979).

Martin Krygier is Lecturer in Jurisprudence in the University of Sydney Law School. Born in Sydney in 1949, he took a first-class honours degree in the arts faculty in government and a degree in law from the University of Sydney and worked on his PhD thesis as a research scholar in the History of Ideas Unit in the Institute of Advanced Studies of the Australian National University. He is a solicitor of the Supreme Court of New South Wales and a member of the editorial board of the Australian monthly journal of letters and ideas, *Quadrant*. He has also recently contributed to *Socialism and the New Class* (1978), edited by Marian Sawer.

Alice Erh-Soon Tay is Professor of Jurisprudence in the University of Sydney, a member of the Australian National Commission of UNESCO and its specialist Committee for the Social Sciences and, during 1979, Visiting Professor in the Max-Planck-Institut für ausländisches und internationales Privatrecht in Hamburg. She was born in Singapore in 1934 and educated at Raffles Girls' School, Singapore, Lincoln's Inn and the Australian National University, where she took her doctorate with a thesis on 'The Concept of Possession in the Common Law'. She has practised in criminal law and lectured in law in the (then) University of Malaya in Singapore and the Australian National University, spent 1965–6 and parts of 1973 and 1978 as a visiting research worker and professor in faculties of law in Moscow, Kiev and Yerevan State Universities and the Academy of Sciences of the USSR, and been Senior Fellow at the Russian Institute and the Research Institute on Communist Affairs of Columbia University, New York, and in the East–West Center of the University of Hawaii. She is the author of numerous articles on common law, jurisprudence, comparative law, Soviet law and Chinese law, and of several contributions to the *Encyclopedia of Soviet Law*, besides being co-author, with her husband, Eugene Kamenka, of two forthcoming books, *Marxism and the Theory of Law* and *Sowjetische Rechtstheorie*. She is an executive member of the

International Association for Philosophy of Law and Social Philosophy and served as President of the Association's Extraordinary World Congress held in Sydney and Canberra in 1977. In this series, she has co-edited and contributed to *Law and Society* and *Human Rights*.

Index

Absolute monarchies, 3, 9, 141
Administration: 1; and legislative reform, 19; based on files, 140; bureaucratic, 139–42, 147; centralization of, 2, 3, 9, 139–42, 147; continuous workflow, 140; craft, 139–40, 144, 152, 154; depersonalization of, 147–9; emphasis on function, 19; European writings about, 11ff; mass, 141–4, 145; of capitalist state, 77–8; of industrial society, 38–42; of new society, 55–7; of proletarian state, 59, 77–80; role in modern society, 35; routinization of, 146; use of specialists in, 78, 150–52
Administrative Factor, The, Schaffer, 32
Administrative imperatives, 35, 59, 90
Administrative institutions: analogy to machinery, 17–19; Austria, 7, 9, 18; France, 3–4; nineteenth-century Europe, 10; Prussia, 7–9; Russia, 85–6
Administrative organization: and domination, 61–3; forms, 1, 6, 12, 15, 62–4, 65–6, 147, 154–5; monocratic versus collegial, 7, 19, 28–9, 64; reform, 16, 19–20
Administrative Reforms of Frederick William I of Prussia, The, Dorwart, 7 *n 10*
'Administrative science', early modern sources, 11–20
Adorno, T., on alienation, 127
Albrow, M., 21, 21 *n 42*, 23 *n 48*, 26, 26 *n 56*, 29, 29 *n 61*, 31 *n 65*
Alexander I, 16, 17 *n 33*
Alienation, concept of, 126–7
Anarchists, 74, 101, 132
Anderson, E. N., 10
Anderson, P. R., 10
Anti-Centralization Union (1854), 27
Aristotle, 122
Asia in the Making of Europe, I, Lach, 122 *n 7*
Aspekte bürokratischer Herrschaft, Schluchter, 127 *n 9*
Athos, A. C., 147 *n 21*
Authority, one-man, 81; *see also* Hierarchical authority

Autocracy, 15
Automation, 148–9; effects on bureaucracy, 150
Avineri, S., 54
Azrael, J. R., 80, 81 *n 17*

Bagehot, W., 33 *n 70*
Bakunin, M., 57–9, 85, 101, 108, 114, 132
Bakunin on Anarchy, 101 *n 27*
Balzac, Honoré de, criticism of bureaucracy, 23, 24, 26
Balzac: les réalités économiques et sociales dans la Comédie Humaine, Donnard, 23 *n 50*
Barker, E., 5
Beamtenherrschaft, 63, 68–9, 72
Beccaria, C., 14
Behaviour in Organizations, Athos and Coffey, 147 *n 21*, 150
Bell, D., 98 *n 22*, 129
Bennis, W., 147 *n 21*, 150
Bentham, J., 13, 14, 16, 18, 19
Berson, J., 132
Between Ideals and Reality, Stojanovic, 107 *n 39*
Beyond the State, Tarschys, 83 *n 19*
Bielfeld, J. F. von, 18
Blau, P. M., 139 *n 8*, 140 *n 10*, 140 *n 11*, 148, 149, 151
Bolshevik Party, Trotsky on, 89–90
Bolsheviks, 68, 72, 79, 81, 89–90, 133
Bolshevism, critiques of, 101
Bonaparte, Louis Napoleon *see* Louis Napoleon
Bonapartism, Marx's analysis of, 47–53
Bosher, J. F., 5 *n 7*, 17–19, 22 *n 46*
Bourgeois Revolution and the Workers' Cause, The, Machajski, 115
Bourgeois society, 48, 74, 99, 113, 116
Bourgeois specialists, 80, 82
Briefe des Freiherrn vom Stein an den Freiherrn von Gagern, 1813–1831, Die, vom Stein, 24
Brockhaus encyclopedia, 29
Brown, R., 121 *n 6*, 128 *n 11*, 131
Bukharin, M., 72, 73, 81, 82
Bukharin and the Bolshevik Revolution, Cohen, 73 *n 11*

Bureaucracy: and capitalism, 48ff, 65, 144–5; as caste, 24, 25, 105–6, 119–20; as form of government, 32; as parasitic, 37, 55, 74, 95–7, 109; as rule by officials, 21–3, 25, 29, 63, 68–9; as ruling class, 95–7, 102, 103, 107, 114–16, 121; autonomy of, 8, 49, 94; centralization and, 27; class analysis of, 92–100, 106–7, 119, 121; concept of, 26, 28, 29, 30, 31–3, 45–57, 72–87, 89–100, 106–7, 109, 135–6, 143, 152–5; contemporary connotations of term, 118; definitions of, 23, 29; Djilas on, 106–7; etymology, 21; features, 148; form and role of, 5, 8, 9, 44, 53, 55, 149; Hegel on, 46; hierarchical nature, 25, 46; indestructibility, 145–6; indispensability 64–8, 70, 91, 141–7; Laski, on Western European, 119–20; Lenin on, 72–87; Marx on, 45–57; military analogy, 25; Mill on, 31–3; nineteenth-century English attitudes to, 26–30; polemic against, 20–33, 45; relationship to corporations, 47; relationship to economic classes, 48–9; relationship to social divisions, 47; relationship to state, 145–6; relationship to work flow, 139, 141, 143; research on, 2; self-maintainance, 144–6, 154; status structure, 67; Trotsky on, 89–100, 106; values of, 67, 120, 127; versus politics, 67–70, 90–91, 120–21, 128; Weber on, 61–70; Weber's ideal type, 4, 19, 63–5, 72, 140

Bureaucracy, Albrow, 21, 23 *n 48*, 26, 29, 31

Bureaucracy, Aristocracy and Autocracy: the Prussian Experience 1660–1815, Rosenberg, 1, 7, 8

Bureaucracy in Modern Society, Blau and Meyer, 148, 149, 151

Bureaucracy: Servant or Master?, Crozier, Downs, and Niskanen, 146 *n 19*

Bureaucratic-administrative welfare state, 130

Bureaucratic collectivism (Rizzi), 98–100, 120

Bureaucratic despotism, 106

Bureacratic dictatorship, 51, 90, 93

Bureaucratic organization: features, 136–8, 152–3; non-state, 2; pyramidal command authority in, 150, 154; role, 136

Bureaucratic Phenomenon, The, Crozier, 145 *n 18*, 147 *n 20*, 148 *n 23*

Bureaucratic Revolution: the Rise of the Stalinist State, The, Shachtman, 107 *n 39*

Bureaucratic socialism, 121

Bureaucratic traits, future of, 149–52

Bureaucratism: as disease, 22, 84, 90; as a social phenomenon, 90; in Soviet state, 82–90

Bureaucratization: benefits, 146–7; features, 136–41, 152; of industrial society, 127 *n 9*; of society, 66–7; of Soviet Union, 91–3; of world, 130–31, 143; Weber on, 61–71

Bureaucrats: 23, 69–70, 74, 83–4

Bureaukratie und Beamtenthum in Deutschland

(Bureaucracy and Officialdom in Germany), 24

Bureaumania, 22

Burke, E., on government as a trust, 13

Burnham, J., 30, 101–4, 110–11, 123

Cameralists, 6, 11–12, 14, 15, 16, 18

Cameralists, The, Small, 14 *n 27*

Can the Bolsheviks Retain State Power?, Lenin, 77

Cannon, J. P., 99

Capital (Das Kapital), Marx, 58, 59, 112, 117

Capitalism, 70, 93–4, 98, 99, 102; bureaucracy and, 48ff, 65, 144–5

Carlyle, T., 27, 28

Carra, J.-L., 22

Catherine II, 13

Centralization, 27, 53–5; *see also* Administration, centralization

Challenge of the Left Opposition (1923–25), The, Trotsky, 89

Chapman, B., 9, 10

China: and oriental despotism, 122–5; European interest in administration of, 18–19; hydraulic society in, 124; Maoist hostility to bureaucracy in, 119

Civil War in France, The, Marx, 52–4, 56, 73, 119

Class: analysis of society, 46–53, 88–9, 121; and analysis of bureaucracy, 92–100, 106–7, 119, 121; bureaucracy as a ruling, 95–7, 102–3, 107, 114–16, 121; Saint-Simon on, 36–7

Coffey, R. F., 147 *n 21*

Cohen, S. F., 73 *n 11*

Colbert, 4

Collected Works, Carlyle, 28

Collected Works, Lenin, 73, 74–86

Collected Works, Marx and Engels, 46, 48

Coming of Post-Industrial Society, The, Bell, 129

Commune, 52–3

Communism, Germany, 95

Communist League, 53

Communist Manifesto, Marx, 52–4, 73, 114, 116, 119, 123, 125

Communist Party, USSR, 84–6, 104, 121

Computerization, 149

Comte, A., 40

Convergence theories, 104

Correspondance littéraire, philosophique et critique, 1753–69, Baron de Grimm and Diderot, 22

Critique of Political Economy, preface, Marx, 47

Crozier, M., 145 *n 18*, 146 *n 19*, 147 *n 20*, 148 *n 23*

Cultural Contradictions of Capitalism, The, Bell, 129 *n 12*

D'Agostino, A., 134

Declaration of the Rights of Man and of Citizens (1789), 5

De Gournay, V., 21–2, 26
Delo Truda (The Cause of Labour), 133
Depersonalization, in society, 127–8; of bureaucratic administration, 147–9
Despotism, 20–21; of intellectuals, 113–21; of state, 122–5; of system, 126–7; *see also* Oriental despotism
Development of Public Services in Western Europe, 1160–1930, The, 5
Dictionnaire générale de la politique, 28
Diderot, D., 22
'Disengagement' of state: 1, 5; France, 12; Prussia, 8, 13; Russia, 12
Djilas, M., 104–7, 109, 111
Dolgoff, S., 101 *n 27*
Domination, Weber's sociology of, 61–2, 64
Donnard, J.-H., 23 *n 50*
Dorwart, R. A., 7 *n 10*
Downs, A., 145 *n 18*, 146 *n 19*, 148 *n 23*

Economy and Society, Weber, 61–71, 142 *n 15*
Eichmann, A., 121, 128
18th Brumaire of Louis Bonaparte, The, Marx, 49, 51–4, 116
Eighth Congress of Soviets, 80
Encyclopaedia of the Social Sciences, Seligman and Johnson, 120 *n 5*
Engels, F., 46, 47, 53, 57, 73, 75; and anarchism, 58; authority in industry, 58; scientific socialism, 116; theory of state, 48
England, bureaucracy in, 9, 11, 23, 26, 29, 33
English Constitution, The, Bagehot, 33 *n 70*
Essay on the Theory of Enlightened Despotism, An, Krieger, 14
Ethical Foundations of Marxism, The, Kamenka, 126 *n 8*
Evans, M., 54

Fascism, 42, 123
Fennell, C. A., 23 *n 49*
Feudal society, Saint-Simon on, 36, 37
Feudalism, 35, 37
Feudalism, Capitalism and Beyond, Kamenka and Neale, 128 *n 11*
Finer, H., 25 *n 54*
First International and After, Marx and Engels, 57 *n 25*, 59
Fiscal, 7, 9
Florence Macarthy II, Morgan, 23
Ford, F., 4–5
France: administration, 11, 43
Frankfurt School, on alienation, 127
Frederick II (the Great), 6, 7, 8, 16
Frederick William I, 6, 8, 9
Frederick William III, 8
Frederick the Great and His Officials, Johnson, 8 *n 11*
Freedom, bureaucratization and law, 130–31
French Finances 1770–1795: from Business to Bureaucracy, Bosher, 5 *n 7*, 17–19, 22 *n 46*
French Revolution, 5, 91

From Max Weber, Gerth and Mills, 69 *n 7*

Gemeinschaft, concept of, 128–31
General Directory, Prussia, 6, 7
General Legal Code, Prussia (1794), 8
German Communist Party (KPD), 95
German Ideology, The, Marx, 48–9, 58
Germany: bureaucracy, 24, 25, 68; bureaucrats, 69–70; bureaucratic collectivism, 98; communism in, 95; monocratic v. collegial administration, 28; state control in, 102
Gerth, H., 69 *n 7*
Gesammelte Aufsätze zur Soziologie und Sozialpolitik, Weber, 66–7, 70–71
Gesammelte Politische – und Finanzschriften, Justi, 17
Gesellschaft, concept of, 128, 130–31
Gillis, J. R., 8 *n 13*, 24
Gorev, B., 134
Government and its Measures, Toulmin-Smith, 27
Government: as a public trust, 12–14; feudal, 37–8; role, 28, 30, 31, 38; Westminster system of, 120–21
Great Elector, the, 6
'Greatest happiness' principle, 14–15
Great Proletarian Cultural Revolution, China, 119
Greenleaf, W., 27 *n 59*
Grimm, Baron de, 22, 143–4
Guarantees of Harmony and Freedom, Weitling, 34
Gurvitch, G., 45 *n 3*
Guy, B., 19 *n 38*

Habermas, J., on alienation, 127
Hagen, von, 7
Hall, R. H., 136–8, 140
Hegel, G. W. F., 45–7, 56, 69, 92, 123
Heinzen, K., 25
Helvetius, C.-A., 14
Herodotus, 122
Heydebrand, W., 139 *n 8*, 140 *n 10*, 140 *n 11*
Hierarchical authority, 136–8, 140, 148–50, 153–4
History of Economic Analysis, Schumpeter, 21 *n 43*
Hitler, A., 51, 121, 123, 128
Hobbes, T., 11, 12, 16, 130
Holy Family, The, Marx and Engels, 48, 133
Humboldt, W. von, 20
Hume, L. J., 9
Hydraulic societies, 124–5

Il collettivismo burocratico, Rizzi, 98 *n 21*
Improvement of Mankind: the Social and Political Thought of John Stuart Mill, Robson, 30 *n 63*
In Defence of Marxism, Trotsky, 96, 97, 99, 100–101
India, hydraulic society, 124
Industrial Revolution, 10

Industrial society, 1, 36–44
Industrialism, 35
Industriels, 37, 41–4
Industry: large-scale and socialist, 58, 78; Marx on, 57–9; Saint-Simon on, 34–45
Inside Bureaucracy, Downs, 145 *n 18*, 148 *n 23*
International (Second), 116
Intellectual Worker, The, Machajski, 101, 114–17, 132–4
Intelligentsia, rise of new class of, 114–17
Italy: bureaucratic collectivism, 98; development of city in, 63; state intervention, 102
Izvestiya, 133

Japan, bureaucratic collectivism, 98
Johnson, A. R., 110 *n 42*, 120 *n 5*
Johnson, H. C., 8 *n 11*, 15
Joseph II, 9
Justi, J. von, 14, 16, 17

Kabinett-System, 8–9
Kamenka, E., 121 *n 6*, 126 *n 8*, 128 *n 11*
Kann, R., 14 *n 28*
Kant, I., 23
Karl Marx, Evans, 54
Karl Marx devant le bonapartisme, Rubel, 51 *n 10*, 51 *n 12*
Kautsky, K., 72, 75
Kraus, C., 23
Krieger, L., 13, 14, 14 *n 29*, 17 *n 34*
Krygier, M., 112, 118, 121, 141, 143, 146
Kulaks, 94
Kuron, J., 107–9

La Bureaucratisation du monde, Rizzi, 98, 99
La Mothe le Vayer, 19
La Plume, La Faucille et le Marteau, Mousnier, 3, 3 *n 4*, 4
L'URSS: collectivisme bureaucratique, Rizzi, 98 *n 21*, 104
Labour, 'mechanization' of, 131
Labours of Sisyphus, The, Zeromski, 131
Lach, D., 122 *n 7*
La Réforme sociale en France, Le Play, 29
Laissez-faire, 30
Laski, H. J., 119–20
Laurat, L., 101–3, 109
Law and Social Control, Kamenka and Tay, 131
Law and Society, Kamenka, Brown and Tay, 121 *n 6*, 128 *n 11*
L'Ordre naturel et essentiel des sociétés politiques, Mercier, 14 *n 29*
L'Organisateur, 38
Le Play, F., 29
Le Tableau de Paris, Mercier, 22
Left Communists, 82
Legislation, eighteenth-century, 16, 19
Lenin: 61, 109; attacks on bureaucratism, 82–6; on economic management, 79–81; on learning from bourgeoisie, 79–80; on non-bureaucratic character of proletarian dictatorship, 75; on specialists, 78–80; single

versus collegial authority, 81; theory of post-revolutionary state and its apparatus, 72–7, 84; views on administration, 78ff
Lenin and the Bolsheviks, Ulam, 82 *n 18*, 85
Lenin's Last Struggle, Lewin, 85 *n 22*, 87
Leninism, 121
Les Employés, Balzac, 23–4
Leviathan, Hobbes, 11
Leviathan, Introduction, Oakeshott, 13
Lewin, M., 85 *n 22*, 86–7, 93–4
Liberal, The, 53
Liga Polska, 132
Limanowski, B., 132
Limits of State Action, The, Humboldt, 20
Lindenlaub, D., 67 *n 3*
Locke, J., 11, 13
Lodz general strike (1892), 115
Louis XIV, 4, 5
Louis Napoleon, 48, 49, 50
Luxemburg, R., 117 *n 3*

Machajski, J. W., 101, 108, 119; analysis of *Capital*, 117; biography, 131–4; themes raised by, 118; theory of new class of *intelligenty*, 114–17; *see also* Makhaevists, 'Makhaevshchina'
Macridis, R., 110 *n 41*
Makhaevists, 132, 134
'Makhaevshchina', 114
Managerial Power and Soviet Politics, Azrael, 80, 81
Managerial society, 102–4, 123
Mao, 119
Maoism, hostility to bureaucracy, 119
Marcuse, H., 127
Maria Theresa, 9, 14
Marx, K.: 35–6, 61–2, 65, 70, 72–5, 85, 88–9, 91, 109, 113, 114, 131; alienation, 126; bureaucracy, and proletarian revolution, 53–7; criticism, 45–6; elimination of, 45–60; in contemporary society, 45–53; bureaucratic mentality (*Gesinnung*), 46; centralization, 53–4; critique of Hegel, 45–7; historical materialism, 47–8; on Bonapartism, 47–53; on constant capital, 117; organization of labour, 57–60; scientific socialism, Machajski's criticisms, 116–17; state, bourgeois society, 45
Marx Critique de Marxisme, Rubel, 54 *n 22*
Marx, Engels and Australia, Mayer, 53 *n 17*
Marxism, 47–8, 88
Marxism and Democracy, Laurat, 101, 103
Marxism and Ethics, Kamenka, 126 *n 8*
Marxism and the Question of the Asiatic Mode of Production, Sawer, 122 *n 7*
Marxist Social Democratic Movement, 115
Marxist theory: 101, 116, 117, 126; class, 88–9, 96, 97, 102; oriental despotism, 123
Mayer, H., 53 *n 17*
Mazarin, 3
Mendoza, 18
Mensheviks, 84

Mercantilists, 11
Mercier de la Rivière, 14 *n 29*, 22
Mesopotamia, hydraulic society, 124
Meyer, M., 148, 149, 151
Michael Speransky: Statesman of Imperial Russia, Raeff, 16 *n 32*, 17 *n 33*
Michels, R., 72, 90
Miliband, R., 51 *n 10*
Mill, J. S., 30–33, 146
Miller, R., 150 *n 28*, 154 *n 30*
Modzelewski, K., 107–9
Mohl, Robert von, 25, 26, 28
Monnier, H., 23
Monocratic versus collegial organization, 7, 19, 28–9, 64
Montyon, J. B. Auget, Baron de, 18
Möser, J., 18
Mousnier, R., 3, 4
Mussolini, B., 123
My Life, Trotsky, 133

Napoleon I, 6, 48
National-Socialist Commune, 132
Natural rights, theorists, 11
Nazism, 123
Neale, R., 128 *n 11*
Necker, 18
New Christianity, Saint-Simon, 43
New Class, The, Djilas, 106
New class theories: 100, 103, 114–15, 118–19, 134; analysis of society, 109; 'bureaucratic', 108, 109; common elements, 109; global, 101–4; on ownership of means of production, 103; socialist, 104–8; 'technocratic', 108, 109
New class theorists, 89, 97, 100–111
New Course, The, Trotsky, 89
New despotism, 113
New International, The, Trotsky, 95 *n 9*
New society, theories of, 34, 35, 43–5, 53–4, 56–7, 61
Ninth Party Congress (USSR), 81
Nisbet, R., 2
Niskanen, W., 146 *n 19*
Nomad, M., 132, 134
Northcote–Trevelyan reforms, 9

Oakeshott, M., 12–13
Obrecht, G., 11
October Revolution, 89, 107
O'Donnel, A., 27
Oeuvres complètes de Saint-Simon et Enfantin, Saint-Simon, 35, 37–44
Of Laws in General, Bentham, 13
Officials: bureaucracy, as rule by, 21–3, 25, 29, 63, 68–9; education and recruitment, 18; France 3–8, 22, 39; organization, 62; power, 66–70; proletarian dictatorship, control in, 75; Prussia, 6–8; role, 1, 11–12, 21; Saint-Simon on, 37–8; socialist society, 56
On Authority, Engels, 58
On Liberty, Mill, 31–3

Organization of labour, Marx on, 57–60
Organizations: forms, 63, 151–5; hierarchical structure, 152
Oriental despotism, 50, 122–5
Orwell, G., 125
Osse, M. von, 11
Ownership, of means of production, 103, 106–8

Paine, T., 13
Paris commune, 55–7, 59, 75, 76, 119
Parry, G., 15–16, 17, 17 *n 34*
Parts of a Lifetime, Djilas, 105–6, 110
Passmore, J., 127
Perfectibility of Man, The, Passmore, 127
Petrine reforms, 12
Philosophes, 11, 13
Philosophy of Right, Hegel, 45, 46
Physiocrats, 14, 21
Pietists, 11
Plamenatz, J., 100, 110
Plans for Political Reform in Imperial Russia 1730–1905, Raeff, 12, 15, 17
Plebs, 63
Pobudka (The Clarion), 132
Poland, socialism in, 115–16
Political and Administrative Aspects of the Scientific and Technical Revolution in the USSR, Miller, 150 *n 28*, 154 *n 30*
Political economy, Marx on, 47
Political Economy of Bureaucracy, The, Stockfisch, 144 *n 17*
Political Institutions and Social Change in Continental Europe, Anderson, 10
Political Power and Social Classes, Poulantzas, 51–2
Political Undercurrents in Soviet Economic Debates, Lewin, 94
Politics, revolutionary rejection of, 34–5
Politics and Vision, Wolin, 2, 35
Post-industrial society, 128–30
Poulantzas, N., 51, 52
Pravda, 89, 133
Praxis, 127
Preobrazhensky, E., 82
Priestley, J., 14
'Principles of Government Reform', (1802), 17
Principles of Political Economy, Mill, 30, 31 *n 64*
Profession of Government, The, Chapman, 9, 10
Proletarian dictatorship, Lenin on, 73–6
Proletariat state, 75–6
Property: education as a form of, 114, 118; ownership of, 108
Protestant Reformation, 141
Prussia: administrative centralization, 3, 6–9; bureaucracy, 8–9, 23, 27, 33; bureaucratic absolutism, 24; bureaucrats, recruitment, 18, 69; judicial system, 7
Prussian Bureaucracy in Crisis, 1840–1860, The, Gillis, 8 *n 13*, 24

Rabkrin, 85–6

Rabochaya revolutsiya (The Workers' Revolution), 133
Rabochii Zagovor (The Worker's Conspiracy), 133
Raeff, M., 9, 12, 12 *n 20*, 14, 15, 16 *n 32*, 17 *n 33*, 17 *n 36*, 141–2
Rational enterprise, 144, 145
Radek, K., 131
Red Guards, 119
Representative Government, Mill, 30, 32
Revolution, Trotsky on, 91–2
Revolution Betrayed, The, Trotsky, 91 *n 4*, 91 *n 5*, 96, 100
Revolutionary Marxist Students in Poland Speak Out, Weissman, 107 *n 39*
Richelieu, 3
Richtungskämpfe im Verein für Sozialpolitik, Lindenlaub, 67 *n 3*
Rigby, T. H., 76
Rights of Man, Paine, 13
Rizzi, B., 98–9, 101–4, 106, 108, 110–11
Robe and Sword: the Regrouping of the French Aristocracy after Louis XIV, Ford, 4–5
Robson, J., 30 *n 63*
Rodbertus, state socialism, 117
Roman Republic, 63
Rosenberg, H., 1, 7, 8
Roth, G., 61 *n 1*, 142 *n 15*
Rousseau, J.-J., 11, 13, 21
Rubel, M., 51 *n 10*, 51 *n 12*, 54 *n 22*
Russia: 68: bureaucratic reform, 15; collegial organization, 7; industrial organization, Lenin on, 80–81; Petrine reforms, 9; rights of citizens, 125, writings on administration, 11; *see also* USSR
Russian Empire, 115

Saint-Simon, C.-H. de R., comte de: 11, 53, 59, 61–2, 77–8, 108; officialdom as 'parasitic', 55; organization of industrial society, 34–45; technocratic element in, 40–41
Sawer, M., 73 *n 11*, 89 *n 1*, 111 *n 43*, 122 *n 7*, 125
Schaffer, B., 32
Schelle, G., 21
Schluchter, W., 127 *n 9*
Schmoller, G., 66
Schumpeter, J., 21 *n 43*, 113
Science and Its Critics, Passmore, 127 *n 10*
Scientific socialism, 114, 116–17
Seckendorff, 13
Second World War, 112
Selected Correspondence, Marx and Engels, 53, 54, 58
Selected Works, Marx and Engels, 47, 49–51, 53, 54, 55, 58, 59
Selected Writings and Speeches, Burke, 13
Seligman, E, R. A., 120 *n 5*
Shachtman, M., 107–8
Shatz, M., 115 *n 2*
Small, A., 14 *n 27*
Smith, A., 38, 43

Sobelsohn, (Karl Radek), 131
Social and Political Thought of Marx, The, Avineri, 54
Social Contract, The, Rousseau, 21
Social Democracy, 116
Social Democrats, Poland, 115
Social Movement in Russia, The, Gorev, 134
Socialism, 42, 70, 101–2, 113–15, 117
Socialism and the New Class, Sawer, 89–90, 111 *n 43*
Socialist Party, Poland, 115
Society: communist, economic management in, 58; concept of hydraulic, 124–5; crisis in, 35; *see also* Feudal society, Managerial society, New society, Post-industrial society
Sombart, W., 65
Sonnenfels, Freiherr von, 14, 16
Sorel, G., 114
Specialization, job, 150, 152, 153
Speransky, Count M., 15, 16, 17 *n 33*, 19
Spitzer, A., 6
Staatsrecht, Völkerrecht und Politik, Mohl, 26
Staatswirthschaft, Justi, 14
Stalin, J. V., 51, 85, 91, 93, 94, 99, 101, 108, 121
Stalin School of Falsification, The, Trotsky, 93
Stalinism and Bolshevism, Trotsky, 90
Standardization, of bureaucratic tasks, 153
Stanford Dictionary of Anglicized Words and Phrases, Fennel, 23 *n 49*
State: apparatus, 1, 11, 75, 77–8, 84, 96; as factory, 40–41; bureaucratic-administrative welfare, 130; capitalist, 1, 70–71, 74–6; capitalist, Lenin on, 76–7; disengagement, 1, 5, 8, 12; economic basis, 95; growth of functions, 1, 10, 102, 112–13, 141, 143; Marxist theory of, 72–4; modern, Marx on the, 48–9; proletarian, Lenin on, 77–8; role, 11–15, 17–18, 48, 124–5; role of workers and socialist, 114–17; Stalin's, 99; workers', 94–5
State in Capitalist Society, The, Miliband, 51 *n 10*
State and Revolution, The, Lenin 73, 76, 80–82, 85
Stauffer, R., 139 *n 8*, 140 *n 10*, 140 *n 11*
Stein, Karl Reichsfreiherr vom und zum, 24
Stinchcombe, A., 139, 140, 154
Stockfisch, J. A., 144 *n 17*
Stojanović, S., 107–9
Struggle Against Fascism in Germany, The, Trotsky, 95
Studies on Voltaire and the Eighteenth Century, Guy, 19 *n 38*
Study in Austrian Intellectual History: from Late Baroque to Romanticism, A, Kann, 14 *n 28*
Sweden, collegial organization in, 7
Szlachta, 116

Talmon, J., 42
Tay, A. E.-S., 121 *n 6*, 128 *n 11*
Taylor system, 81

Technik, 127
Technocracy: concept, 109; totalitarian, 42
Theory and Practice of Modern Government, Finer, 25 *n 54*
Theory of Social and Economic Organizations, The, Weber, 141
Tocqueville, A. de, 5, 51, 92
Tönnies, F., 126, 130
Totalitarianism, concept of, 123–5
Toulmin-Smith, J., 27
Transformation of Communist Ideology: the Yugoslav Case, The, Johnson, 110 *n 42*
Trotsky, L., 51 *n 10*, 88, 101–3, 105–8, 133; and Marxism, 89, 93; bureaucracy, class or caste?, 92–7, 103, 111; 'bureaucratic collectivism', views on, 98–100; on betrayal of revolution, 98, 100; post-revolutionary bureaucratism, USSR, 89–94; theory of workers' state, 94–5
Tucker, R., 73 *n 13*
Turgot, A. R. J., 21
Twilight of Authority, The, Nisbet, 2

Über die Liebe des Vaterlands, Sonnenfels, 16
Udy, S., 138, 140
Ulam, A., 82 *n 18*, 84–6
Un Petit Mot de réponse, Carra, 22
Union of Soviet Writers (USSR), 121
Union of the Youth of Poland, 131
Unperfect Society: Beyond the New Class, The, Djilas, 107 *n 38*
USA: bureaucratic collectivism, 98; role of state, 112; state intervention in, 102
USSR: 93, 100–101, 120; 'automated system of control', 150, 154; bureaucracy, 2, 29, 95–7, 104–5, 120–21; bureaucratic collectivism, 98; legal framework, 120–21; post-revolutionary development, 91–2; post-revolutionary organization, 82; revolution in, 93–5; state intervention in, 102; Stalin and, 99; totalitarianism in, 121
Utilitarianism, Liberty, Representative Government, Mill, 30 32

Verein für Sozialpolitik, 66, 69
Vermischte Schriften, Kraus, 23
Vincent de Gournay: Laissez-faire, laissez-passer, Schelle, 21
Vol'sky, A., 133
Vorontsov, Count, 15

Wagner, A., 66
Weber, M., 41, 51, 75, 90, 92, 119, 126, 140, 151; administrative organizations, 61–3; *Beamtenherrschaft*, 63, 68–9; bureaucracy, and socialism, 70–71; indispensability, 64–6, 141–6; inescapability, 66; bureaucratic domination, 67–9; bureaucratization of society, 66–7, 136; bureaucrats, power, 67–8; critiques of, 127 *n 9*; ideal type of bureaucracy, 63–4; domination, sociology of, 61–3
Weissman, G., 107 *n 39*
Weitling, W., 34, 114
Werke, Marx and Engels, 46, 54, 55
Western Europe: Laski on bureaucracy in, 119–20; role of state in, 112
Wittfogel, A., 123, 124
Wittich, C., 61 *n 1*, 142 *n 15*
Wolin, S., 2, 34–5
Wright Mills, C., 69 *n 7*
Writings, Trotsky, 91 *n 4*, 92, 95–7, 98, 100 *n 24*

Yugoslavia: 100; bureaucratic despotism, 106

Žeromski, S., 131, 133